PALESTINIAN LAWYERS AND ISRAELI RULE

Palestinian Lawyers and Israeli Rule

Law and Disorder in the West Bank

by George Emile Bisharat

 University of Texas Press, Austin

First Edition, 1989
First Paperback Printing, 2012
Requests for permission to reproduce material from this
work should be sent to Permissions, University of Texas
Press, Box 7819, Austin, Texas 78713-7819.

♾ The paper used in this publication meets the mini-
mum requirements of American National Standard for
Information Sciences—Permanence of Paper for Printed
Library Materials, ANSI Z39.48-1984.

Library of Congress Cataloging-in-Publication Data

Bisharat, George Emile, 1954–
    Palestinian lawyers and Israeli rule : law and disorder in
    the West Bank / by George Emile Bisharat. — 1st ed.
        p.   cm.
    Bibliography: p.
    Includes index.
    ISBN 978-0-292-73984-0
    1. Lawyers—Israel.   2. Palestinian Arabs—Legal
status, laws, etc.—Israel.   3. Rule of law—Israel.
I. Title.
LAW ‹ISRAEL 7 Bish 1989›
349.5694—dc20
[345.694]   89-9143
                                                  CIP

To Maurice and Mary Bisharat

Contents

Figures

Tables

Acknowledgments

The bulk of this study is based on field research conducted in the West Bank between January 1984 and March 1985. My stay was funded by a grant from the International Doctoral Research Fellowship Program for the Near and Middle East of the Social Science Research Council and the American Council of Learned Societies, with funds provided by the Ford Foundation and the National Endowment for the Humanities. I wish to record my gratitude to these institutions for the special opportunity they provided me.

The idea to study the legal profession in the West Bank grew out of my experience working with lawyers there in the summer of 1982. I had received funding from the Harvard Law School's fledgling Human Rights Program to work with Law in the Service of Man (LSM), a Ramallah-based human rights organization. I would like to register my gratitude to both the Human Rights Program for its support and the lawyers and other LSM staff for their patience and interest. I owe special thanks to Mona Rishmawi, Raja Shehadeh, Ali Jaradat, and Jonathan Kuttab, who were additionally helpful on my return to the West Bank in 1984.

I was the recipient of kindnesses from many quarters during my period in the field. John C. Viste, director of the Jerusalem office of Amideast, and Ismat al-Atireh were extremely helpful and supportive. I became an affiliate of the Arab Studies Society in Jerusalem. I owe special gratitude to the society's directors, Faisal al-Husseini and Ishaq al-Budeiri, for their solicitude. I discussed my research on numerous occasions with Salim Tamari, Mahmoud Mi'ari, and Lisa Taraki, all from the Department of Sociology and Anthropology of Bir Zeit University, and received much valuable guidance from them.

As a whole, my informants, the Palestinian lawyers of the West Bank, were amazingly open and cooperative, given the difficult circumstances of occupation. My deepest thanks are due to all of them. It is not easy to single out individuals, but some went to extraordinary lengths to ensure both my comfort and the success of my research project. Mursi Hajir, acting head of the West Bank branch of the Jordanian Lawyers Union (JLU), extended me the full cooperation of his office. Abdurrahman Natshe, Ibrahim Sha'baan, and George Mikhail Musa, members of the JLU, were also extremely helpful. The Steering Committee of the Committee of Arab Lawyers was gracious and supportive as a body. Several of its members, including Bahij al-Tamimi, 'Adnan Shu'aibi, Osama 'Awdeh, and Mary Rock, deserve mention. Special thanks are reserved for two other Steering Committee members, 'Ali Ghuzlaan and Shukri Nashashibi. Both of these men demonstrated the utmost patience and conscientiousness in their efforts to have me understand the world of the lawyers of the region, and I am deeply grateful to them.

Two other lawyers played unique roles in my experience in the Occupied Territories. Abu Maher acted as my surrogate grandfather, kind, wise and accepting. Abu Wa'il was like an uncle and presented me a model of human strength and dignity under duress. My respect and fondness for these men run very deep.

Gratitude is also due my thesis committee at Harvard University: Thomas Barfield, Charles Lindholm, Sally Falk Moore, and my adviser, Nur Yalman. Tom Barfield was unfailingly cheerful and accessible. Chuck Lindholm was kind enough to read the text with great care, and made many useful substantive editing suggestions.

Sally Falk Moore has been a source of encouragement and inspiration throughout my studies at Harvard. She was particularly sympathetic of the challenges of straddling the fields of law and anthropology, and her concern and interest in me was warming and invigorating.

Nur Yalman is unique in my academic career. He is the antithesis of the "aloof intellectual." His genuine and universal regard for people is more than a veneer of courtesy, and his caring was a large part of the sustenance that kept me working steadily and, for the most part, happily through the writing stages of my thesis.

I would like to acknowledge several other personal and intellectual debts here. Laura Nader, through the course I took with her as an undergraduate at the University of California—Berkeley, did much to stimulate my interest in legal anthropology, and I am extremely grateful for her continued interest in my work. Jim Ferguson and Roberto Kant de Lima of the "Bacardi School of Anthropology," formerly situated at Harvard, have been the most treasured of intellectual companions. They are chiefly responsible for my conviction that anthropology can be exhilarating, meaningful—and just pure fun.

My family has been my reserve of love and strength all my life, and no less so these last few years. My deepest debt, however, is to Jaleh Bisharat, who has given her love and support unstintingly, and in so many ways.

Note on Transliteration

I have opted not to employ any of the various technical systems of transliteration from Arabic to English, but instead to render phonetic transliterations of Palestinian colloquial words as accurately as possible. In most cases, I have represented long vowels in Arabic by doubling their equivalent in English, although I have not done so if a standard transliteration for the word is available.

1. Introduction

In December of 1987, the West Bank and Gaza Strip erupted in civil unrest. By the following December, the *intifada*, or uprising, showed little sign of abating. More than three hundred Palestinians had been killed in clashes with the Israeli army. Some fifteen Israelis, both soldiers and civilians, had also been killed. Almost five thousand Palestinians were being held in prisons and detention centers as a result of the unrest, including seventeen hundred under "administrative detention." Those under administrative detention could be held up to six months without formal charges or judicial hearing.

To many observers, the vehemence of Palestinian opposition to continued Israeli military occupation came as a revelation. For a number of years preceding the uprising, life in the Occupied Territories had settled into a semblance of normality, its residents wearing a mask of superficial quiescence. Israeli claims that an improved standard of living for residents of the Occupied Territories had blunted resentment against the occupation; that material satisfaction had subdued the longing for self-determination seemed plausible. Such assumptions have been severely shaken by the months of violence since witnessed in the area.

One objective of this book is to deepen our understanding of Palestinian society in the Occupied Territories through a detailed examination of one of its vocational sectors—the legal profession. This book is the product of field research conducted in the West Bank in 1984 and 1985, a period of relative quiet in the region. Yet the frustrations leading to the uprising in 1987 were apparent even then. The account given here of daily experience under occupation for one segment of the Palestinians of the West Bank thus gives fuller dimension to the images that flicker across the television screens of Western viewers.

I do not maintain that the Palestinian lawyers of the West Bank are any more representative of their society than are other occupational groups. It is clear, however, that a number of the challenges confronting the contemporary West Bank lawyer are merely particular manifestations of general social problems facing the whole of Palestinian society in the Occupied Territories. This is notably true, for example, of the indeterminacy of the political future of the Occupied Territories. As this study will show, uncertainty concerning the future of the region has been extremely damaging to the interests of the lawyers. But virtually all other groups have likewise been damaged, although in different ways.

Moreover, as frequent intermediaries between Israeli military authorities and Palestinian citizens, lawyers stand close to the fault line dividing Israeli and Palestinian society. Their professional experience thus reflects many of the stresses that result as those societies shift and chafe against one another.

Another important point should become evident to the reader: Palestinian society of the West Bank does *not* exist solely in relationship to the Israeli occupation. A number of prior studies of the region have understandably focused on that relationship, and fruitfully so. Yet left without complement, they have tended to impart a somewhat limited view of Palestinian society. Of course, documenting the impact of Israeli rule on the West Bank's legal profession is indeed a major preoccupation of this work. But I have also tried to convey the richness and complexity of the life of the lawyers and of their surrounding society, which exist independently of the Israeli presence. Certain social dynamics influencing the condition of the profession will be shown to bear little or no relationship to the occupation.

The many unique features of the contemporary West Bank legal profession also should not obscure fundamental similarities with the legal profession in other Third World societies. In a number of these societies, the legal profession in its "modern" or contemporary form was the offspring of legal reforms enacted in the nineteenth and twentieth centuries. The goal frequently underlying these measures was to centralize authority by extending a unified system of law and courts, which were often structured after European models. In some cases, the reforms were imposed directly by European colonial rulers; in others, they were voluntarily undertaken by the "modernizing" elites of still-independent states.

Students of legal anthropology—the cross-cultural study of law and other modes of dispute processing—have long been interested in the phenomenon of the imposition of Western-style laws and legal systems in non-Western societies. In the last twenty years, many works in legal anthropology have examined the response of small, typically rural communities to the intrusion of national systems of law and courts. Most have documented that villagers and townspeople throughout the world have submitted to supralocal authority only with the greatest reluctance and have struggled covertly to preserve informal institutions and, through them, autonomy in the conduct of local affairs.

The modern Palestinian legal profession emerged with the Ottoman Empire's adoption of a European-modeled system of laws and courts in the nineteenth century. For Palestinian lawyers, the extension of the power of national courts has simultaneously implied the extension of the ambit of their own power and the broadening of their opportunities for financial and social advance. Viewing matters from the vantage point of an occupational group closely associated with state power, in contrast to the communities typically studied by anthropologists, may be a modest aid in rounding out our vision of the continuing struggle between central and local authority in many societies of the world.[1]

The Story of Abu Munif

The incident that first stimulated my interest in the role of the Palestinian legal profession in the West Bank occurred in the summer of 1982, when I was funded by the Harvard Law School's Human Rights Program to work for six weeks with Law in the Service of Man. The latter was founded in 1980 in Ramallah (approximately ten miles north of Jerusalem in the West Bank) by a group of local Palestinian lawyers to protect human rights and uphold the principles of the "rule of law" in the region. Its members seemed dedicated, competent, and undaunted by the challenging environment in which they were forced to operate. I was impressed with, and could not help but share, their sense of mission. Having no awareness of the conflicts that I would later discover to have split the local legal profession into intensely hostile factions, I assumed that their enthusiasm and integrity were typical of the Palestinian lawyers practicing under the occupation.

Tension between Israeli settlers in the West Bank and the indigenous Palestinian community was at a peak that summer. After some discussion about my project with LSM's directors, we agreed that I would research allegations of vigilante activities by Israeli settlers in the region. I commenced by collecting affidavits from Palestinian victims of settlers' violence.

One day I was taken by an employee of a voluntary organization to visit a Palestinian peasant farmer who lived adjacent to Ofra, an Israeli settlement to the northeast of Jerusalem. Some months before, residents of the settlement had come to the peasant's fields at night, had cut down some twenty olive trees, and had uprooted a larger number of grapevines. Shortly thereafter, the settlers (armed with rifles and submachine guns) had entered the man's land during the day with a bulldozer and had started to clear ground, apparently in preparation for laying a roadbed to the settlement. The farmer and one of his sons attempted to stop the settlers, and both received beatings for their efforts. Complaints to the police had temporarily halted further attempts, although no arrests had been made.

The day before we arrived to hear the Palestinian farmer's description of these events, he had been served with an order from the Israeli military government for the expropriation of his land. The settlers would apparently have their access road after all.

When queried as to his planned response to the expropriation order, the farmer merely shrugged resignedly, signifying that, in fact, he had no plan. The agency worker with whom I had come exhorted him to hire a lawyer to appeal the seizure. It was not clear whether the peasant was unaware of the existence of the appeals process for such expropriations, or had simply judged his chances of success to be nil. In any case, the agency worker made a spirited argument in favor of exploiting any legal recourse the farmer had, and we left only after he had agreed to contact a lawyer who was renowned for his expertise in land cases.[2]

I had begun to feel vaguely uncomfortable during the course of our conversation with the peasant and as we drove off, this feeling intensified. I was not at all convinced that we had done the right thing in encouraging the peasant to seek legal assistance, given the slim chance he had of succeeding in protecting his land. Appeals against land expropriation orders are reviewed by a special military administrative tribunal, and orders are seldom reversed. Didn't the peasant's "fatalistic" attitude toward his predicament reflect a fairly accurate assessment of the constellation of power in which he lived as one of its subordinate fixtures? Was there any point in seducing him into trusting legal procedures, into believing in the "rule of law" (an ideological precept that seemed to me to mask the exercise of power even in my own American society), when everything in his past and present experience instructed him to fear and despise state authority? Was anyone really to benefit from this, other than the lawyers— who, in addition to their fees, would gain status as "champions" of the nationalist cause of saving the land from Israeli control—and the military government—which would gain legitimation as a law-abiding member of the international community?

The direction and scope that my field research took on my return to the region almost two years later were necessarily different and more elaborated than these initial questions. But to a significant extent, my work was framed and informed by them for the duration of my stay in the West Bank. Nor did I ever resolve the profound sense of contradiction and irony about law, legal institutions, lawyers, the occupation, and myself in relation to them that I first felt so strongly that hot summer day.

A Profession in Crisis

Much of what I had seen during my initial stay in the West Bank suggested, perhaps paradoxically, that the circumstances of Israeli occupation afforded Palestinian lawyers significant opportunities for the advancement and consolidation of their social position. The Arab-Israeli war of June 1967 brought Palestinian society into contact with an alien Israeli military administration. The new authority bore many of the external features of a Western-style bureaucratic and legal system, rationalized by an ideology of the rule of law. The indigenous Palestinian society, on the other hand, was organized on a kin and highly personalized basis. In this respect, the relationship between Israeli occupiers and Palestinian occupied had some of the structural features of a classic colonial situation.

In a number of non-Western societies, colonial rule provided both the occasion for the foundation of the legal profession and circumstances propitious for lawyers to achieve substantial social power and status. Throughout most of the Eastern Arab world, the legal profession in its contemporary incarnation took form only after the demise of the Ottoman Empire and the imposition of British and French rule in the Levant.[3] In Egypt, where a British occupation had been established even earlier, lawyers rose to social and political prominence under the aegis of their foreign custodians, even while spearheading nationalist political resistance against them.[4]

A similar pattern of prosperity coupled with leadership in nationalist movements is recognizable in the development of the legal profession in India, Ghana, Kenya, and a number of other Third World countries.[5] As Reid noted of the legal profession in Egypt and the Fertile Crescent:

> At a time when the overriding problem facing the Arab world was colonial domination, the lawyers were well equipped to lead. Whether nationalist, neutralist, or collaborationist, it was the lawyers who could meet Westerners on their own terms in

dealing with law suits, administrative procedures, diplomacy, and constitutions. They could turn Western notions of democracy and the rule of law and the Western techniques of party organization and propaganda against their imperial masters.[6]

In contrast, the legal profession in the Third World has often not fared as well in the aftermath of the departure of colonial administrations. The causes for this postindependence decline have been multiple and have varied from country to country. Evacuation of colonial rulers opened new routes to competing careers, and broader access to legal and other education undercut the prerogatives of wealth, family, or caste. In a number of countries, including several in the Arab world, the legal profession was brushed aside by new military elites, who were bent on rapid "modernization" of their societies and were determined not to be inhibited by the niceties of legal form in reaching that goal. Lawyers, and the landowning and commercial cliques that formed an integral part of their clientele, were often seen as impediments to social and political change.

In Palestine itself, the legal profession acquired its modern form and rose to what appears in retrospect to have been the zenith of its social power during the British Mandate period (1923–1948). Lawyers were among the most prominent leaders of the Palestinian community in cultural affairs and also assumed leadership roles in the unsuccessful struggle for Palestinian national independence.[7]

Superficially at least, the advent of Israeli occupation and the subsequent establishment of a legally oriented system of administration in the West Bank would seem to have reproduced some of the conditions that had fostered the growth and prominence of the legal profession in a number of other colonial societies. On this basis, the occupation might have been expected to favor the West Bank's legal profession in its quest to advance and consolidate its social position.

From the outset, the Israeli occupation administration worked explicitly to provide legal rationales for its existence and actions. The watchful eye of the international community no doubt necessitated this approach. Perhaps equally weighty were the constraints imposed by Israel's own sense of itself as a democratic nation that respected and upheld the rule of law. The legal form of the military government immediately established in the West Bank had been meticulously crafted even before the 1967 war. Nor was the fledgling Israeli administration long in generating a flood of legislative changes in the form of military decrees. Among them were orders constituting an entirely new system of military courts and administrative tribunals to supplement the court systems already functioning in the West Bank. The substance of the decrees ranged broadly from matters of security to environmental management, intensified state regulation in some spheres of life, and introduced it to others never before subject to state law. Moreover, the occupation administration had at its disposal the army units stationed in the region. It thus enjoyed more effective instruments of law enforcement than any recent state authority.

The increase in state regulation, especially in extensive security regulations employed by the occupation administration, has resulted in more frequent interactions between individuals and formal state authority, and thus in an increase in potential occasions for the intermediation of lawyers. Thousands of Palestinian detainees have been processed through the Israeli military courts since 1967, contributing to the emergence of a whole new field of legal practice, that of "security" or "political" cases, and bestowing on lawyers the opportunity to assume key roles as defenders of the national resistance against occupation. The legal struggle for control of land in the West Bank between the Israeli military government and entrepreneurs, on one hand, and Palestinian owners, on the other, also cast Palestinian lawyers as potential champions of a sacred national cause, that of protecting the tangible land base for the establishment of a Palestinian state. In a number of respects, then, the circumstances of occupation appear to have placed a social premium on the technical expertise in which the legal profession holds a monopoly.

Other developments brought about by occupation simultaneously worked to subvert the social position of existing "notables," or prominent community leaders. Wealthy landowners, businesspeople, local government officials, and others who were closely linked to Jordan and had been the principal arbiters between state authority and the local population during the era of Jordanian rule saw their ties to Jordan partially neutralized by the shift of effective authority to the new Israeli administration, diminution of community dependence on land, and the growth of Palestinian nationalism and its organizational expression, the Palestine Liberation Organization (PLO). The same developments simultaneously favored the emergence of younger "counterelites" drawn from intellectual and professional backgrounds. They characteristically espoused liberal and nationalist ideologies and proclaimed their allegiance to the PLO.

To a number of observers, the shifts in the relative power of these social groups seemed well advanced by the early seventies. Their accounts of political change in the West Bank under Israeli occupation frequently centered on the theme of the displacement of the traditional leadership by young members of the new intelligentsia.[8] Lawyers were typically categorized as part of the ascendant counterelite.[9]

The ethnographic data presented in this work suggest a different phenomenon: the fortunes of local lawyers have declined steeply during the period of Israeli occupation. It is no exaggeration to describe the current state of the legal profession as one of severe crisis in internal morale, public esteem, and, it would seem, real social power, to the extent that the profession's existence as a corporate group in West Bank society has been significantly jeopardized. The crisis is most acutely felt by the lawyers themselves, but is evident to an outside observer as well, particularly when the profession's current social position is compared to its position in the past. In the words of one of my informants, "There was a time, especially in the Mandate years, when to be a lawyer was to be *somebody*, to be looked up to as a learned person, as a defender of peoples' rights, as a guardian of justice. After all, ours is one of the noble professions! But today we fight among ourselves in an unseemly manner. The authorities scoff at us, and the community holds us in contempt."

Thus my principal aim here is to answer the question: What accounts for the profession's actual decline and social marginalization during the period of Israeli occupation, when conditions appear to have granted it significant opportunities for advancement? Equipped with an answer to this question, we may be in a better position to address others, such as: What role does the West Bank's legal profession play in legitimating or delegitimating the Israeli occupation? Does it defend or defuse national resistance to Israeli rule? What conclusions may be drawn from the West Bank case about the role of Western-inspired legal professions in other non-Western societies? How can knowledge of the role of the legal profession be integrated with anthropological understandings of institutions of dispute processing in "developing" societies?

Profile of the West Bank

The West Bank comprises that 22 percent of former Mandate Palestine that fell under Jordanian control in the first Arab-Israeli war in 1948. The area had been slated under the UN Partition Plan of 1947 to become part of a proposed Palestinian state. Full implementation of the Partition Plan was aborted, however, with the outbreak of fighting between the newly declared state of Israel and the armies of the surrounding Arab states. The lands reserved for the Palestinian state were totally absorbed by Israeli forces advancing from the coastal region to the east and by Jordanian forces pressing from the interior to the west. The city of Jerusalem was also divided between these two states into western and eastern portions. The West Bank, including East Jerusalem, was formally annexed by Jordan in 1950, its residents becoming citizens of that state. It remained under Jordanian rule until Israeli military occupation in 1967.

The region, historically part of the Palestinian hinterland, straddles the rocky spine of the mountain range running north-south and dividing the coastal plain of historical Palestine from the more arid areas to the east. It also includes the fertile lands of the Jordan Valley to the west of the Jordan River, now the de facto border between Israel and the Occupied Territories, on one hand, and Jordan, on the other. The distance between northernmost and southernmost points in the West Bank is approximately 150 kilometers (approximately 100 miles), Jerusalem being situated somewhat south of the midpoint. The east-west girth of the region averages approximately 50 kilometers (approximately 30 miles).

The climate is typically Mediterranean, with a long dry season stretching roughly from April to November. Rainfall is sparse overall and tends to be concentrated in the winter months. Not infrequently, it falls in cloudbursts and, with hillsides mostly denuded of forests in past centuries, much soil is lost to runoff. Most of the populated areas of the West Bank lie at an elevation between 450 and 900 meters (approximately 1,500 to 3,000 feet) above sea level. Winter temperatures routinely approach freezing, and snowfall is not quite an annual event. But areas on the fringe of the coastal plain in the vicinity of the towns of Tulkarm and Qalqilya or below sea level in the Jordan Valley are decidedly milder.[10]

The total Palestinian population of the region is approximately 870,000, including 120,000 residents of East Jerusalem.[11] The remainder are distributed in the three other major urban areas of Nablus, Ramallah, and Hebron, and in the medium-sized towns of Jenin, Tulkarm, and Qalqilya in the north, Jericho in the Jordan Valley, and Bethlehem just to the south of Jerusalem. An indeterminate number of the residents of these cities and towns are refugees from areas of Palestine that fell under Israeli control in the 1948 war. In addition, some 85,000 refugees live in sixteen camps set up in 1948 by the United Nations Relief and Works Agency (UNRWA), the UN body charged with ameliorating the plight of the Palestinian refugees.[12] But some 70 percent of the population continues to inhabit the several hundred villages of the region, which range in size from several hundred to 5,000 residents. Demographic divisions between town, camp, and village dwellers are also social categories

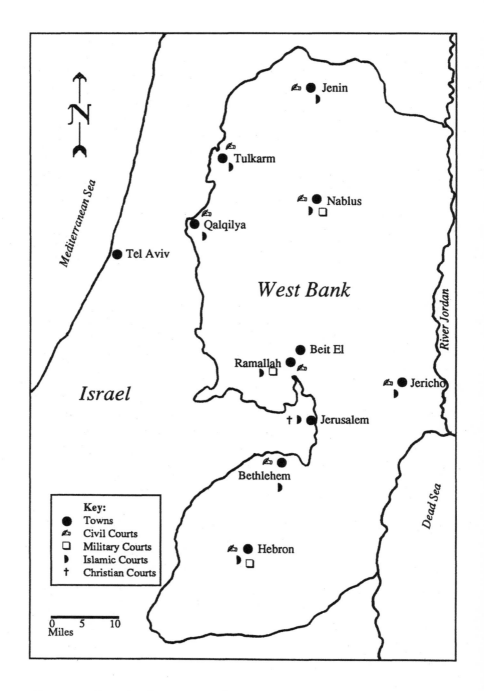

Figure 1. West Bank Towns and Courts

preserved in the terms *"hadari"* (a town resident), *"qarawi"* (a villager), and *"laji^ʾ "* (refugee).[13]

The Palestinian population is ethnically homogeneous and speaks a colloquial dialect of Arabic.[14] The vast majority is Sunni Muslim; a Christian minority of perhaps 8 percent, composed of several sects, is centered in Jerusalem, Ramallah, and the Bethlehem area. As in the Middle East in general, religiosity within both Muslim and Christian communities is strong, especially in the rural areas; even in the towns and cities, religion and sect constitute important components of social identity.

At the inception of occupation, the West Bank's economy was predominantly rural, supporting a dominant group of medium- to large-scale landowners. Some resided in the villages, while others had been absentee for generations. Most of the remainder of the village population derived its livelihood directly from agriculture, typically as small owners or sharecroppers. The *hamula,* or extended lineage, was the salient social and economic unit of rural Palestinian society.[15]

Landowners were linked, often by kinship ties, to an urban stratum composed of merchants and small industrialists. The latter engaged primarily in the finishing of agricultural products and in small-scale crafts production. A small middle stratum of petty merchants, civil servants, salaried clerical workers, and professionals of middling success and a lower stratum of laborers, drivers, clerks, and others rounded out the urban social structure. Clear awareness existed of differences in the wealth and status of individuals and extended kin groups in both the rural and the urban environments. It is perhaps most accurate to say that there was a "sense" of class rather than any articulation of it as such.[16]

Although it is clear that the period of occupation has brought radical change in the structure of the West Bank's economy and major transformations in social structure as well, the character and direction of that change is a matter of controversy.[17] A general phenomenon, which is indisputable, is the growing integration of the West Bank's economy into that of Israel.[18] A substantial level of infrastructural development linking the two regions (in transportation, electrical services, and so on) has advanced this process. Another of its major dimensions is the daily flow of migrant wage laborers from the West Bank to Israel, at times reaching as many as 120,000 per day. Availability of wage labor has diminished community dependence on access to land and brought a corresponding diminution in social and political subservience to those who control land.

Migrants have also departed in increasing numbers to the Arab countries and to the West. Their remittances have become another vital source of West Bank prosperity.[19] So the reduced dependence on land and landowners has come at the expense of new dependence on external sources of employment. In the mid-eighties, the confluence of hyperinflation and simultaneous downturns in the economies of Israel and of the Arab oil-producing states (where many Palestinian migrants had found work) thus was wreaking ruinous financial effects on the residents of the Occupied Territories. Their dependence was exacerbated by the stagnation that characterized the local industrial sector.[20]

Migration abroad has also had a profound social impact on West Bank society. Many migrants are young men, often among the most able and best educated of their communities; some scholars term their exodus a "brain drain."[21] The growth in the Occupied Territories of a number of Palestinian institutions of higher learning during the past twenty years has contributed to a general rise in the level of education in the region, but many of their best graduates still seek their fortune abroad. The precise effects of this steady brain drain are incalculable, but the loss of this particular segment of the population works to the detriment of a group such as the legal profession, depriving it of an ostensibly sympathetic and potentially influential ally.

The Israeli government has pursued twin policies of land expropriation and settlement of Israeli citizens in the Occupied Territories. A nearly contiguous series of high-rise apartment complexes were built ringing Jerusalem to the east. They contain the city's Arab population and segregate it physically from the remainder of the West Bank. An estimated 40 percent of the region's land mass has come under Israeli possession and supports some one hundred Israeli civilian settlements. The Israeli settler population of the region was estimated in early 1987 to have reached fifty thousand.[22]

Settlements constitute distinct administrative, economic, and social enclaves interacting only minimally with surrounding West Bank society. Aside from such concrete effects on Palestinians as the loss of lands they might have used for agriculture or for residential construction, the political and symbolic impact of Israeli land acquisition and settlement policies is profound. In fact, from the perspective of West Bank Palestinians, the ongoing struggle for control of land (and water resources, without which agricultural land is nearly useless) constitutes the most basic clash between their own and Israeli interests. The military government's facilitation of Israeli land acquisition more than anything else distinguishes it from prior governments (Ottoman, British, and Jordanian), which taxed and conscripted the Palestinians, but never expropriated their lands on a massive and systematic scale.

Recent years have witnessed the blossoming in the West Bank of what locally are termed "nationalist institutions" (*mu'assassaat wataniyeh*)—municipal councils, charitable societies, professional associations, women's groups, institutes of higher learning and research, trade unions, and so on. These nationalist institutions attempt to provide social services akin to those normally offered by the state. They are founded by Palestinians to strengthen the community—so as to enable its members to resist pressures toward migration—and to establish the infrastructure of a future Palestinian state. Leaders of these entities have become influential spokespersons for the community under occupation.

The nationalist institutions gained a major source of support with creation of the *amwaal as-sumud*, or Steadfastness Fund, created at the Baghdad Conference of Arab States in 1978. The goal of the conference was to organize aid to the Palestinian communities under occupation and thus to encourage their "steadfastness" on the land. Commitments to the fund by the Arab oil-producing states ran to hundreds of millions of dollars. Although the full pledges were never consistently paid, significant sums were injected into the local economy for several years.[23] A Joint Committee (*al-lajna al-mushtaraka*) based in Amman and composed of representatives of the Jordanian government and the PLO was charged with disbursement of the steadfastness fund. As a consequence, that agency gained a major say in the direction of local-level politics in the West Bank.

Indeterminancy and Overcontrol

For more than twenty years, the status of the Occupied Territories has remained unresolved, their residents hostage to the will of larger external political forces. The indeterminancy of the political future of the region has exerted manifold influences on the experience of the general community under occupation and has had a specific impact on the local legal profession. It is difficult to exaggerate the toll on individual and collective morale of life in a kind of legal and political limbo, a state of "permanent impermanence." Prospects for a resolution of and relief from occupation have, on occasion, seemed tantalizingly good, but have never reached fruition; they have simply multiplied local frustrations. Hopes are pinned to every new "peace plan," "initiative," or "proposal" for a resolution to the Arab-Israeli conflict, only to be dashed or simply dissipated once again in countless meetings conducted by the stream of diplomats shuttling between the various capitals of the region and the West. The situation has given rise to a sense of uncertainty, powerlessness, and insecurity, which pervades the experience of Palestinians at all levels—as individuals and as members of a community—in day-to-day decision making and in longer-term planning, in school, business, and social life. The emotional drain caused by the community's continual oscillation between euphoria and despair is palpable.

Of course, the indeterminacy of the region's political future is not completely open-ended: the identities of the three primary contenders for authority, Israel, Jordan, and the PLO, are known. To these may be added a fourth, namely, the Palestinians of the West Bank themselves. But the permutations in ways to divide rule among these four contenders, in schemes for autonomy, annexation, confederacies, and the like expand future possibilities exponentially. It is critical to note here that West Bank Palestinians must orient their activities to the mere possibility that any of these contenders may accede to power. As the interests of Israel, Jordan, and the PLO are so highly divergent, it is nearly impossible for individuals or social groups in the West Bank to cast their lot with one of the three external powers without offending one or both of the others. Thus the indeterminacy of the region's future for many years has been strongly conducive to paralysis at the local level.

It is also of fundamental importance to remember that the West Bank's ongoing legal categorization as an "occupied territory" has funded Israel with the rationale to continue ruling there through the medium of a military government. The Israeli government thereby accrues the political benefit in the world community of complying with international law while retaining a discretion for action in the West Bank far greater than that which it enjoys within Israel itself.[24] It simultaneously averts a dilemma that would surely flow from formal annexation of the Occupied Territories, namely, whether to deny rights of citizenship to the 1.3 million Palestinians residing there and suffer the attendant political costs in the domestic and international spheres, or to grant them such rights and accept the consequences of the swell of Israel's Arab minority to perhaps 35 percent or more of the total population of the country. While Israel has sought control of land and resources in the West Bank, it has never seriously aspired to rule its Palestinian community *as a legitimate authority.* Although the military government periodically endeavors to promote a local Palestinian leadership sympathetic to its interests, its policies have never truly been pitched to winning the loyalty of the residents of the West Bank and Gaza Strip to Israel. Rather, its aim has simply been to win local compliance, in its minimal form, hardly more than the abstention from violent resistance to Israeli rule. With stability and authority guaranteed ultimately through military might, the Israeli occupation administration for most of its duration has faced only the few minor political constraints to its actions emanating from the dynamics of either Israeli or international politics. Only since the uprising in December 1987 has Israeli rule faced serious challenge from within the Occupied Territories themselves.

The indeterminancy of the situation has also been crucial in preserving an important measure of Jordanian control over the West Bank. This is true not only because Jordan is one of its several potential future sovereigns. In the absence of a resolution, Jordanian civil departments and agencies in the West Bank continued to function until 1988 under a superimposed layer of Israeli military administration. For the first twenty-two years of occupation, West Bank residents held Jordanian passports, were subject to conscription into the Jordanian military, and were treated, for all practical purposes, as citizens under Jordanian law. The structural arrangement that emerged after 1967 afforded King Hussein of Jordan a considerable array of powers with which to manipulate West Bank affairs: salaries paid to many West Bank civil servants could be increased or withheld, travel of goods or people through Jordan could be allowed or denied; property and other assets held by West Bankers in the East Bank could be seized or frozen; and the like.[25]

This situation was altered considerably with King Hussein's surprise announcement in July 1988 that he would henceforth sever all ties with the West Bank in deference to its residents' preference for PLO leadership. Salaries of West Bank civil servants are no longer paid, and Jordanian passports held by West Bank Palestinians are to be considered "temporary" travel documents valid for only two years instead of five. Educational opportunities for West Bank residents at Jordanian universities have been curtailed in favor of East Bank residents. Food and other goods coming from the West Bank are taxed as foreign imports. The Jordanian parliament, with representatives from both banks, was dissolved. Nonetheless, Jordan continues to wield considerable power over the West Bank, a point these measures may have been designed to emphasize.

Indeterminacy in the West Bank is therefore linked closely to the phenomenon described here as "overcontrol." By this I mean simply the intensification of governmental or quasi-governmental authority brought about by the jurisdictional overlapping of two or more states or other entities in a single locale. The West Bank is subject to the direct authority of one state, Israel, which enjoys extensive powers to regulate community affairs, and to the indirect authority of another state, Jordan, whose instruments of control, while far less effective than Israel's, are still formidable. Finally, the West Bank Palestinian community is subject to the authority of a quasi-state entity, the PLO, which not only aspires to sovereignty, but at present commands some quasi-governmental resources, including both money and the power to impose political discipline through the use of violence.

Several things are noteworthy about overcontrol. First, the legitimacy of the three authorities within the Palestinian community ranks inversely to the degree of their real, effective powers, that is, tangible resources such as military might, money, and administrative institutions. Israel, with clearly the greatest effective power, has virtually no legitimacy whatsoever as the government of the people of the West Bank. Jordan, with substantially less effective power, possesses a limited legitimacy in the West Bank (especially among urban notables and, to some extent, the rural population). The PLO, with the fewest tangible resources and the least effective power, is far and away the most legitimate force in the region.[26] Hence there is a radical disjuncture between legitimate authority and governing efficacy.

Second, *all* of these authorities are external and have interests that range, in relation to the general interests of the West Bank Palestinian community, from somewhat distinct (the PLO) to diametrically opposed (Israel), at least as viewed from the local perspective.[27] The intrusion of all of these tendrils of external control leaves the local community with limited autonomy of its own and deprives its institutions of social control (such as the police and courts) of most of their capacity to regulate affairs according to locally defined needs and interests. The result is a bizarre combination of immediate intervention and smothering control in matters that implicate the interests of the three external authorities ("overcontrol"), coupled, at times, with a breakdown of the system of social accountability and virtual anarchy in realms in which only or primarily local community interests are at stake.

Organization of the Study

The object of the next three chapters is to delineate the various contexts in which the West Bank legal profession exists and operates. Chapter 2 documents the formation of the modern Palestinian legal profession from the late Ottoman period to 1967; it thus establishes the historical context in which the profession now functions. Chapter 3 describes aspects of indigenous Palestinian society and culture that complicate the legal profession's task of collective self-legitimation. In short, it details the present-day social and cultural context of West Bank legal practice. Chapter 4 documents the structure, style, and policies of the Israeli occupation administration, an example of what I characterize as "Orientalist despotism," thereby delineating the political-administrative context in which West Bank lawyers practice. Chapters 5, 6, and 7 present a detailed ethnography of the contemporary West Bank legal profession. Chapter 5 looks at the social identities of West Bank lawyers in relation to the processes by which entry to the profession is gained. Chapter 6 deals with the social organization of the profession: the forms in which law is practiced, the structure of offices, and the human and tangible resources that are at the profession's disposal. Chapter 7 focuses on the content of contemporary West Bank legal practice, the kinds of litigation and other activities in which the lawyers engage.

Chapters 8 and 9 take up two major problems specifically afflicting the legal profession at present. The first is the general deterioration in the West Bank's formal court system, which is the primary domain of the West Bank lawyers. The second is the disintegration of the legal profession itself, the consequence of disagreements over the strike declared by lawyers in the early months of the occupation, and the subsequent erosion of the profession's status as a corporate group in Palestinian society.

Chapter 10 attempts to sum up the argument that I have offered in response to the question posed at the beginning of this study. I also offer some suggestions as to the broader theoretical conclusions that may be implied herein.

A qualification must be registered at this point. The list of informants on whom I relied excludes an important category of persons: officials of the Israeli military government. Although their insights surely would have broadened the perspective of this book significantly, I was not long in the region before abandoning any hope that I might have access to them. Given the general political tension in the region and the specific suspicions that are generated by anyone seeming to pose in any way as a kind of "intermediary" between the occupation administration and the Palestinian community, I concluded that my research could be conducted practically on only one side of this stark social divide. The reader must be aware, as I am, that the perspective presented here is that of the Palestinian community and, more particularly, of its lawyers. While I have endeavored to present this perspective honestly and comprehensively, it is of necessity only one among several views of a complex social reality.

2. Imposition of the Modern Legal Profession

As in other parts of the Arab and Third worlds, the origins of the modern legal profession in the West Bank are historically linked with the nineteenth-century intensification of European commercial penetration in the region and the establishment (in the case of Palestine, in the early twentieth century) of direct European colonial rule.[1] While a secular legal profession had begun to develop slowly in the Fertile Crescent coincident with the establishment of new secular courts during the reforms of the late Ottoman period, the British Mandatory government deliberately fostered the growth of a Western-modeled legal profession in Palestine. Lawyers were groomed for positions in the civil service and schooled carefully in British precepts of law and government. This chapter therefore maps the "imposition" of the Palestinian legal profession, the legacy of which greatly influences the position of lawyers in contemporary West Bank society.

The Emergence of the Secular Court System in Ottoman Palestine

Prior to the nineteenth century, the only formal courts in existence in Ottoman Palestine were the *shari'a*, or Islamic law, courts, located in most of the larger towns and cities. A chief *qadi* (judge) in Jerusalem was appointed from Istanbul and rotated annually to avoid the consolidation of local affiliations and bases of power. The *shari'a* courts exercised broad powers of jurisdiction, encompassing as they did virtually all kinds of litigation as well as a range of administrative transactions and extending to the members of all religious communities resident in Palestine. In addition, they functioned as a public records office of sorts, with every important public or private document entered into their *sijills*, or record books.[2]

The *shariʿa* courts did not oversee disputes or transactions pertaining to taxation or military affairs; such matters fell within the purview of provincial governors or special military judges.[3] Tribal adjudication (*al-qadaʾ al-ʿashaʾiri*), following *ʿurf*, or customary law, also transpired in rural regions, especially in the southern fringes of Palestine, which bordered on Bedouin territories.[4]

Beginning in the mid-nineteenth century, Ottoman authorities embarked on a wide-ranging program of military, administrative, educational, and legal reforms that had the twin aims of centralizing political authority and modernizing and rationalizing state bureaucracy. Collectively known as the Tanzimat, these reforms led to the gradual diminution of the power and authority of the *shariʿa* courts throughout the empire, including those in Palestine.[5]

It is important to recall the economic and structural changes that the Ottoman Empire was then undergoing. In one sense, the Tanzimat were the political-administrative expression of the effort to transform Ottoman society into a modern capitalist society patterned after its European competitors. This was particularly evident in a series of laws pertaining to land tenure. These were clearly designed to eliminate impediments to transfers and investments in the agricultural sector.[6] These changes were crucial in stimulating the development of the modern legal profession throughout the Arab provinces.[7]

One of the immediate goals of the Tanzimat in the specific realm of law was the elimination of the "capitulations," agreements that since the early years of the empire had granted various European powers the right to try their own subjects in disputes arising within the empire. Ottoman administrators self-consciously modeled legal reforms after European institutions and practices, hoping thereby to answer foreign criticisms of the imperial system of justice and to "raise" its standards to levels demanded by Western diplomats.[8] A commercial code and a penal code based on the French equivalents were promulgated in 1850 and 1858, respectively, and codes for civil and criminal procedure, also French-inspired, followed in 1870 and 1879. The movement for codification also produced the Land Law of 1858, which reorganized and explicated prior substantive law pertaining to immovable property in the empire, and the Majalla, the Ottoman civil code promulgated in stages culminating in 1876, which was based on the relevant rules of the Hanafi school of Islamic law.[9]

Enforcement of the new codes was entrusted to new "reglementary" (*nizamiyeh*) courts, founded earlier to hear litigation between

Muslim and non-Muslim claimants. As the power and jurisdiction of the secular court system expanded, so did the authority and functional significance of the Islamic courts diminish. *Shariʿa* courts were reorganized in 1866, and their jurisdiction progressively narrowed to exclude all criminal and most civil cases. By the late nineteenth century, only their authority over matters of personal status and inheritance remained. Their role as public records offices was progressively attenuated as well, with the creation of civil agencies such as the Land Department.

Precursors of the Modern Legal Profession

While Islamic law formally conceives of no class of specialists in the representation of parties in litigation and, in many places (including the West Bank), litigants in Islamic courts are still entitled to plead their own cases, an informal but distinct group of courtroom pleaders arose early in Islamic history. Defending another's interest in court was treated formally as simply an application of a general contract of agency (*wakala*), and the term used to refer to those who did so was the general term for agent (*wakil*). The training of the *wakils* was purely informal; some, apparently, were former clerks of the courts, and others simply skillful orators.[10]

It is reasonable to assume that the emergence of the *nizamiyeh* courts and the deluge of new foreign laws effected by the Tanzimat considerably stimulated the demand for the services of the *wakils*. As a group, however, they had developed a reputation for chicanery, which led the central government to take its first steps to regulate the practice of law.[11] An 1876 decree required those engaged in legal representation before the courts to register with the Ministry of Justice. Ottoman administrators, conscious of the pressing need for formal training for judges and administrators of the new court system, had already founded the Istanbul law school (Hukuk Mektebi) in 1871. In 1884, the requirement of matriculation from a law faculty was decreed for practitioners before the *nizamiyeh* courts. But law graduates were so few that the government was quickly forced to make provisions for an examination, the passage of which would substitute for a formal degree.[12]

Opportunities for formal legal training for residents of the Fertile Crescent expanded with the establishment of government law schools in Baghdad in 1908 and Beirut in 1912. But among licensed *wakils* in Palestine and elsewhere in the Fertile Crescent, those with formal legal training remained a scant minority until the end of the Ottoman Empire.

The Mandate Legal System

Directly prior to the establishment of British rule in Palestine, the region was divided administratively into the *sanjaqs* of Jerusalem, Acre, and Nablus, each of which was further subdivided into judicial districts, or *qazas*, which totaled thirteen.[13] In each *qaza* sat a *nizamiyeh* court of first instance constituted of three judges, typically one professional serving as the president and two lay assessors appointed from among the local notables. Each *sanjaq* also had a five-member court of appeals. Numerous magistrates presided in lower-level courts distributed in the smaller towns.

British rule was established in Palestine in 1917, when troops led by General George Allenby advanced from Egypt to oust Turkish forces from the region. In 1920, after several years of military administration, Palestine was assigned to Great Britain as a Mandate under the League of Nations in the postwar conference in San Remo.[14]

Among the first of the new Mandatory government's actions was the simplification of the rather cumbersome administrative and judicial structures it inherited from the Turks. The country was first divided into seven districts, which were further divided into subdistricts. In 1922, these were amalgamated into four districts, still subdivided into smaller units.

The British preserved the basic three-tiered judicial system originally established with the *nizamiyeh* courts in the nineteenth century; however, they reduced the number of courts and administrative districts. Magistrate courts, exercising jurisdiction over minor criminal and civil cases and actions for recovery of possession of real property, were maintained in each subdistrict. Larger towns such as Jerusalem, Jaffa, and Haifa had two such courts. District courts composed of a British president and two local judges and exercising jurisdiction over most civil and criminal cases not cognizable in a magistrate court existed for each of four judicial districts. District court members went on circuit, hearing cases on alternate days in the different subdistricts within their jurisdiction. Arabic was usually the language of the magistrate courts. In designated trilingual areas (such as Jerusalem, Jaffa, and Haifa), official documents and oral pleadings could be in Arabic, Hebrew, or English, each of which was designated an official language.

A Supreme Court was formed of two British judges and four local judges: two Muslims, one Christian, and one Jew. The court sat in Jerusalem, both as a court of appeals to review the decisions of the lower courts and as a high court holding original jurisdiction to hear complaints against allegedly illegal or unjust actions by government officials. British justices of the Supreme Court formed courts of criminal assize when sitting with district courts to hear criminal cases bearing the death penalty. The civil court system was rounded out by special land courts set up in Jerusalem and Jaffa to adjudicate disputes over ownership of immovable property, and by tribal courts in the south, which tried minor disputes in accordance with "customary law."[15]

In the realm of substantive law, the British began by maintaining the corpus of Ottoman legislation previously in force in the region, with the proviso that the English common law and the doctrines of equity would be applicable in the absence of prior statutes. But the Mandate administration used its charter to assume full legislative authority. This authority was progressively exercised to supplement and repeal many Ottoman laws, replacing them with statutes based on British models. A number of new proclamations were issued in the areas of torts, corporate and commercial law, and labor law, and an entirely new criminal code was promulgated. Both criminal and civil procedural law were altered to conform to their English counterparts. British administrators declined to institute the jury system in Palestine, in view of the already high levels of communal tensions that had arisen between Palestinian Arabs and immigrant Jews.[16]

The Ottoman system of religious courts survived relatively intact, as the fourteen *shariʿa* courts in Palestine continued to function. But the last vestige of their jurisdiction over non-Muslim citizens was eliminated and vested in either Christian ecclesiastical or Jewish rabbinical courts or directly in the civil courts.

A mere recounting of the structure of the civil court system under the Mandate fails to convey the impact it exerted on local society. As elsewhere in the empire, British colonial legal institutions in Palestine were rich with decorum.[17] Judges, either British or Palestinian, presided in robes and wigs, enforcing an atmosphere of great solemnity. Local advocates were likewise obligated to wear robes in court. Judicial salaries were very high and served as a concrete index of the social value accorded the bench by the British administration.[18] Many of my informants who had practiced during the Mandate years, all of them strong nationalists, spoke glowingly of the British-supervised legal system:

> The one good thing the British gave us was a strong court system. These were *real* courts—you had a sense of the majesty of the law when you entered them. Judges and lawyers treated each other with respect, which was not a personal respect, but which came from an appreciation of the nobility and impor-

tance of their respective professions. And it wasn't just a matter of appearances—we saw for the first time what it was like to live under the rule of law. The idea that a judge could issue a decision against the government, and that administrative officials would then honor the decision, and not simply flout it—this was totally new to us.[19]

In the case of Palestine, of course, British colonial policy was guided by a stronger-than-normal didactic aim. The League of Nations' mandate system was predicated on the notion that the mandatory powers had been entrusted with a temporary responsibility of tutelage intended to prepare the subject populations for self-government. Thus, by the terms of the Mandate, the British were charged with a legal obligation to foster the development of local administrative and political institutions, among them the judicial system.[20]

This obligation doubtless provided much of the impetus for the foundation of what became known as the "Jerusalem Law Classes." This was essentially a law school for training administrative employees, especially those of the Judicial Department, and local advocates.[21] The Jerusalem Law Classes were organized under the auspices of Englishman Norman Bentwich, who in a variety of official capacities functioned as the highest legal officer in Palestine in the twenties. The classes were directed by Francis Goadby, fresh from a similar post in the Royal School of Law in Cairo. He was supervised by a Law Council, which included justices of the Supreme Court, the attorney general, and other administrative officials.

The classes opened in 1920 with some forty-five students, approximately equal numbers of whom were Arabs and Jews. Admission was originally conditioned on passage of a special examination that tested proficiency in English and general knowledge of history, geography, arithmetic, and other topics. The majority of students were of the "internal" category; that is, they resided in Jerusalem. Government employees outside of Jerusalem were permitted to enroll as "external" students, however, and received mimeographed notes of lectures and came to Jerusalem periodically to sit for exams.

Until 1924, the Law Classes offered a three-year course of study covering the Ottoman Majalla and Land Law, general areas of civil and criminal law and procedure, *shariʿa* and rabbinical law, and political science.[22] Classes were held in the evening to permit attendance by government employees. Most lecturers were drawn from the local judiciary or Judicial Department, or were distinguished members of the legal profession. After 1924, the curriculum was gradually expanded and a fourth year required; before the end of the Mandate, an elective fifth year was added. Graduates of the four-year program were granted a Certificate and normally entered the civil service; fifth-year graduates were granted an additional Diploma and typically engaged in private law practice.

Class sizes grew quickly until yearly admissions numbered approximately 120. Applications for the Law Classes soon outstripped capacity, a reflection both of the prestige of the degree and of the lack of alternatives for higher education in Palestine.[23] Administrators gradually took steps to restrict admissions. After 1926, the special entrance examination was abolished in favor of a requirement that applicants hold the Palestine Matriculation, a secondary school certificate difficult to earn, given the underdevelopment of the educational system at the time. In 1929, the admission of external students was vastly reduced. By the mid-thirties, the English proficiency examination was made competitive, to facilitate further screening of applicants. Tuition fees for the Law Classes also proved prohibitive for many citizens.

Needless to say, these obstacles exerted different effects on different segments of the Palestinian Arab population. Sons of wealthy Muslim notable families formed a high proportion of the five hundred or so Arabs who graduated from the Law Classes in the Mandate years.[24] Christians were also disproportionately represented among the graduates, advantaged as they were by the proximity of their communities to Jerusalem and by access to education in private denominational schools run by foreign missionaries. Self-perceived religious-cultural proximity between themselves and the British during this period encouraged Palestinian Christians to associate themselves closely with the administration and positioned them to advance in the legal profession in its formative stage.

The Legal Profession under the Mandate

For all intents and purposes, the legal profession functioned without effective government regulation until the end of the Ottoman period. This situation changed quickly under British administration. The Advocates Ordinance was passed in 1922, requiring lawyers appearing before the civil courts to register with the Law Council.[25] Eighty-three advocates from the Ottoman period were authorized to continue practicing, but admission from that point onward required proficiency in two of the three official languages (Arabic, Hebrew, and English), as determined by an exam, and either a Certificate from the Jerusalem Law Classes or a law degree from a recognized foreign institution, and passage of the Foreign Advocates Examination.[26] A two-year *estage*, or period of apprenticeship with a licensed attorney, was also required of all new entrants to the profession.

Exclusivity of access to the legal profession and the respect accorded it by the Mandate administration combined to elevate its image in the eye of the Palestinian public. The number of practitioners from notable families attested to the worthiness of the field of law and bestowed on the profession the already high social standing of its members. Lawyers such as ʿAwni ʿAbd al-Hadi, Musa ʿAlami, and ʿAbd al-Latif Salah were among the most prominent civic personalities in the Palestinian community during the Mandate years.

Many lawyers were involved in political activities, thus solidifying a connection between law and politics and surrounding the profession with the semisacred aura of nationalist values. ʿAbd al-Hadi, for example, founded the pan-Arab Istiqlal (Independence) party in 1932, and served as its representative on the Arab Higher Committee until his exile in 1937 by the British.[27] Indeed, lawyers had the highest representation of any profession on the Arab Higher Committee for the duration of its existence.[28] In the words of one observer:

> Upper class families educated their children in law in order to protect their families' businesses and interests and to represent them in the political domain after graduation. The high representation of the law-educated in the Arab leadership bears witness to the relatively high esteem in which lawyers were held in the Arab society of Palestine. Lawyers were seen by the people as men having access to political and social power. Many ambitious young men had sought social advancement and recognition through the legal profession. In other words, the legal profession was a springboard to political prominence.[29]

Jewish lawyers in Palestine had, since the early days of the Mandate, organized themselves in voluntary local bar associations in Jerusalem, Tel Aviv, and Haifa and in 1928 had formed the country-wide Palestine Jewish Bar Association (PJBA).[30] The PJBA addressed itself to nonpolitical concerns, such as defending the professional against the trespasses of "petition writers" and accountants and establishing and enforcing a schedule of minimum fees. It also involved itself in political matters, once prohibiting its members from addressing any court in English and refusing to accept documents except in Hebrew, to protest legislation judged to be unfavorable to Jewish community interests. The PJBA also protested bitterly against the Defence Emergency Regulations, enacted by the British to aid in suppressing the Zionist paramilitary organizations that became active in the last years of the Mandate.[31]

Probably spurred by the example of the Palestine Jewish Bar Association, Palestinian lawyers began belatedly to organize regional Arab Bar Associations in Jaffa, Jerusalem, and Haifa, which then united in a single ABA in a meeting in Ramallah in 1945.[32] There is little evidence that the association ever undertook any substantive activities.[33] The ABA did campaign fairly vigorously for legislation granting it legal status, making membership compulsory, and giving it disciplinary powers over its members.

In fact, while the British recognized both the Jewish and Arab bar associations informally, they balked at the prospect of vesting either with disciplinary powers, which were being exercised by the Law Council, or at strengthening their institutional power. Draft ordinances from the Jewish and Arab groups were entertained by British administrators in the late forties, but pretexts were always found for declining to enact them.[34] The underlying concern of the British was that official bar associations would become vehicles for political expression all the more effective for the legal powers they wielded. Administrators succeeded in dodging the issue until the end of the Mandate, so the birth of formal professional associations had to await the establishment of Israel, on one hand, and the incorporation of the West Bank into Jordan, on the other.

In retrospect, the Mandate period would seem to have marked the apogee of the social and political power of lawyers in Palestinian Arab society. Concentrated in the major cities of Jaffa, Haifa, and Jerusalem, lawyers commanded both substantial income and a central position in the life of the community.[35] From their vantage point at the time, probably little hinted that things might ever be different. Today, memories and anecdotes from this "golden age" plague West Bank lawyers, sharpening their consciousness of the distance of their collective fall.

The Era of Jordanian Rule

Jordan gained control of the West Bank during the hostilities of 1948 and annexed the region shortly thereafter. With this act, King Abdullah of Jordan joined a more urban, educated, and organized Palestinian community with a well-defined national consciousness and sense of purpose to a far less sophisticated and developed East Bank community.[36] Moreover, with the exodus of an estimated 450,000 Palestinians from areas formerly in Palestine to refugee camps in both the East and the West banks, the Jordanian regime found itself in control of a population in which Palestinians outnumbered the original inhabitants of the East Bank by a considerable margin.[37]

With little legitimacy in the West Bank, King Abdullah adopted a policy of co-optation of traditional West Bank elites and repression of oppositional tendencies. Members of notable families were courted with government positions or were permitted to mediate between their West Bank clientele and sources of government patronage. As Jerusalem had been the center of nationalist political activity under the Mandate, Amman focused its efforts on winning loyalties in Nablus and Hebron and among followers of the minority Nashashibi faction within the nationalist movement.[38] Palestinian organizations such as the Arab Higher Committee were dissolved, and the Defense Emergency Regulations, still in force from the Mandate years, were used to arrest and jail West Bank political activists.[39]

Administrative arrangements were also manipulated to inhibit the development of a unified West Bank political leadership. The status of Jerusalem as the West Bank administrative center was deliberately downgraded, as all West Bank districts were made directly subordinate to Amman. A system of "equal" representation for the two banks in the Jordanian parliament actually overrepresented the sparsely populated East Bank. Jordanian soldiers were permitted to vote in the district in which they were stationed on election day, which permitted the government to shift votes according to need. Finally, discriminatory economic policies also fostered West Bank dependence on the East Bank.[40]

King Abdullah succeeded in gaining a conditional legitimacy among residents of the West Bank, among whom there was consensus in favor of some Arab rule, and differences only as to its specific form. Conflict between the two banks was also mediated by the ideology of Arab nationalism, which emphasized the common destiny of the Arab countries and advocated their unity in a single nation, and which was at its peak strength in the Arab world in the fifties and sixties. Still, the West Bank was at times a base of strong opposition to the Jordanian regime, as evidenced by public demonstrations in favor of Prime Minister Suleiman Nabulsi in his 1957 confrontation with the monarchy.[41]

Developments in the Palestinian legal profession paralleled social and political trends within the society at large. Some Palestinian lawyers in areas subsumed by the new state of Israel remained there, eventually resuming practice in the Israeli legal system. Others fled to adjacent regions, a few settled in the West Bank, and still more in Amman. The influx of Palestinian lawyers into the Jordanian legal profession apparently provided sufficient momentum to over-come the regime's resistance to the establishment of a bar associa-tion. One was organized soon after the passage of the Law of the Union of Nizami Lawyers (*qanun niqabat al-muhaamiin al-nizami-yiin*) in 1950.[42] Henceforth all lawyers practicing before the secular courts were required to become members of the Jordanian Lawyers Union (JLU).

A West Bank lawyer, 'Abd al-Latif Salah, was elected first *naqib*, or head of the JLU and was re-elected for a second one-year term. Through the 1950s, only one East Banker broke the monopoly held by West Bank lawyers over the office and that for a single one-year period.[43] Agitation by West Bank members resulted in the opening of union branch offices in Jerusalem and Nablus in 1964. In both banks, the JLU became a stronghold of the radical nationalist Ba'th party (and remains so today in the East Bank), and clashes with gov-ernment officials were frequent. West Bank lawyers, among them some of the most prominent, were also active in the National Front, an oppositional group associated with the Communist party, and sev-eral earned prison terms and temporary exile for their involvement.

Initially, Jordan maintained the court system and laws in force in the West Bank at the time of its annexation. But a program to unify the two banks legally was begun in the 1950s under a special Judicial Council. The unification, for the most part, took the form of repeal-ing the British-modeled Palestinian statutes in favor of new codes that owed more to Ottoman and civil law traditions. The Court Es-tablishment Law of 1951 created the Jordanian court of cassation (or appeals court) and High Court, hence constituting in essential form the three-tiered system familiar in Palestine for the whole of the kingdom.[44]

Despite what Palestinian lawyers viewed as "regressions" in sub-stantive law,[45] and the "backwardness" of Jordanian courts, they flourished in Jordan no less as practitioners than as union poli-ticians. With superior training and a strong sense of professional pride instilled during the Mandate years, Palestinian lawyers rapidly rose to the forefront of the profession. The condescension with which they regarded East Bank jurists was palpable in the comments of one informant whose practice straddled the periods of British and Jordanian rule:

> In the Mandate period, there was a very advanced legal system. The Jordanians came along, with a very, very primitive system of law. They were ignorant of the rule of law, and generally not legally oriented. I never really enjoyed going to court in Jordan,

although I often traveled to plead before the court of cassation in Amman. But the judges were naïve and good-hearted and eventually began to understand that the power of the government was not absolute. The lawyers there were even worse— hardly more than petition writers. Do you know that it was *us* [Palestinian lawyers] who taught them to keep case files? They didn't even keep case files before we showed up!

Their own high level of self-esteem was apparently matched by the esteem in which others held them. Toward the end of the Jordanian era, Palestinian lawyers, either in the West Bank or relocated in Amman, handled the lion's share of major cases for clients on both banks.

Conclusions

The modern legal profession in Palestine is historically tied to the increase in bureaucratic complexity begun in the late Ottoman period and manifested in the establishment of the *nizamiyeh* court system and the reception of massive bodies of European law. The spread of private property, which led to more numerous transactions and disputes involving land, and the emergence of more elaborate forms of economic organization were an integral part, indeed a primary aim, of the reforms and greatly stimulated the demand for legal services. The foundation of the modern profession was thus one dimension of the general imposition of Western law and legal institutions initiated by the Ottoman Empire's Westernizing leadership.

These developments were only accentuated under the British administration, which also solidified the position of the legal profession through its careful fostering of legal institutions and their ideological rationale, the concept of the rule of law. This was done through conduct, in the genuine respect accorded to judges, attorneys, and the legal system as a whole, and by indoctrinating Palestinian jurists through the Jerusalem Law Classes. The momentum established during the Mandate period continued into the era of Jordanian rule and permitted Palestinian lawyers to weather changes in their legal and political environment, and even to emerge as leaders in the profession.

The economic prosperity and high social status of the legal profession during the periods of British and Jordanian rule were not so much illusory as tenuously founded. By virtue of the origins and mode of development of the institutions that constitute their very raison d'être, lawyers have typically stood on one side of a series of overlapping oppositions that run through the social history of the region: local authority versus central state authority; Islam versus "Westernization" and secularism; indigenous clientelism versus purportedly "rational" bureaucracy; and uneducated, rural, lower social stratum versus formally educated, urban, upper and middle strata.

As an imposed profession, a creature essentially of foreign state authority wielded first by the Westernizing Ottoman Empire and second by the British colonial administration, the legal profession has shallow roots in Palestinian civil society. It has therefore remained vulnerable to the will of the state, or at least to that of a strong state. Whereas the Mandatory government was strong, it saw fit to promote the profession. The Jordanian regime, less powerful, was forced to accommodate it, sometimes begrudgingly. The Israeli military government, for a variety of reasons, has not been so constrained. This vulnerability on the part of the legal profession has been a key factor in the decline it has suffered during the period of Israeli occupation.

It is crucial to recognize that underlying mandatory government policy toward the legal profession was a specific aim to develop a political and administrative cadre for an independent Palestinian state. For the British, a legally trained corps of civil servants was the sine qua non of proper and orderly government, and they set about creating such a body with vigor and purpose. As will be seen subsequently, this feature of Mandatory rule distinguishes it sharply from the later Israeli military government, the policies of which are informed to a great extent by precisely the opposite aim: to prevent the emergence of any cadre capable of leading a Palestinian state.

The establishment of the profession through a process of imposition also explains the dissonance between the ideological and cultural orientations of lawyers and the beliefs and values of indigenous Palestinian society. The next chapter surveys some characteristics of West Bank society and culture and examines the ways in which they complicate the legal profession's task of collective self-legitimation.

3. The Social and Cultural Context

The contemporary West Bank legal profession has been forced to function in a social and cultural context lacking many of the institutional and ideological props that supported the development of the profession in other societies.[1] Outside the limited segment of the town-based population, which shares their educational experience and outlook, legal practitioners frequently encounter attitudes and behavior that baffle and sometimes infuriate them. Viewed from the perspective of many of their clients, the lawyers, with their inevitably Western-style dress, technical language, and often aloof manner, simply add to the sense of alienation, powerlessness, and confusion that the courts and the law inspire.

The dissonance between indigenous beliefs and values and the ways and ideology of the lawyers has significantly complicated that group's task of collective self-legitimation.[2] In fact, it impedes recognition of the value of legal services. This chapter will discuss those aspects of local culture and society that most impinge on the work of lawyers and review alternatives to which citizens may resort in the event of dispute or need for intermediation with state authority.

Attitudes toward State Authority

West Bank Palestinians have never experienced anything but foreign rule. Loyalties thus have been affixed to family, village, and nation—but never to state as such.[3] Historically, the most direct local interactions with state authority have been through tax collectors and military personnel, the latter often seeking unwilling conscripts from the villages. The predominant and lasting image of the state, moreover, is that of a power virtually unchecked, whether by law or by forces in civil society. In the face of this, Palestinians have tended to adopt strategies of instrumentalism and avoidance in coping with government authority.[4]

Undercurrents of ambivalence toward the state are sometimes evident in interactions between citizens and state bureaucrats. The latter, at least if of high rank, are imperious, impatient, and deliberately inaccessible. Fear and obsequiousness mark the comportment of a citizen in the presence of a government official, but these transform instantly into contempt in the wake of the official's departure.

The circumstances of Israeli occupation have, in many respects, sustained these tendencies and even strengthened them. The age-old practice of tax evasion is now pursued with a nationalist fervor; many times, I faced the rhetorical question, "Should we let them rob us to better pay for the slaughter of our relatives in Lebanon? or the settlement of our lands here in the West Bank?" There are ever-new reasons for avoiding formal authority; a number of lawyers mentioned, for example, that since 1967, numerous disputes over land trespasses have not reached the courts. Lawyers referred to a military order by which land shares inherited by Palestinians categorized as "absentees" during the 1967 war would revert to the control of the military government's custodian for absentee property. Heirs with an absentee sibling feared that government discovery of their situation would lead to the seizure of that sibling's share and so had no recourse to formal authority in the event of trespass.

Law in Palestinian Culture

Disputes are affairs of great interest in Palestinian communities. In fact, it is typical that many people, even anonymous bystanders, intercede in streetside quarrels and attempt to mediate between the disputants, who themselves seem to welcome a public hearing. Thus what may begin as a private confrontation often rapidly assumes the dimensions of a community event. Gratitude is showered on the mediator who can produce a resolution on the spot and a boost is given to his status in the community. Conflicts that are not immediately resolved become the topics of discussion and speculation. Those with knowledge of the relevant principles of *shariʿa* or *ʿurf* (customary law) hold forth, it being an occasion for public display of religiosity and general wisdom.[5]

Consider the assessment of one lawyer-informant, who sighed to me despairingly:

> Ours is a society that lacks legal culture [*al-hadara al-qanuniya*]. We lawyers may use this phrase—the rule of law [*siyadat al-qanun*]—but I don't know how much it conveys outside of these offices. You see, ours is a simple people, under-

developed, legally speaking. It never occurs to them to do
something properly from the beginning, to come to a lawyer to
get a lease agreement drawn up, for example. Instead, they go
to the bookstore and buy a form for a few piastres. They fill it
out themselves—incorrectly, of course, since they're ignorant
of the laws. Only when they have a problem, and a lot of
money is suddenly at stake, do they show up in my office.
Then I have to listen to their insults for telling them their
lease is unenforceable.

What the juxtaposition of the lawyer's view and the prior description suggests, of course, is that the public's intense interest in disputation does not translate into awareness and involvement in the
law of the lawyers and the state. State law, or *qanun*, especially concerning civil matters, is not a general reference point that serves to
orient and guide normal transactions among individuals. The resort
to lawyers for legal planning, or the prospective structuring of relations, for example, is confined to the minute segment of the West
Bank population engaged in relatively sophisticated commercial
transactions. Even this, according to lawyers, has been a fairly recent development.[6]
The notion of the constraint of state power by law, an essential
feature of the ideology of the rule of law, claims adherents among
educated portions of the population, but is totally alien to the majority. This was illustrated by a conversation I witnessed between Riad,
a Palestinian agricultural economist educated at the American University of Beirut, and Abu Munif, a Palestinian farmer who had received a notice for the expropriation of part of his land just one day
prior to our visit to his home:[7]

> **Riad:** When did you get the expropriation notice?
> **Abu Munif:** The *mukhtar* [petty village official] brought it to
> me yesterday.
> **R:** Are you going to appeal it?
> **AM:** Well . . . I, don't know . . . what's the use? They'll take
> it anyway.
> **R:** Abu Munif! You can't think like that! [Abu Munif is si-
> lent, fidgeting with the corner of his headdress]. Abu Munif!
> We can't give up our land to the military government without
> a fight! Don't you know that the courts stop them sometimes
> and give lands back to their owners?
> **AM:** God knows, I'm just a *fellah* [peasant].
> **R:** Are you concerned about the cost?

AM: Well . . . lawyers and courts and these things are expensive.

R: But don't you know of the legal aid center in Jerusalem [run by the American Friends Service Committee; see chapter 6, note 17]? They give money to people with cases like yours. You know where it is, don't you?

AM: Yes, I've been there once.

R: Abu Munif, promise me that you'll go to the center and see a lawyer tomorrow. [Abu Munif shifts his feet, looks away]. You've been to see Darwish [a prominent Jerusalem lawyer] before, haven't you?

AM: Yes.

R: Abu Munif! You must promise me you'll go tomorrow!

AM: (weakly) All right . . . I guess I can go see Darwish Bek tomorrow. [*bek* was a Turkish honorific title and is still used to signal deference to notables]. (Taking a gulp of coffee, and more resolutely) Thank you, Riad Bek, may God protect you.

Abu Munif's distrust of state authority and resignation to its dictates were patent in this exchange.[8]

Corruption and *Wasta*

"Corruption" for the purposes of this discussion may be defined as the improper exploitation of official capacity for personal gain.[9] It is a phenomenon specific to societies in which "office" and "persons" are well differentiated and in which the obligations of office are, at some junctures, contradictory to or at least limiting of personal interests. The term in Arabic for corruption is *fasaad*, and at the formal level, everyone knows that *fasaad* is "bad" and to engage in it is "wrong." But what is stated publicly and explicitly is denied implicitly by certain aspects of indigenous tradition.[10]

Bribery is the most obvious form of corruption. Attitudes toward bribery were described by an ethnographer of a West Bank village during the Jordanian period:

> The belief that most government officials are corrupt had led the villagers to offer bribes whenever they ask for a favor. Their willingness to offer bribes has encouraged even the most insignificant officials, including doorkeepers in government buildings, to ask for bribes openly. The villagers tolerate such corruption, and indeed, seem to envy those who are in a position to receive these bribes. They speak in open envy of the

wealth acquired by bribery and even encourage their children and friends to enter government service because they believe it is a way to get rich quickly.[11]

The institution of *wasta*, or intermediation, may be seen as a milder but even more ubiquitous variant of corruption. It too is formally regarded as "improper," especially by lawyers and other educated members of the society, but far less so than bribery.[12] Even among the educated, however, *wasta* is widely practiced, and those who have successfully manipulated it to their advantage will boast of it, however subtly. Typically, it takes the form of intercession by an influential member of the community on behalf of a less influential one seeking a benefit or favor from some state agency. As we have seen, it was a fundament of Jordanian policy to manage its relationship with the West Bank through manipulation of channels of intermediation, exchanging favors for loyalty through *wasta*.

There is much evidence that West Bank Palestinians continue to conceive of interactions with formal authority within the framework of the same *wasta* mentality. Many informants, like the following, complained, "Clients always think that everything can be done by *wasta*, even when I explain patiently to them that there are *laws* that have to be followed. It's like they don't even hear me— they sit there, and then when they get up to leave, they kind of wink and ask me just to try to 'fix' things." Some lawyers, especially of the younger generation, described solicitation of this kind as demeaning and offensive to their professional pride. Others, however, appear to present themselves to clients deliberately as *wastas*. From the perspective of the public, then, it is not always possible to distinguish between lawyers qua lawyers and lawyers qua *wastas*.[13]

It was striking in this light that Abu Munif referred to his lawyer, Darwish—perhaps one of the best-trained lawyers in Jerusalem, with a strong sense of professionalism and critical of the *wasta* approach—as "*bek*," strongly evocative of the style of traditional patron-client interactions.

Corruption and *wasta*, no matter the actors involved, are powerful solvents to the legal profession's claims to legitimacy based on mastery of technical expertise. While there may be an art to the game of bribery and manipulation of ties to authority, lawyers have no monopoly or even advantage in its exercise. Corruption and *wasta*, hence, constitute alternative systems of intermediation—mildly illicit and disapproved of in a formal sense, but no less functional for that fact—which often yield stronger guarantees of satisfaction than the legal routes proffered by the lawyers. Meanwhile, in West Bank society and, one might surmise, elsewhere, predictability of outcome heavily influences choices between alternate modes of dispute processing and intermediation.[14]

Negotiability in Everyday Life

The institution of *wasta* can be seen as a particular manifestation of a broader reality in Palestinian society, which may be described with only slight exaggeration as the "infinite negotiability" of all social transactions.[15] The terms of these transactions are seldom fixed by general rules. For example, West Bank butchers post a single price for a kilo of meat, uniform for all cuts and qualities. The value customers actually receive will vary according to their relationship with the butcher (whether friends or relatives or regular customers), their vigilance against cheating, and their willingness to protest aggressively if given a cut containing large proportions of bone and fat.[16]

The practice of *wasta* is one way in which the principles of negotiability and particularism are applied in the specific realm of relations between citizens and the state. Needless to say, this bears important implications for the manner of citizens' responses to state authority. For members of society with access to *wasta*, laws function less as the real guidelines to social action than as cues to the opening bargaining position of the government. In fact, transactions with state authority often assume the form of negotiations without the resort to *wasta* in its classic form. Tax assessments, for example, are often fixed in negotiations between an official and a person's accountant; formal regulations serve only as the baseline of discussion.[17]

Negotiability is not simply the trademark of transactions within traditional sectors of the population. According to some West Bank entrepreneurs with whom I spoke, business relationships are typically characterized by great fluidity. Contracts do little more than bind parties to a relationship, and this only lightly; their detailed terms undergo constant revision and renegotiation throughout the life of the contract.[18]

These beliefs and practices impinge on the functioning of the legal profession in a number of ways. Many lawyers complained of a maddeningly cavalier attitude among clients toward formal requirements and documents.[19] More important, however, is the way in which they subvert the profession's claims to relevance and competence. After all, if the formal laws and regulations are not the operative principles of much of social interaction, either among citizens or between citizens and the state, then expertise in them is an instrument of marginal utility, and the lawyers who monopolize those rules are little more than masters of a fool's game.

Honor

Palestinian society participates in the ethos of honor and feuding common to a number of circum-Mediterranean societies.[20] Honor (*ʿarad*, from the classical Arabic *ʿird*) is an attribute of collectivities, especially families and clans (*hamayil*), and of the individuals who constitute them. It is linked to social hierarchy: members of higher-status families and clans have more "honor" than those of lower status. But every individual is vested with an initial minimum increment of honor, which may be increased or diminished by the person's deeds. Such deeds strongly reflect on the honor of the collectivity, although appropriate actions can sometimes insulate the group from the errant behavior of a member.

Women, in particular, are repositories of family honor; men are charged with protecting them against offense and, in the event of the latter, with avenging the group's honor against the offender. In common parlance, a *qadiyat ʿarad*, or "case of honor," is synonymous with a sexual assault against a woman. But an offense against any individual, male or female, is also seen as an offense against his or her family or clan. A transgression of sufficient gravity—the rape of a woman or the murder of a man, for example—triggers a period in which members of the aggrieved's family may justifiably take vengeance against any member of the offender's family.[21]

Dissonance between the ethos of honor and its surrounding customs, on one hand, and the ideology and practices of the formal court system, on the other, is manifested in a number of circumstances. The formal court system conceives of offenses primarily in their material dimension, and its procedures assume a rational plaintiff who will take initiative to maximize a material or economic interest. In the ethos of honor, damage to the body or property, whether intentional or accidental, is an offense against the *person*, the proprietor, so to speak, of either the body or the property, in other words, against his or her honor. Moreover, the indigenous system contemplates an offended party who will act in the first place to defend his or her honor. Of course, the very essence of honor is that it is of a different order of value than the material. Indeed, one's honor is best displayed precisely when it is maintained in conflict with a material interest. An example serves to illustrate the complications that arise from the incongruity between this system of thought and that which rationalizes the formal court system.[22]

Abu Munif lived with his immediate family next to the Israeli settlement, Ofra, northeast of Jerusalem. One morning he awoke to discover that some twenty olive trees and sixty grapevines had been cut down or uprooted. Several days later, armed settlers appeared with a bulldozer, preparing to cut an access road to the settlement through his land. He and his son were knocked down in the scuffle that ensued, but he succeeded in staving off the settlers temporarily, and at the cost of only a few bruises and scratches. On the advice of Riad, the agricultural specialist who worked in the area, Abu Munif hired Darwish, a prominent lawyer. Darwish astutely involved the press in the case and eventually won an order from the military government halting the settlers' spontaneous act of expropriation. Complaints to the police, however, resulted in no arrests of the settlers.

In the course of our conversation, I queried Abu Munif on the option of filing a civil suit against the settlers in a local West Bank court to seek monetary compensation for the very considerable economic damages he had suffered. At first he seemed not to be aware that such a course of action existed. As Riad and I explained it further, however, it became clear that whether or not he *had* considered it before, he would not hear of it now. He appeared proud not to have sought monetary compensation.

Several principles are worth noting here. First, in the logic of the honor system, willingness to enter into procedures leading to a resolution assumes social proximity and implies an affirmation of the equivalence of the parties to the dispute.[23] It is much more honorable to sustain a loss of some kind than to enter into procedures with a party of inferior status, which would convey the social meaning of granting one's status to the other and assuming the other's status for oneself. By this reasoning, Abu Munif fared best by refusing flatly to enter into any dealings with the Israeli settlers, who are feared and despised by West Bank Palestinians.

Second, Abu Munif followed the expected route of an aggrieved party by withdrawing, "sitting fast" on his honor, one might say. In the system of honor, it is for the offending party or members of his or her family—for it is they who are fair game for vengeance until they initiate a process of resolution—or for the "good citizens" of the community, anxious to restore its harmony—but *not* for the offended party—to sue for peace. This, of course, is precisely the opposite of the practice in the formal court system, where it is the duty of the damaged party to prosecute the claim.

There is also a strong sense that right needs no justification or defense, that justice is self-evident. To take affirmative action to defend oneself is thus to betray a lack of confidence in the righteousness of one's position.[24] Finally, for Abu Munif to have proceeded with a civil claim for monetary damages would have signaled that an economic value was all that was at stake, that he had no honor, or that it could be purchased.[25]

The formal court system fails to recognize some transgressions against honor—for example, a sexual innuendo uttered to a woman constitutes a serious offense to honor, but is not cognizable in the civil courts—and fails to recognize important dimensions of cases that are otherwise formally cognizable. It also calls on individuals to act in ways that contradict their sense of propriety and dignity. Finally, the social unit with which the formal courts transact is the individual, whereas the true unit of conflict, especially in the state of feud, is a collectivity, the family or the clan. "People don't say *'fulaan'* (so-and-so) committed a crime; they say *'ibn fulaan'* (son of so-and-so)," one informant apprised me.

This does not mean that Palestinians are absolutely deterred from bringing actions in the civil courts. They do so, but perhaps with vague discomfort and somewhat less frequency than they might but for the dissonance between indigenous values and a formal court system of alien design. Of course, all of these cultural restraints are weaker among the urban-based populations, where the ethos of honor is subdued.

But its echoes may occasionally be sensed even in the conduct of the most educated and apparently Westernized members of the society. Notions of honor account for much seemingly irrational behavior on the part of clients, behavior that is often thoroughly confounding to lawyers. And yet these notions infuse even some of the lawyers' actions as well, as shall be seen in coming chapters.

Tribal Adjudication

In light of the uneasy fit between the system of honor and that of the government courts, it should not be surprising that informal modes of dispute processing coexist with the formal system.[26] One of the most important of these modes is the complex of institutions and customs grouped roughly under the rubric of *al-qada' al-'asha'iri*, or "tribal adjudication."[27] In fact, this term seems to apply to a number of somewhat distinct practices, sometimes described as "levels."[28] There is merit in a digression of some length to describe tribal adjudication, for a glimpse of local beliefs and practices and a sense of the atmosphere surrounding them will greatly sharpen the reader's awareness of their differences with the ideology, procedures, and ambience of the civil courts.

The most widespread type of tribal adjudication is also the least formal, in the sense that it involves no true specialists or distinct body of rules and customs. Two shop owners in the *souq*, or indigenous market, who become embroiled in a minor commercial dispute, for example, will repair to a respected, often elderly, member of the local merchant community. He will act as an ad hoc *qadi ʿashaʾiri* (tribal judge) and mediate a resolution between them based on a mix of trade customs, possibly augmented by a smattering of legal knowledge, common sense, and general notion of justice. Tribal judges may handle a wide range of ordinary matters, including disputes over land or other property, altercations, and others.

Those who prove adept at this gradually become identified for their skills, and peers begin to resort to them regularly. Their services are never more than occasional, and their only compensation is the boost to their status delivered by their fellows' tacit recognition of their wisdom.[29] People in this category in the West Bank apparently number in the hundreds.

A second level is that presided over by a specialist termed the *"manqaʿ al-damm."*[30] Perhaps twenty or so of these "blood judges" preside in the West Bank. Although they may treat less serious cases, and do so on a routine basis, they are distinguished from the tribal judges by their competence to deal with cases of death, whether by murder or accident. The principles they apply are drawn from *ʿurf*, customary law, which the judges themselves often claim to be applications of the *shariʿa*, or Islamic law.[31] One of their principal functions is to determine the amount of the *diya*, or "blood money," that the family of the victim receives from the family of the perpetrator.

The third and "highest" level is the domain of the *manshad* (roughly translated, the "one who is implored"), who may deal with all manner of disputes, but is uniquely qualified to view cases of *ʿarad*—offenses against the chastity and purity of women. I was told that compensation in *ʿarad* cases routinely runs into thousands of dinars. The jurisprudence of the *manshad* is likewise the *ʿurf*, which is also carefully represented as consistent if not identical with *shariʿa*.[32] Only three of these highest judges currently operate in the West Bank.[33]

In all but the simplest and least weighty cases (which are sometimes resolved on the spot by the *qadi ʿashaʾiri*), procedures unfold in stages. In the immediate aftermath of a killing, for example, the family of the perpetrator seeks out a judge of sufficient caliber and arranges payment to the victim's family for the ʿatweh, or truce, which is initially for 3 1/3 days.[34] The ʿatweh suspends the right of vengeance held by the victim's family and may be renewed periodically while attempts for a settlement are being made.

The next step is the organization of the *jaha wa al-wajaha* (or simply *jaha*), an assemblage of the *wujuh*, or notables and family heads of the entire town or area. The group, which may include up to fifty cars and several hundred participants, travels in procession to the home of the victim's family. On arrival at the victim's home, where members of his ʿashira, or tribe, have assembled, a feast is prepared using nothing but food and implements brought by the *jaha*. Following the feast, what is essentially a bargaining session ensues, orchestrated by the judge, with the object of reaching a *sulh*, or settlement. All of this is done with great ceremony and numerous ritual pronouncements. One session was described to me by the presiding blood judge as follows:

> After the feast, I got up and made a sort of general introduction, stating that the presence of all the people there demonstrated their honor and love of peace, and reminding them with a *sura* from the Qurʾan that the Prophet cherished forgiveness. Next, representatives of the families of the victim and the perpetrator got up and in turn sang the praises of the other side, mentioning anecdotes that testified to the other's honor. Finally, the *sahib al-damm* [possessor of the blood claim], the father of the murdered boy, got up and asked for compensation of twenty thousand JD. Of course, this is far more than he expected—the point is to humiliate the other family by forcing them to "beg" for reductions. They started out asking a reduction "for God's sake," so I knocked off two thousand. Then they asked "for Muhammad's and Jesus's sake" [one party to this dispute was Christian]. I kidded them—"I already gave you the father, what more do you want with the son?" But I knocked off another one thousand. Then they asked "for King Hussein's sake," and then for the sake of this great *jaha*, and so on, until a settlement was finally reached at thirty-five hundred JD.

Other sanctions may be imposed along with the imposition of the blood money requirement, including the exile of members of the offenders' families from their village and the closing of their business for months. Adherence to the judgment is guaranteed by the investiture of the entire process with the honor of its participants, and sometimes by the pledge of a specific *kafil*, or guarantor, for a party.

Unless an agreement is reached during the initial period of the *'atweh*, the judge who conducts these ceremonies is entitled to a payment called the *rizqa*, paid by the party at fault. The more esteemed judges often return the proffered amount, vastly contributing to their honor by doing so. The resolution is often capped off with publication of the *sulh* in the local Arabic newspapers. On rare occasions, parties are unable to reach a settlement, in which case the *qadi 'asha'iri* is entitled to impose an authoritative judgment.

Interaction with the Formal Court System

The system of tribal adjudication is not closed, but, rather, functions at a kind of wary distance from the formal court system. Although some of the cases that are processed in it are not cognizable in the civil courts (such as, for example, a verbal insult to a woman), most, in fact, are, and in criminal cases, in which the state has acted to prosecute an offender, the two systems frequently function in parallel. This occurs in some civil cases as well: since the institution of no-fault insurance in the region in 1976, awards from government courts in cases involving injuries from car accidents are substituted for the *diya*, but all other aspects of the ritual are followed.

It is not unheard of, especially in the Hebron area, for tribal judges to clash with the civil courts and attempt to impose their judgments in cases in progress in the courts. But the judges in the civil courts generally appear to tolerate the competing system, sometimes even consciously accommodating it by delaying actions in a case while awaiting a *sulh*. A provision of Jordanian law permits agreements concluded according to specified standards to be registered as a judgment of the civil court, thereafter enforceable through the Execution Department like any other court judgment.

This provision has led to an interesting and subtle process whereby the laws of the formal court system are infiltrating tribal adjudication, since an incentive has been created for tribal judges to adapt both procedures and substantive judgments to conform with those of the civil courts.[35] One lawyer, from a younger generation of a family that has produced many tribal judges, had been increasingly plied for his opinions on points of secular law by his uncle, a *manshad*:

> You see, Sheikh Zuheir doesn't want to render a judgment different from that of a civil court. The reason for this is that people look to enforcement when deciding where to take their claim. If the court's judgment differed from Sheikh Zuheir's,

then people would go to the court, since Sheikh Zuheir's judgment would be unenforceable, at least through the Execution
Department—which is a distinct advantage, especially in commercial cases, or land cases, in which the element of honor
isn't so strong. On the other hand, if Sheikh Zuheir's is in accord with the law, then he retains the principal advantage of
the 'asha'iri system—speed.

The lawyer's comment hints that, while honor may be the dominant
and explicit value governing the conduct of dispute processing within
Palestinian village society, there are subterranean elements of pragmatic strategizing as well, from both the plaintiff's and the mediator's angles.

Islamic Courts

The jurisdiction of Islamic courts is narrow but exclusive, including
only cases of personal status and inheritance. There is no overlap
with the jurisdiction of any other court. Strictly speaking, then, the
Islamic courts are not alternatives to the civil courts, and the direction of a dispute to one court system or the other is merely a function of its subject matter (fig. 2). However, it is relevant to note the
marked difference in the relative willingness of disputants actually
to take appropriate cases to the respective court systems. This difference was most pronounced among disputants of rural and lower-
class backgrounds, precisely the sector that is least at home in the
civil courts, but that seems not the least hesitant to bring conflicts
before the Islamic qadi.[36] The reasons for this are no doubt diverse,
but among them certainly are the greater moral legitimacy of the Islamic courts within the community and the greater familiarity and
intelligibility of their laws and procedures.[37]

Other Alternatives for Dispute Processing and Intermediation

There are a number of other modes in which Palestinians of the
West Bank process disputes, ranging from the almost-casual to the
semiformal. I experienced the casual end of the scale when I was involved in a minor traffic accident in which my car struck that of a
young Palestinian man. After more than half an hour of wrangling,
he suddenly demanded, "Do you know of any older person here in
the neighborhood?" He was willing to abide by any resolution that
such an older member of the community proposed.

In fact, I knew no such person in the vicinity. Khaled, the young

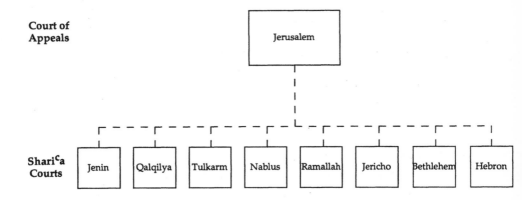

Figure 2. The Islamic Court System in the West Bank

man, did not want to go through the bureaucratic process of filing an insurance claim and instead demanded that I pay for repairs to his car out of pocket. I preferred the formal route, as I was fully covered by insurance. A friend of Khaled's eventually happened by and among us we negotiated an agreement by which I paid for the repairs, to be performed, however, by a friend of mine who was a mechanic.

A number of formal bodies—chambers of commerce, village councils, and others—contain clauses in their charters or internal regulations that authorize them to engage in arbitration or general methods of dispute resolution among their respective constituencies. Trade unions have recourse to several special arbitrators, civil servants who work out of the offices of the Labor Department. In some areas, such as Bethlehem, the unions apparently make regular use of the services of the arbitrator based in that town.

Citizens with some administrative problem or need have recourse to a number of alternatives for intermediation. In the towns, mayors frequently intervene with authorities on behalf of individual constituents in a wide variety of circumstances. In recent years, associations named Village Leagues have been charged by the Israeli authorities with responsibility for the processing of many kinds of licenses and permits.[38] A host of characters whittle away at the low end of the scale of services that might otherwise be performed by lawyers: in rural areas, petty village officials, and sometimes teachers (who are sought out for their literacy), assist citizens in transactions with officialdom by drafting letters, filling out forms, and sometimes conveying them to the proper authority.

Entrances to the town courts are inevitably staffed by a "petition writer" (*katib al-istid'a'at*), an entrepreneur whose sole qualifications are often ownership of a battered table and antique typewriter, minimal literacy, and self-training in the drafting of legal documents and filling out of court forms. Larger courts are often adorned with a coterie of petition writers. Their fees seldom exceed five dinars, and they are the preferred champions of only the pettiest claims and interests.

Public Perceptions of the Legal Profession

One sign of the recent and exogenous origins of the legal profession in the West Bank is that local folk culture preserves no images of it in the form of the parables, maxims, or stereotypes concerning lawyers that are sometimes found in other societies. There appears to be no sense that a particular mode of behavior or speech is specifically "lawyerly," nor any personality type purportedly suiting an individual to law practice. The names of several Jewish Israeli lawyers who have defended many West Bank Palestinian detainees and landowners in the Israeli military courts have become household words in much of the region, but there is little to indicate that the general public otherwise has much consciousness of the legal profession as a distinct group in society.

Some inferences about the public's perception of the legal profession may be derived from the vocational preferences and choices of its individual members. Here one immediately confronts a salient feature of contemporary Palestinian society, that is, its high valorization of university education.[39] Within this generally favorable predisposition toward higher education, one may further discern a clear hierarchy of preferences among fields of study and subsequent vocational practice. The natural sciences and the related professional fields of medicine and engineering rank high; law, commerce, and the social sciences are at the low end of the scale.[40]

This hierarchy is common to the postwar Arab world and is reflected in the differing admissions standards of the various faculties of Arab universities: those of medicine and engineering are especially stringent, while law has become one of the dumping grounds for the educational system's less-qualified students. In addition, law is the only professional degree that may be studied by correspondence through the *intisab*, or external studies system sponsored by a number of universities in the Arab world.[41]

Recent easing of access to legal education has led to the rapid influx of large numbers of individuals of diverse social background—particularly members of the middle class—in the legal profession of the West Bank. Their collective entry has done less to elevate their individual social status than to lower the prestige of the profession as a whole. They have, one might say, conferred their own social position on the profession rather than the reverse.[42] As one eminent lawyer sniffed disdainfully to me, "Now *anyone* can get a law degree." Public perceptions of the profession—of its capabilities, competence, and general social authority—have, in large part, been determined by the social status of its members.

It should be mentioned that the trend toward higher levels of education in West Bank society in the long term favors the consolidation of the social position of the legal profession. But the brain drain characteristic of recent years has done much to deflate the local impact of increasing education. And whether such an environment actually develops is a function of many factors, of which education is only one.[43]

Conclusions

The West Bank legal profession's task of collective self-legitimation, progressing according to an alien ideological and institutional charter, has been hindered by a number of beliefs and customs prevalent in Palestinian society. Indigeneous attitudes toward the state and its law, concepts of honor and ways of defending it, negotiability in transactions among citizens and between them and the state, and alternative modes of dispute processing and of intermediation that are frequently more successful than actions through the formal authorities and sometimes more in accord with local values—all of these factors represent formidable obstacles to the consolidation of the social position of the legal profession. The many respects in which the advent of Israeli occupation only led to an increase in the obstacles faced by the lawyers of the West Bank and to the generation of newer and more daunting obstacles is the topic of the next chapter.

4. Orientalist Despotism

The aim of this chapter is to examine the structure and style of the Israeli military government in the West Bank, to review some of its policies, and to set the political-administrative context within which the local legal profession currently operates. Since its establishment in 1967, the Israeli military government in the West Bank has evinced a dual character. It has demonstrated consistent attention to legality, reflected in the style and form of the foundation of the military government itself, the establishment of a system of military tribunals of various kinds, the subjection of acts of the military officials in the West Bank to review by the Israeli High Court, and a general tendency to seek legal form and justification for administrative actions. This legalistic bent naturally expresses Israeli values and conceptions of democratic government and the rule of law, although they are modified to fit the exceptional circumstances of occupation.

The character of the Israeli military government as perceived by the Palestinian community, however, is strikingly different. Since 1967 the military government has steadily extended and intensified its intervention into the affairs of Palestinian society, subjecting individual West Bank Palestinians to increasing state regulation in almost every aspect of their daily lives. The community experiences the regime as intrusive, omnipotent, capricious, and unpredictable except in its unrelenting hostility to Palestinian interests. Nowhere is the contradiction between community interests and government practice more graphically symbolized than in Israeli policies of land acquisition and settlement of Jewish civilians in the West Bank.

The dual character of the military government—law-oriented, at one level, but arbitrary and unconstrained as experienced by its subject population—is one of the distinctive features of what may be described as "Orientalist despotism."[1] I use this term with a sense for the significant continuities *and* discontinuities between realities under the present regime and conditions believed to have prevailed under stereotypical traditional "despotisms." A number of the features generally associated with classical despotic rule obtain in the modern West Bank, such as the insecurity of private property from government, the absence of legal predictability due to the intervention of political authorities in the judicial process, and a bureaucracy riddled by political favoritism.[2]

But these conditions are not brought about under the rule of an indigenous sultan, in command of a powerful and "autonomous" state.[3] Rather, the structural and political unaccountability of the Israeli military government to its subject Palestinian population is the product of the unique circumstances of occupation and the indeterminate status of the region. Neither is the occupation administration a traditional patrimonial or even "neopatrimonial" bureaucracy, rather it is the extension of a modern bureaucratic Israeli state.[4] Despite its orientation toward formal legality and rational bureaucracy, the military government often functions in a style analogous to that of a patrimonial regime. This is in part due to the conscious policy of Israeli administrators, who are informed by an Orientalist vision of Palestinian society, to manage affairs within local society through "traditional" forms of patronage, thus the sobriquet Orientalist despotism.[5] This suggests that a syndrome analogous to the stereotypical Oriental despotism, but with distortions and even some exaggerations of the traditional model, has been created by a new and different conjuncture of circumstances.

The implications of this situation for the lawyers of the region have been devastating. Public trust in the efficacy and integrity of the courts has plummeted. Political favoritism and patronage have undermined the value of technical legal expertise. Law, as it is used by the military government, is perceived locally as simply another instrument for the control and dispossession of the Palestinian community. In both reality and public perception, the services of lawyers have been devalued and their claims to social legitimacy undermined.

The Establishment of Military Government

In occupying the West Bank, the Israel Defense Forces (IDF) assumed for themselves the formidable task of governing an Arab population of perhaps seven hundred thousand, which was alien if not actively hostile to its new rulers.[6] It was not, however, a task for which the military command came unprepared. Following their experience in occupying the Gaza Strip after the 1956 Suez War, Israeli military officers were convinced of the necessity of formulating contingencies for similar situations. By the early sixties, they had organized training courses in military administration, published a pamphlet entitled "A Manual for Legal Personnel in Military Administration," and had gone as far as to appoint specific officers to positions as "governors" of prospective areas to be occupied.[7] The leader in this effort was Meir Shamgar, then military advocate general, who describes the preparation of his unit as follows:

> Before the war the officers of the platoon (regular and reserve) had taken special courses of the Military Advocates' Corps, studying in detail the laws of war and had carried out skeleton exercises in military government problems. All sections were equipped with movable emergency kits including basic legal textbooks and other material necessary for the performance of their duties, and inter alia a large set of precedents of military government proclamations and orders, vital at the initial stages of military government, as well as detailed legal and organizational instructions and guidelines. These facilitated, from the outset, the legal and administrative activity of the sections, according to a previously planned scheme.[8]

Indeed, on the outbreak of the June War in 1967, these specially trained units advanced virtually simultaneously with the combat troops and, in some cases, were deployed before military actions had even commenced. Platoons were assigned to each of the three areas occupied by Israeli forces in the fighting (the Gaza Strip, the Golan Heights, and the West Bank) and their leaders were designated legal advisers to the regional commanders of the IDF in the respective areas. On June 7, the regional commander in the West Bank headquartered in Jerusalem issued a proclamation prepared by the Military Advocate's Unit announcing that "the Israel Defense Forces entered this region today and assumed control of the rule and preservation of security and public order in the region."[9]

On June 28, 1967, exactly three weeks after Israeli troops entered the West Bank, the Knesset promulgated legislation empowering the government to annex the city of Jerusalem, which act was accomplished the following day.[10] Headquarters of the military government for the West Bank, renamed Judea and Samaria, was transferred to Beit El, approximately fifteen miles to the north of Jerusalem and adjacent to the Palestinian town of Ramallah. Military rule was lifted from Jerusalem, which was henceforth treated legally and administratively as a part of Israel. Its Palestinian residents were required to carry special Israeli identity cards, corporations and other legal entities were obligated to reregister under Israeli law, and Jordanian civil administrative offices were closed.

The Structure of Military Government

The early structure and policies of the military government were described by their principal architect, Defense Minister Moshe Dayan, as "governing without administration," which commentators have accurately identified as simply another phrase for the classic colonial practice of indirect rule.[11] The aim, as an IDF weekly magazine described it, was to create the possibility that an Arab "could be born in a hospital, receive his birth certificate, grow up and be educated, get married and raise his children and grandchildren—all without having to resort to an Israeli employee or civil servant, or even having to see one at all."[12]

The practice bore the personal stamp of Dayan, who was renowned for his impatience with bureaucracy and his preference for flexible and pragmatic policy-making. Furthermore, indirect rule was appropriate to Israeli requirements: it minimized expenditures of human and material resources, ensured less friction between the army and the West Bank community, and thus hastened the "normalization" of life in the Occupied Territories. "Normalization," to the extent possible under the circumstances, had been adopted by Dayan as the principal aim of the military government pending a disposition of the territories in peace negotiations.

The policy also rested on a sort of new social contract, which called for residents' being granted considerable latitude in community affairs, economic life, and the like, as long as they refrained from resistance to the occupation beyond mild civil protest. Dayan was apparently fond of reminding his lieutenants that "they don't have to love us or be good Zionists—we just want their cooperation." While tolerance would be visited on those who complied, Dayan demanded an "iron rule" in matters that touched on security. He supervised, for example, a program of summary demolition of houses belonging to people suspected of having aided the Palestinian armed resistance.[13] This gave birth to a tacit distinction, observed by both the military government and the population of the West Bank, between "national" politics (or matters pertaining to the medium- and long-term fate of the region and its inhabitants), a domain fraught with tension and conflict, and routine daily administrative functions, in which considerable cooperation was initially achieved.[14]

The chief executive officer in the West Bank military government was a military governor, ensconced in the new IDF headquarters in Beit El. True to the formula devised by the military advocate general, he announced on June 7, 1967, that "every governmental, legislative, appointive and administrative power in respect of the region or its inhabitants shall henceforth be vested in me alone and shall only be exercised by me or by persons appointed by me for that purpose or acting on my behalf." [15] He was assisted by district governors deployed in each of the seven districts into which the region was divided. Enforcement of general security in the region was charged to regular units of the army, while internal security fell to units of the Border Guards and to personnel from the General Security Services (Israel's domestic intelligence agency). The Jordanian civilian police force was maintained, although directed by a stratum of Israeli officers and largely restricted to the bailiwick of petty crimes and traffic offenses.

Coordination between Israeli civil authorities and the West Bank military government went through several permutations, but by September 1968, a satisfactory formula had been reached with the establishment of a Cabinet Committee on the Territories. This committee includes senior members of the Israeli government and exercised primary decision-making responsibility for policies vis-à-vis the territories. Employees of the various Israeli ministries were seconded to a civilian branch of the military government and served in either of two departments: Administration and Services, or Economics and Finances. [16] Formal structure notwithstanding, the minister of defense has tended in practice to wield the greatest power over the government of the territories, especially when that office has been held by a strong personality like Moshe Dayan.

Even in its least obtrusive stage, military rule was jarring to West Bank Palestinians, to say the least, and the military's intervention in the life of the community only relatively minimal. In the first place, many wanted no part of the new social contract. They opted instead to defy the occupation and ran afoul of laws barring membership in "hostile organizations," incitement and "adverse propaganda," participating in illegal meetings, as well as engaging in more active and violent forms of resistance. The eleven hundred military court trials for violations of security regulations conducted in the first year of occupation only hint at the level of friction between the occupiers and the occupied. [17]

As expectations of an imminent settlement diminished and the likelihood of a lengthier occupation increased, Dayan himself began to call for more active intervention in civil life. An extensive system of licenses and permits was instituted, which increased citizens' contact with state authority. The military government liberally availed itself of its powers of legislation by enacting extensive changes in the substantive laws and administrative structures of the region.[18] In the first year of occupation, 259 military orders pertaining to the administration of justice alone were promulgated.[19] Many legal changes were accomplished in the form of military orders "amending" Jordanian law, but some preserved preambles and little else while replacing all substantive content with new clauses, often modeled after Israeli law.

Economic Policies

Early decisions on Israeli economic policies toward the Occupied Territories were to have far-ranging impact on the economy and social structure of the West Bank. The war severely disrupted the economy of the region, especially since it occurred just before the summer harvest, as West Bank vegetables were being readied for export to traditional markets in the East Bank, Iraq, and the Arab countries of the Gulf. Israeli officials were keenly aware that an impoverished population would be a restive population and saw restoration of economic activities as a key aspect of the program of normalization. Fearing massive crop spoilage and widespread economic ruin, an ad hoc decision was quickly taken to permit the normal flow of trade across the Jordan River to continue. The decision eventually evolved into the "open bridges" policy and has remained a fixture of Israeli policy ever since.[20]

Economic integration of Israel and the West Bank was promoted by a number of measures, including the lifting of travel restrictions between the two areas and the functional elimination of the former border, or Green Line, between them.[21] This permitted a deluge of curious Israeli tourists to descend on the West Bank. They bought curios and mementos, thus injecting a large amount of much-needed cash into the local economy. It also stimulated a reverse flow of Palestinians into the labor-short and soon-to-be-booming Israeli economy. What began as a trickle soon developed into a flood. Customs duties between Israel and the West Bank rapidly went the way of the old border posts, as West Bank markets were opened to Israeli goods and, to a lesser extent, vice versa.[22]

Some of the consequences of these policies have already been noted. Here it is sufficient to emphasize the manner in which they solidified Israeli control over the region while preserving an important measure of Jordanian power at the same time. Control of the flow of goods and people across the bridge into the East Bank and, in the case of Israel, across the Green Line armed the political authorities on both sides of the Jordan River with a powerful protective and punitive weapon, which neither hesitated to use to its advantage.[23] Hence both the people and the economy of the West Bank have, in a sense, been kept hostage by two captors.

Local Government and Institutions

The Israeli military government slowly activated the remnants of the Jordanian civil departments, such as those responsible for justice, education, health, agriculture, and income tax, assigning them to the supervision of the civil servants from counterpart ministries in Israel who served in the civilian branch of the military government.[24] The Israeli administration mediated its relations with the Palestinian population through a number of local institutions, the most important of which were the twenty-five municipalities in the region. Mayors and, to a lesser extent, municipal councils became the conduits through which the military government communicated with the West Bank community and the unofficial spokespersons for Palestinian interests in the area.[25] Municipalities were vested with control over the dispensation of vital privileges to the community, including family reunification permits, exit visas, and other licenses. It was to the mayors that military authorities voiced displeasure in the event of political unrest and on whom they relied to communicate threats of retaliation to the broader community. Mayors became the champions of political detainees by appealing to the military governor for clemency, of citizens facing house demolition or land expropriation, and of townships suffering curfew or other forms of collective punishment. As a number of observers have noted, municipal leaders were catapulted into unprecedented regional prominence, their role undergoing a qualitative transformation from strictly administrative to broadly political and national.[26]

The tentative modus vivendi struck between the military government and the municipal leaders survived as long as most local offices were held by pro-Jordanian notables. But a major transformation in local politics occurred with the 1976 municipal elections, which brought to power representatives of "nationalist blocs" supportive of the PLO in a majority of West Bank townships. The elections initiated a six-year period of tension and conflict between municipal leaders and the military government. In 1978, the municipalities gained a source of independent financing with the establishment of the Steadfastness Fund, and some embarked on projects designed to wean their growing infrastructural dependence on Israel. Mayors became the guiding lights of the new National Guidance Committee, set up the same year to coordinate resistance to the occupation. In 1980, attempts by an Israeli terrorist network on the lives of three prominent West Bank mayors, which left Bassam Shakaʿa of Nablus and Karim Khalaf of Ramallah maimed, only elevated them to the status of national martyrs. The stage was clearly set for a showdown with the military government.

Several other local institutions have functioned in a manner parallel to the municipalities, although on a far more modest scale. Ninety-six rural councils represented smaller villages to the district commissioner under Jordanian rule. Half ceased operations in 1967, but many were reactivated by the military government and several new ones created; eighty-five remain in existence. *Makhateer* (sing., *mukhtar*), petty village officials who since Ottoman times had served as liaisons between their *hamayil* (clans) and state authority, were retained to inform constituents of government actions and with the power to authenticate documents.[27] Finally, in the towns, elected chambers of commerce have provided channels of communication between the military government and the West Bank business community.

Civil Administration

In November 1981, the military government promulgated Military Order No. 947, creating a "civil administration" in the West Bank. The military command in the region was dissolved and its area commander redesignated the commander of Israeli defense forces in Judea and Samaria. He was assigned to the Central Command just as the head of any other military unit in Israel. In most respects, these measures seemed only to formalize the preexisting division of the military government into one strictly military and another civilian branch.

Palestinians locally and abroad scrutinized the measure in its relation to the broader movements in the region associated with the Camp David Accords, signed into treaty by Egypt, Israel, and the United States in 1979. One part of the accords called for negotiations to establish and define the powers of a "self-governing authority" in the West Bank, which would administer the region for a five-year "transitional" phase while the question of political sovereignty was settled.[28]

The shift to a civil administration was interpreted by many Palestinians as Israel's attempt unilaterally to predetermine the powers of the proposed self-governing authority according to its own vision. The Camp David requirement for the withdrawal of the Israeli military government had been technically met with the dissolution of the West Bank Command, although jurisdiction over military affairs continued to be exerted by the Central Command. The civil administration, already segregated, was ready to be handed over to indigenous officials as a discrete package.[29]

As West Bank political leaders fully realized, the success of this plan also rested on the emergence of individuals willing to accept the offices and powers defined for them by the Israeli authorities, a role for which indigenous leaders had no intention of volunteering. On the contrary, the new civil administration was condemned as roundly as the Camp David Accords themselves, and mayors and other community notables organized a boycott, steadfastly refusing any dealings with the Israeli administration in its new form.

After several months of mayoral pronouncements of opposition to the civil administration, its head, Menachem Milson, dismissed first three and then six of the noncooperating mayors and their municipal councils and replaced them with Israeli military officers. The remaining mayors and councils, in solidarity with their fellows, immediately suspended operations. Public protests erupted throughout the West Bank, ending only after three weeks and the deaths of twenty-two Palestinians in clashes with the Israeli army.

Both sides have since been unrelenting. The Israeli government has declined to restructure its administration in the West Bank, and members of the community still avoid dealings with it to the extent possible. Some in the Palestinian community have second-guessed the decision of its leadership to boycott the civil administration, for if the Israeli scheme for the region was foiled, it was at the expense of the surrender of the significant institutional resources afforded by the municipalities. In several towns, Palestinians have quietly accepted appointments by the occupation authorities, but at best have been castigated and isolated from their communities as traitors.

In a more celebrated case, Zafir al-Masri, scion of a wealthy and politically influential Nablus family, accepted appointment to the mayorship of his home city in 1986, only to be gunned down in the street within weeks of taking office.[30] The gulf between the Israeli occupation authorities and the West Bank Palestinian community has widened, stretching those who have tenuously bridged it and causing others, almost as graphically as the analogy suggests, to fall into the abyss.

Changes in the Formal Legal System

Israeli occupation brought sweeping changes to the West Bank's legal system. These changes obviously had direct and wide-ranging consequences for the local legal profession, not to mention the broader community. The most immediate and overt of these changes was the military government's establishment of a system of military courts, accomplished in the first days of occupation through Proclamation No. 3, the "Security Provisions Order." The order contains chapters that detail rules for the constitution of military courts, establishes their laws of procedure and evidence, and outlines their substantive law in the form of security regulations.[31] The military courts also exercise concurrent criminal jurisdiction with the civil courts of the region and are authorized to enforce the Defense Emergency Regulations, inherited by Jordan from the Palestine Mandate and never formally repealed.[32] Both these and the new security regulations grant the military government wide extrajudicial powers to impose exile, house arrest, "administrative" detention, curfews, collective punishment, house demolition, and other sanctions.[33]

Military courts are of two kinds: single-judge courts, empowered to try offenses bearing punishments of up to five years of imprisonment or petty fines; and three-judge courts, which preside over more serious offenses. All judges are Israeli military officers, appointed by the area commander. Those sitting singly or as presidents of three-judge courts are required to have formal legal training. No appellate judicial level is provided, although informal appeals can be directed to the area commander.[34] Military courts are authorized to sit anywhere deemed appropriate; at first, they convened on occasion in a number of the smaller towns in the region. With the passage of time, however, most cases are now referred to courts in Nablus and Ramallah, and somewhat less frequently in Hebron.

A second system of military administrative tribunals was created early in the occupation and has risen in significance as more and more fields of citizen-state interaction have fallen within its purview. These tribunals, typically staffed by three Israeli military officers (at least one of whom has expertise in a particular area of substantive law), are not bound by rules of procedure or evidence other

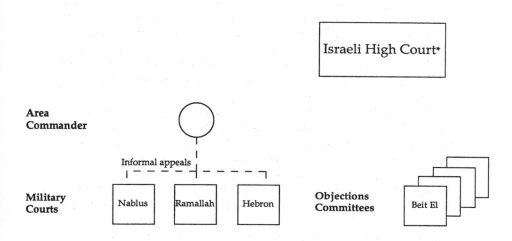

*Regular channels of appeal from the military courts and objections committees to the Israeli High Court do not exist. However, the High Court exercises personal jurisdiction over all military government personnel and may review complaints against their actions.

Figure 3. The Military Legal System in the West Bank

than those selected by the tribunals themselves. They operate far more informally than the military courts.

Initially, the tribunals were set up to provide aggrieved citizens with some legal recourse against the military government and its employees.[35] "Military objections committees" convened on demand to hear claims against the military government pertaining to such diverse matters as income and value-added tax assessments, pension rights of civil servants, customs duties, registration of patents and companies, licenses for vehicles and drivers, and other matters. Undoubtedly, the most important category reviewed by the objections committees, however, is claims concerning land, especially expropriation of land owned by Palestinians (fig. 3).[36]

The Jordanian civil court system was preserved by the occupation administration, although it was subjected to radical and more subtle transformations. The latter relate principally to the cumulative effect of minor but constant erosions in the authority of the civil courts and the not-coincidental growth in power of the military courts and administrative tribunals, whose jurisdiction had expanded in part at the expense of the jurisdiction of the civil courts.

The radical transformations ensued either as natural consequences of occupation or as by-products of the annexation of Jerusalem. For example, Israeli occupation meant that the supervisory powers of the Jordanian Ministry of Justice and the Supreme Court, both in Amman, no longer reached the Occupied Territories. Thus all the powers formerly exercised by the Ministry of Justice and its various officials and bodies, including supervision of the administration of the civil courts and training and appointment of judges and prosecutors, were vested in an Israeli military officer holding the new position of officer in charge of the judiciary.[37]

Occupation also resulted in the imposition of Israeli law in Jerusalem. Jordanian magistrate and district courts there were replaced with Israeli civil courts. The West Bank was consolidated into two judicial districts, with district courts in Nablus and Ramallah, and the Jordanian court of appeals was transferred from Jerusalem to Ramallah. Ramallah, now the seat of two magistrate courts, the district court for the southern half of the West Bank, the court of appeals, and housing the main offices of the public prosecutor, replaced Jerusalem as the judicial capital of the region. The court of appeals became de facto the highest indigenous court in the land, a status somewhat reinforced by the military government's vesting it with the powers of review of the Jordanian High Court (fig. 4).[38]

Not surprisingly, these radical transformations met with bitter opposition from the fifty or so Palestinian lawyers who had remained in the area following the 1967 war.[39] After some deliberation, a strike was declared, and local lawyers refused to engage in any transactions with either the civil courts or the new military courts. A few months later, the military government responded with a military order authorizing Israeli lawyers to appear in the civil and military courts of the West Bank. The striking lawyers remained steadfast, gaining the official endorsement of the Jordanian Lawyers Union (JLU) in Amman and with it a monthly stipend to compensate them for their loss of income.

Although the strike has never been formally suspended, by 1970 a small number of lawyers had returned to work. Despite expulsion from the JLU and condemnation by their peers, the working contingent of the profession has grown steadily, through further defections from the strike and the entry of new attorneys who choose to work. Other post-1967 law graduates opted to honor the strike at an even greater rate, swelling the ranks of the strikers. In light of the

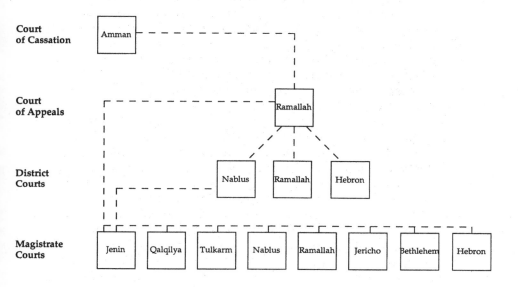

Figure 4. The West Bank Civil Court System

JLU's backing of the strike, its powers of certification and discipline were assumed by the officer in charge of the judiciary.[40]

In contrast to the civil court system, the Islamic and ecclesiastical courts largely escaped Israeli intervention and have been permitted to function in a relatively undisturbed fashion.[41] In the first place, their narrow jurisdictional range over disputes concerning personal status implicates few Israeli interests. Second, Israeli authorities generally approach their dealings with non-Jewish religious institutions in gingerly fashion, to avoid tipping the incendiary potion of religious agitation into the cauldron of nationalist sentiment.[42] One consequence of the preservation of the institutional integrity of the religious courts is that the lawyers' strike has never applied to them, so a few otherwise "striking" lawyers still engage in religious court litigation.

Although no Israeli courts have territorial jurisdiction in the West Bank, in a variety of circumstances they nevertheless hear cases arising there. Most important, the Israeli High Court, on the admittedly tenuous theory that it possesses personal jurisdiction over military government personnel operating in their official capacities, reviews appeals by residents of the Occupied Territories against acts of the military government claimed to violate international law. By an agreement based on political considerations, this theory has never been challenged by the Israeli attorney general.[43]

The scope of the High Court's review has been very narrow, as its justices have afforded military officials scarcely limited discretion in a broadly construed realm of "security." The military government's powers of legislation have never been directly examined by the High Court. As military courts have been disinclined to consider the issue, and the West Bank civil courts squarely considered it and eschewed any jurisdiction, the military government has been left to legislate free of any judicial review.[44] Occasional victories concerning administrative acts of the military government, including a few major ones, have still been eked out by a few West Bank Palestinians.

Israeli courts commonly try civil disputes in the West Bank arising from road accidents, as many insurance companies providing coverage to its residents are based in Jerusalem or elsewhere in Israel. It is common for contracts between Israeli and West Bank businesspeople to include a "forum clause," which specifies that any disputes arising from the agreement must be litigated in Israel. Israeli courts-martial try Israeli soldiers based in the West Bank for any violations of law or security regulations. Israeli citizens in the Occupied Territories submit to rabbinical courts in Israel in matters of personal status. Finally, an Israeli law permits Israelis "registered in the Population Register" to be tried in Israeli courts under Israeli laws for criminal offenses in the Occupied Territories if their alleged acts would have constituted offenses if committed in Israel.[45]

Administrative Practices and Style

Mere descriptions of formal institutions seldom convey, and often conceal, the ways in which the institutions actually function, and so must ordinarily be supplemented with further observations of administrative practices and style. It is doubly necessary to do this in the case of Israel's military government in the West Bank, as the gap between formal structures and empirical reality has been seldom recognized by casual observers or even more serious students of the region. It is unquestionably true, for example, that some Israeli administrators brought "an ideology of duty and service towards the Arab population,"[46] and that they instituted more "procedural standardization," narrowed discretionary latitude of local officials, and discouraged *wasta*, thereby "broadening access to government services."[47]

While the range of intermediaries through which the military government deals with the community has tended to be narrowed to those in positions of formal authority, the fundamental criterion for the dispensation or withholding of benefits and the imposition of sanctions has always been political rather than bureaucratic, and discretionary rather than rule-bound.[48] Compliant mayors, for example, received material support for municipal projects, while defiant ones were starved of funds.

Moreover, especially recently, the military government has cultivated new intermediaries wholly dependent on it for power and influence.[49] The extension of state regulation and required licenses and permits for virtually everything have simply given the military government more currency with which to withhold or bestow favors. New realms of discretionary power have proven fertile soil for the exercise of patronage, but also for the proliferation of corruption in the form of bribery.

Citizens are typically ignorant of many military government regulations and policies. In part, this results from the linguistic and cultural gap that separates them from their rulers.[50] But military orders of a legislative nature are frequently distributed late and haphazardly. Other decrees of more administrative and specific character are often issued verbally to the parties concerned, sometimes by Israeli military officers known only by their first names. The structural confusion brought about by the division between the military and the civilian wings of the government occasionally leaves citizens at the mercy of bodies working at cross purposes and issuing conflicting directions.[51]

Inconsistent and summary law enforcement practices contribute to the popular image of the military government as an arbitrary, unpredictable force. Several examples may demonstrate this. Military Order No. 854, decreed in July 1980, eliminated the distinction in Jordanian law between lower and higher educational institutions, thereby purporting to introduce direct Israeli supervision of the administration of the Palestinian universities in its most minute aspects. In fact, many of the provisions of the order have never been fully implemented, and the relationship between the military government and the university administrations instead continues to be constantly negotiated and renegotiated.[52]

Approximately ten years ago, Israel imposed an initial 5 percent value-added tax (VAT) on all goods and services. In Israel this was done by normal Knesset legislation, in the West Bank, by a military order amending the Jordanian law on customs and duties. Subsequent military orders increased the VAT rate, on par with increases in Israel, to its present 15 percent. In the beginning, according to informants, low-level officials charged with collecting VAT payments, often Palestinian employees, took a "soft" approach, cajoling merchants and others to pay symbolic amounts, fixed by negotiation. The screws of enforcement were gradually tightened, with steadily higher proportions of assessed rates actually being collected. During the period of my research, authorities responsible for the collection of VAT and income tax assessments undertook an intensive enforcement campaign, which often employed summary methods. Tax officials, now typically Israelis instead of Palestinians, would appear in shops, businesses, and professional offices, unannounced and without uniform or other identification, and confiscate cashboxes and business records, carting them off to administrative offices with violently distraught proprietors in tow. One lawyer in Nablus described to me the plight of one of his fellows:

> The tax authorities came to this lawyer's office, and demanded that he pay one thousand JD—about three thousand dollars— in VAT tax. This was crazy—*nobody* makes enough money here to deserve that kind of assessment. He told them that he wasn't doing much work and didn't have that amount. So they took him to prison! They kept him there for a few hours, asking him periodically for that amount, but he persistently refused. Without his knowledge, they went to his wife, told her that her husband was in prison, and said that he would be released only upon payment of the one thousand JD. She ran around frantically, raising the sum from relatives, and paid the amount a few hours later—whereupon the husband was released.

Though the policies behind these various law enforcement practices may vary, the messages they convey are mutually reinforcing: the laws on the books are not the operative principles of administration; on the contrary, in some cases there is room for these to be negotiated; but ultimately, the consistency and manner of law enforcement rest solely on the will of the authorities.

Settlements and Land Acquisition

Israeli policies concerning the settlement of its own citizens in the West Bank fall into three phases. In the early years of occupation, the Labor party government's settlement activities were focused on the establishment of a series of *nahals*, or military-agricultural encampments, at the easternmost perimeter of the Jordan Valley, and a second string of purely civilian settlements along the spine of the highland ridge that runs north-south through the West Bank.[53] Annexed Jerusalem was heavily settled, with a number of large highrise complexes ringing Arab portions of the city to the east.

A second phase of Israeli settlement in the region was ushered in with the fall of the Labor party government in 1977 and the accession to power of the Likud bloc led by Prime Minister Menachem Begin, a strong proponent of settlement in the Occupied Territories. Immediate steps to retroactively authorize several illegal settlements established by the Gush Emunim were coupled with declarations of the government's intention to assert permanent Israeli sovereignty over all of the Occupied Territories.[54] When the Camp David Accords raised the specter of the return of some form of Arab rule to the West Bank, the Begin government sought to implement a plan intended to secure permanent Israeli control thereby increasing the Israeli settler population to one hundred thousand in the following four years.[55]

A potential stumbling block to the program of settlement in the West Bank arose when the Israeli Supreme Court overturned a military order requisitioning private land owned by Palestinians for use as an Israeli civilian outpost at Elon Moreh. But a survey subsequently commissioned by the government revealed that a majority of Palestinian landholdings in the West Bank were unregistered, and that many might be of the *miri* category of state lands. After a pause, then, Israeli government acquisition of land in the region resumed, primarily through the new process of "realizing state lands."[56] At approximately the same time, the government also rescinded an order (in force since 1967) barring the purchase of land in the West Bank by Israeli individuals and land companies.[57]

A shift in Israeli settlement policy was compelled by the 1982 invasion of Lebanon and the subsequent occupation of the south of that country, which severely strained government resources.[58] The Labor-Likud National Unity government, which emerged from the Knesset elections of 1984, deemphasized settlement while the difficult problems of the national economy were being addressed. Still, by 1983, more than one hundred Israeli settlements had been erected in the West Bank, and the program of land acquisition by 1987 had led to direct Israeli control of at least 40 percent of the West Bank land mass. The total population of these settlements was most recently estimated at fifty thousand.[59] Despite the recently slowed pace of settlement, construction of a major new road system speeding traffic between Israel and the West Bank, for which much expropriation of private land was planned, continued apace during the period of my research.

There is no feature of Israeli rule that symbolizes more dramatically for West Bank Palestinians the diametric opposition between their own interests and aspirations and the aims of the military government than the latter's program of settlement and land acquisition in the region. The land base in historical Palestine is a national trust, the material foundation for a future Palestinian state, and its defense is assumed as a virtually sacred responsibility. It is the firm conviction of many West Bank Palestinians that the military government is little more than a weapon for the seizure of their lands, and a muzzle for their protests against that process. This facet of policy also distinguishes the Israeli occupation from all prior regimes, which taxed and conscripted Palestinians, but never dispossessed them of their lands on such a massive and systematic scale.

Settler Vigilantism

In the late seventies and early eighties, friction between the Israeli settlers and the indigenous population of the West Bank had reached dangerous levels. Settlers, who had been authorized by the military government to bear arms for self-defense, participated alongside the army in efforts to quell civil disturbances and accounted for a number of woundings and deaths of Palestinian demonstrators. Settlers also vandalized Arab property in their vicinity, sometimes even enclosing adjacent lands with barbed-wire fencing and joining it to the settlement.[60]

A number of confrontations were provoked by incidents of stone throwing. Palestinian youths took to hiding along the winding rural routes along which settlers and other Israelis passed and bombarding their car windshields with stones, sometimes causing serious injuries and even a few deaths.[61] After one stone-throwing incident, as many as twenty settlers rampaged through Ramallah, shattering windows of stores, homes, and over 150 parked vehicles.[62] Several Palestinian teenagers were shot to death while fleeing after stone-throwing incidents, and others were apprehended by settlers, detained, and physically abused in the settlements before being delivered to military authorities. Settlers were also suspected in a few mysterious abductions of Palestinians, whose mutilated corpses were later found dumped next to rural roads.

It requires only a few of these events to induce terror in the hearts of a civilian population, particularly in a confined space such as the West Bank. The pervasive unease that afflicted the West Bank population for several years prior to my arrival had been greatly exacerbated by the appearance of official diffidence toward the settlers' violence, and even active collusion in it. Civilian police, in the Palestinians' view, had been "neutered" by the occupation authorities, and persistent complaints to military authorities about settler abuses appeared to fall on deaf ears.

Indeed, it was often impossible for residents even to determine whether it was military personnel or settlers who stopped and interrogated them, shot at them, searched their homes, and the like. Settlers often represented themselves as military personnel, an appearance supported by the articles of army dress they often sported. Confusion was increased by one order exempting settlers from service with their normal army reserve units in Israel and grafting them onto units in the West Bank. Another order functionally "deputized" settlers, permitting them to demand identification from citizens and to arrest persons suspected of violating security regulations.[63] It was never thereafter evident whether settlers involved in repressing demonstrations, for example, were doing so in a military or a civilian capacity, and thus to what standard in the use of arms they should be held and in what courts, should they cause serious injury or death.[64]

From the perspective of the settlers, of course, taking the law into their own hands was a necessity imposed by the military government's abdication of responsibility to protect them from the hostile Palestinian population. Settlers representing their respective communities met and resolved to organize their own "regional security committees." In doing so, however, they finally aroused sufficient alarm in Israel to stir the government to action.[65] A special commission ordered by the attorney general's office submitted a report in May 1982, citing grave deficiencies in the administration of justice in the Occupied Territories, especially as it pertained to curbing settler violence.[66] In April 1984, the General Security Services announced that it had infiltrated a Jewish terrorist organization operating in the West Bank and had narrowly foiled the group's plan to booby-trap buses belonging to a Palestinian bus company.

For the remainder of the period of my field research and after, Palestinians were treated to the spectacle of the trials of the Jewish terrorists in the Jerusalem District Court. Although it seemed clear that settler vigilantism had been dealt a strong blow, it had not wholly abated. And the sentences meted out to the Jewish terrorists seemed ridiculously light to most Palestinians when measured by the standards applied to them in the West Bank military courts.

The Village Leagues

Israel's strategy with respect to other Arab populations under its rule has been to accentuate indigenous sectarian and "ethnic" divisions and to forge alliances with minority groups—such as with the Bedouins of the Negev or the Druse in northern Israel, and the Christian and Shi'a Muslim militias in Lebanon. A similar tack was inhibited in the West Bank by the relative ethnic and sectarian homogeneity of population of the Palestinian highlands.[67]

This was no major liability while the cooperative pro-Jordanian mayors held office, or even for some time afterward. But interest in a compliant local leadership became acute with the conclusion of the Camp David Accords, which called for Palestinian participation in negotiations to define and establish the "self-governing authority" in the West Bank. Shortly thereafter, Menachem Milson was appointed civil administrator of the region. He was determined to combat what he saw as PLO patronage by matching it with the military government's own.

Milson's strategy sought to exploit class and sectoral divisions between the urban and village populations in place of the usual ethnic and sectarian ones. The agency chosen for this was a preexisting network of Village Leagues (*rawabit al-qura*), established first in 1978 in villages in the Hebron area with the ostensible aims of promoting rural development, resolving disputes locally, and representing the interests of villagers to the administration. Political aims were specifically eschewed. League leaders sought legitimacy by fueling villagers' resentments against the urban community and by accusing municipal leaders of corruption in the distribution of the Steadfastness Funds, which had flowed into the region in recent years.[68]

By early 1982, with the support of the civil administration, the leagues had spread to all districts of the West Bank. Their membership of several hundred appeared to comprise mostly men of lower middle class origins, from both towns and villages. A large number, even among the leadership, seemed of marginal social status, frequently with reputations for idleness and criminal pursuits.[69]

The civil administration charged the leagues with implementing such projects as drilling wells or extending electricity to villages and permitted league members to pose as benefactors to their peers. Citizens from the entire region, not simply its rural reaches, were compelled to resort to the league in their area for family reunification or travel permits, civil service positions, construction licenses or cancellation of orders for demolition of unauthorized buildings, driving licenses, reductions of jail sentences—in short, the host of services and benefits under the control of the civil administration. At one point, Israeli administrators entertained the notion of establishing league "courts," which would be modeled after the informal al-qadaʾ al-ʿashaʾiri, or tribal adjudication.[70] League leaders, moreover, began to present themselves, and to be represented by the Israeli government, to the outside world, as local alternatives to PLO leadership in the West Bank.

The leagues were violently denounced by all politically articulate segments of the local population as quislings, and their members were socially shunned. It was not long before the head of the Ramallah League, who was suspected of having sold lands belonging to his *hamula* to the Jewish Agency, was assassinated, presumably by operatives of the PLO. The civil administration responded by arming and training league members, who, for the next few months, were seen by local residents riding routine patrol in Israeli army jeeps.

The leagues-cum-militias proved an even less disciplined force than the Israeli settlers. During 1982 and 1983, league members roamed the streets of West Bank towns and villages in private cars, identifiable only by the Uzi submachine guns they wielded, stopping and interrogating civilians, confiscating books from students, and beating, harassing, and intimidating whomever they chose. League members exploited their position to prosecute purely personal vendettas against local rivals, and many confrontations occurred between league members and the community at large.[71]

The situation was clearly approaching chaos when the leader of one league was directly implicated in the murder of a villager who refused to permit his home to be linked to the league-installed electrical lines in his village. The killer was arrested and eventually convicted, and from that time on the leagues suffered an eclipse. The army retrieved many of the arms it had supplied them. Some league leaders apparently reevaluated their close relationship with the Israeli administration and attempted to distance themselves from its policies.

By the time of my arrival in the area in February 1984, mention of the leagues scarcely evoked comment by politically aware informants. In their role as a political alternative to the PLO, at least, the leagues were universally seen as a spent force. But for some time, they had greatly contributed to a sense of insecurity and fear in the community, which still lingered. And their powers as intermediaries between citizens and state authority remained largely intact.

Conclusions

The advent of Israeli occupation introduced an alien regime to the West Bank that evinced a strong legalistic orientation, and yet, together with the very unsettledness of the prevailing political situation, produced some of the effects associated with traditional stereotypes of Oriental despotism. I call this syndrome "Orientalist despotism." The cumulative effect of the transformations in substantive law, court structures, and administrative system has been the greater intrusion of governmental control into the lives of all West Bank Palestinians. But the actual statutes and military orders as issued are often not understood to be the operative principles of interaction between state and society, which, on the contrary, may sometimes be negotiated.

Insofar as the Palestinians' experience with state authority is mediated through the occupation administration, nothing has invalidated their perception of authority as omnipotent. Law, far from limiting the power of the state, is merely another way of exercising it. To the extent that the impact of state power may be limited or deflected, the principal mode for accomplishing this is still through intermediation, or *wasta*, and usually at the price of political compliance.

So the Israeli military government is perceived as being arbitrary and distant in the manner of all prior state authority. Especially in its policies of settlement and land acquisition and in its abetting of the settlers and Village Leagues, it is viewed as harboring aims and ambitions for the region in fundamental opposition to the interests of the Palestinian community. Meanwhile, native institutions—the civilian police, the courts—are recognized as mere shells of their former selves, possessing no power independent of the military government and now slated either to stand aside for or to participate actively in the implementation of the Israeli military government's agenda.

West Bank lawyers have been perfectly able to distance themselves ideologically from the military government; indeed, they are some of its sharpest and most vocal critics. But their effective power to resist the military government and to defend the community, or even to serve citizens in private disputes or other affairs, has been substantially diminished in the current circumstances. At the root of this is the fact that the lawyers are structurally dependent on formal institutions of the state—the courts—the integrity and efficiency of which are beyond their control. The quality of services they are capable of providing the public is, therefore, only in part a function of their own performance. When the courts and the more general formal system are not answering community needs, or are not working in conformity with the rules in which lawyers hold expertise, then the latter are left with little to offer their fellow citizens, and still less to justify the prerogatives they seek in wealth and social position.

We have investigated the historical, sociocultural, and political-administrative contexts in which the West Bank lawyers operate. Let us now turn to a direct examination of the legal profession itself.

5. The Social Composition of and Entry into the Profession

This chapter is the first of three that together constitute a detailed ethnography of the contemporary West Bank legal profession. I shall first describe who the lawyers are, in social terms, how and in what form they conduct their practices, and what the actual content of their work is. This chapter will consider the first of these questions, focusing on the social identities of the lawyers. The social and political capacities of the profession are, to a significant extent, determined by the power and status of its individual members. Identifying them is thus a key step in understanding the conditions that characterize contemporary West Bank legal practice.

The present composition of the West Bank's legal profession is a function of the processes by which membership in that group is attained. We must therefore examine both the formal requirements governing entry to the profession and the general social forces determining which members of society are capable of meeting these formal requirements.

Numbers and Distribution of West Bank Lawyers

In 1985, the number of legal professionals in the region, both striking and working, was about five hundred, including approximately ninety young lawyers engaged in an obligatory two-year apprenticeship under the supervision of older "master" lawyers. This represents an increase of 1000 percent since the advent of occupation in 1967, at which point, according to informants who had been practicing at the time, there were only fifty-odd lawyers in the entire West Bank.[1]

In view of the strike, however, the number of lawyers actually engaged in the full-time practice of law probably has only slightly more than tripled. Striking lawyers were represented by about 250 master lawyers and 70 apprentices, of whom no more than 5 to 10 could be said to be practicing full time in law-related fields, whereas another 20 or so were working part-time, usually in the religious courts. The remainder either supported themselves with the stipend received from the Jordanian Lawyers Union, income from other assets or savings, or had entered non–law-related vocations. Working lawyers were represented by 165 master lawyers and 23 apprentices, although perhaps 10 to 15 of the officially licensed master lawyers had permitted their practices to lapse.[2]

About 70 percent of lawyers maintaining offices do so in Nablus, Ramallah, Jerusalem, or Bethlehem—arranged on a north-south axis less than fifty miles long. Perhaps another 15 percent are based in Hebron, the largest town in the southern West Bank, while the rest are based in Jericho, and the northern towns of Tulkarm, Qalqilya, and Jenin. No more than a handful maintain offices in more than one locale. The primary reason for this distribution is the location of courts and administrative offices. Ramallah, for example, has become the judicial center of the West Bank, as well as the seat of the military government for the entire region. Nablus has a local magistrate court, military courts, and the civil district court for the northern half of the region.

Social Origins and Characteristics

Social identity and status in West Bank Palestinian society is a composite formed of such elements as kin group membership, social class background, gender, religion or sect, and placement in the demographic scheme of townspeople/villagers/refugees, as well as specific town, village, or camp of origin. These elements frequently overlap and are mutually reinforcing.

In the rough hierarchy of lower (*adna*), middle (*wusta*), and upper (*'ulya*) classes generally recognized in the towns of the West Bank, the majority of West Bank lawyers, especially in the larger towns of Nablus, Ramallah, and Hebron, are of middle-class background. These are the sites in which the middle class is most fully developed.[3] A small minority is of lower-class background. But a disproportionate share of the older lawyers and of the members of a roughly identified elite within the profession are members of upper-class notable families. In some of the smaller towns from which many of these major families originated, such as Qalqilya, Jenin, and Tulkarm, their members virtually monopolize the practice of law.[4]

Several trends are suggested here. First, access to the legal profession has widened as educational opportunities have increased for West Bank Palestinians of diverse social background. Still, access to the profession, and even more so the level of success subsequently achieved within it, continues to be significantly influenced by kin and class status. This appears to be more strongly the case in the smaller towns and may express the greater continued force of "traditional" social divisions in them. It also hints of the greater difficulty small-town people encounter moving into the profession, because they lack the economic resources and more extensive contacts outside the hometown enjoyed by members of the major families.

West Bank lawyers, as might be expected, are overwhelmingly of the demographic and social category of townspeople. The preponderantly urban origin of lawyers doubtless reflects this sector's better access to and higher valorization of education, its disdain of manual labor, and other general advantages conferred on its strategic placement in the milieu in which lawyers are called on to operate.

Interestingly, refugees may be the group that has contributed the second highest number of contemporary legal practitioners. Lacking land and other tangible economic resources, refugees have perhaps invested more heavily in education than have most villagers.[5] In contrast, students from the villages face more pressure from their families to discontinue their studies to work the fields or orchards, to tend flocks of grazing animals, and otherwise to contribute to the household economy. Accordingly, fewer are able to break the bonds to family and village and to achieve higher levels of education.

A disproportionately large contingent of about 20 percent of the West Bank legal profession is composed of individuals belonging to one of the four or five major Christian sects that claim Palestinian adherents. Together these represent approximately 8 percent of the Arab population of the region. An even higher proportion of the most prominent and older lawyers of the area are Christians. As I have noted, this trend began during the Mandate period, the result of advantages Christian Palestinians enjoyed in access to higher education and geographical proximity to administrative centers; these advantages have continued into the present. While the proportion of Christians within the profession appears to be diminishing somewhat, several Christian families have established as much of a tradition of eminence in legal practice as has been possible in the span of two or three generations, with current upholders of the tradition clearly destined to become well-known and successful lawyers.

The West Bank legal profession is overwhelmingly male. Among the 320 striking lawyers in the region, I was able to ascertain the presence of 2 women *estagiares,* or trainees, both of whom were

Muslims. Among some 188 working lawyers, I encountered 2 women *estagiares*, a third formally finished with her apprenticeship but still in transition into independent practice, and 3 fully accredited and independently practicing women master lawyers. The oldest was about thirty-six years old, and was the only one married among the entire group of 6 women lawyers. The younger 2 had been in practice for less than two years, while the oldest had been working for approximately ten years. All but one of the 6 working women lawyers were Christian, a reflection of that group's urban status, educational experience, and cultural orientation, which is more "liberal" and "Western" in its attitudes toward women.[6]

The average age among the striking faction tends to be slightly higher than that among the working faction. Age distributions within the two factions are represented in table 1.[7]

Table 1. *Age Distribution of Working and Striking Lawyers*

Age	Working Lawyers (N = 188) (%)	Striking Lawyers (N = 320) (%)
25–35	40	20
36–45	35	30
46–55	15	30
56 and over	10	20

Formal Regulation

Legal practice in the West Bank is regulated under the Jordanian Law of the Union of Nizami Lawyers, passed in 1952, and its subsequent amendments. The first function of this law was to define both the criteria for gaining certification as a lawyer in the civil court system and the parameters for the practice of law. Second, it founded the Jordanian Lawyers' Union and charged that body with administering entry to the profession and enforcing regulations governing the practice of law, backed ultimately by the power to expel errant members.[8]

The primary requirements for admission to the legal profession are that the candidate (1) be a Jordanian citizen, currently holding the status of permanent resident; (2) hold a degree from an accredited institute or university in the country of issue; (3) present a certificate from police authorities that he or she has never been charged with a felony or crime of moral turpitude, nor been subject to any disciplinary action related to honor; and (4) have completed a two-year apprenticeship according to terms specified in the law. The law grants a monopoly to lawyers to represent clients in all civil tribunals (courts, departments of prosecution, administrative agencies, and so on), to draft legally enforceable contracts, and to provide legal counsel.[9]

After the Israeli occupation, previously licensed West Bank practitioners were permitted to continue their civil court practice and to plead before the new military courts. Initially, almost all declined to resume working, to honor the strike, which had been declared by local initiative but soon received the official sanction of the JLU. The military government countered with a military order authorizing Israeli lawyers to appear in the civil and military courts of the West Bank. Meanwhile, the JLU's responsibilities for oversight of admission to the profession and disciplining its members were assumed by the military government through its officer in charge of the judiciary. From that point to the present, lawyers aspiring to resume or begin practice in the civil or military courts in the region have had to seek certification from the officer in charge of the judiciary. New lawyers who opt to observe the strike seek admission to the bar through the JLU's local West Bank branch office. Membership, however, confers no rights to appear before any tribunals under the military government's supervision.[10]

A special note must be made regarding Palestinian lawyers legally resident in the portions of the municipality of Jerusalem formerly held by Jordan, but annexed by Israel in 1967. Formally, they, like all other Palestinians living in Jerusalem, are no longer treated by Israel as residents of the West Bank.[11] While the right of Jerusalem's lawyers to appear in West Bank tribunals has been uninterrupted since 1967, they have been required to become members of the Israeli Bar Association in order to practice in the Israeli civil courts now operating within the city of Jerusalem. Given their lack of mastery of either the Hebrew language or Israeli law, and the strong community opprobrium attaching to actions smacking of acquiescence to the permanence of Israeli occupation, very few Palestinian lawyers from Jerusalem have exercised their right to membership in the Israeli bar.

Recruitment

In chapter 3 I noted that, while Palestinians have placed a high premium on education, specifically, on higher education, legal study ranks low in their general hierarchy of preferences, and law faculties in Arab universities have served as dumping grounds for the educational system's less highly motivated and accomplished students. The relative accessibility and lower prestige of legal education no doubt partially explain the diffident responses given by a number of my informants to inquiries into their reasons for joining the profession. Only a small number described having felt a strong desire to practice law (an "inner feeling," as one informant described it), or spoke of having fostered an ambition to become a lawyer from youth. Those who did so tended to come from the elite of the profession.[12]

The single feature of law practice consistently mentioned as having appealed to informants was its independent character. A number of lawyers, half in self-criticism, explained this by alluding to the alleged difficulty Arabs encounter in cooperating with one another: "You know the Arabs—everyone wants to be a sultan!" as one lawyer said ("Kull wahid biddu yikuun sultan!").

In an otherwise highly politicized environment, relatively few informants seemed to have entered the legal profession motivated by explicit notions about legal practice as a form of political activity, or with a specific agenda for political change to be effectuated through law. This was true even of lawyers who had become active in so-called political or security cases, in which Palestinians were being charged with offenses against the Israeli occupation. Many of these lawyers, of course, had subsequently developed a keener appreciation of their actual and potential political roles as legal practitioners.

It is important to note that in the West Bank there are no institutions or agencies that centralize information about vocational opportunities. Secondary schools, for example, provide no career counseling. Apart from pragmatic and financial considerations, then, career choices are made on the basis of individual preference and, to a significant extent, family influence and pressure.[13] Most individuals appear to embark on legal careers (and probably other careers) in a void of information about the realities of legal practice, including that pertaining to actual opportunities in the field. A number of informants, for example, had entered law school after 1967 and the imposition of the lawyers' strike, but had been completely ignorant of the reasons for or even the existence of the strike until after the completion of their studies.

In a number of cases, it was evident that the model of a particular individual's success in the profession was responsible for the pursuit of law by kin or fellow villagers of the next generation. The most obvious examples of this were the number of lawyers whose fathers and sometimes grandfathers had practiced or were still practicing law, or had been members of the judiciary. Though small in number, almost without exception, lawyers with a tradition of family involvement were among the most successful and eminent in the profession. As we shall see, this reflects the substantial tangible advantages conferred on close relatives of established lawyers.

Occasionally, the impact of a single individual's professional achievements has spread beyond that person's immediate family. One extended family from the Hebron area had produced fourteen lawyers on the inspiration, one of them claimed, of their uncle, who had apparently been an extremely successful lawyer during the Mandate period. Another informant explained the disproportionately large number of lawyers hailing from a particular small village northeast of Jerusalem as having been due to the model provided by one of its residents. The man had achieved great financial success and social prestige in a long and illustrious career in the legal profession.

Legal Education

Legal education in the Arab world is based on the continental European model. In large part, this is the consequence of the strong French influence infusing the Egyptian legal and educational systems, which, in turn, have served as models for the remainder of the Arab world. Thus the initial degree, the B.A. or "license" (usually also the last sought by legal practitioners) is granted after the completion of four years of postsecondary study.[14]

Once having decided to pursue a law career, a student must select an institution in which to study. Although there are now some ten institutions of higher learning in the West Bank, none as yet contains a full faculty of law.[15] Thus since the demise of the Jerusalem Law Classes with the termination of the Mandate, students have had to study law abroad or through a system of correspondence, or *intisab.*[16]

Material considerations weigh heavily at all stages of decision making concerning how and where to study law. The feasibility of study outside the West Bank is greatly enhanced, for example, if the student has relatives in a university city with whom he or she might live.[17] In some cases, grants for study abroad are linked either formally or informally with particular universities.[18] Expense is almost surely the primary reason why more West Bank lawyers have not pursued legal education in Western Europe and the United States.[19]

Beyond material considerations, individuals who choose to enter the profession under the influence of a specific role model are probably also influenced by that person's institution of study. Egypt, the eastern Arab world's center of legal (and other) cultural production, draws the greatest number of law students from the West Bank. Perhaps two-thirds of the region's lawyers are graduates of Cairo University, Ain Shams University, or Alexandria University. Many West Bankers from the north have family affiliations in Syria (manifesting the historical orientation of that area toward Damascus because of earlier trade patterns, political relationships, and other factors) and thus travel there to study law. This is matched in the south by Hebron's orientation toward Gaza and thence to Egypt.

The principal institution through which West Bank residents have studied law as correspondence students is Beirut Arab University (BAU), an affiliate of Alexandria University in Egypt. Perhaps as many as one-quarter to one-third of the lawyers in the area during my fieldwork had studied through BAU. Approximately equal numbers of these had completed four years of external study or had combined some years of external study with some of resident study (commonly the first two years external study and the last two years in residence at Alexandria University).

The system of education by correspondence is significant for having made legal study accessible to several categories of West Bankers for whom professional training would otherwise have been out of reach. These include members of the poor and lower middle class, women (for whom study abroad is socially and practically problematic), and employed persons seeking a second career.[20]

Among laypersons of at least middle-class educated background, there is again a clear hierarchy among the various universities. Within the legal profession, the hierarchy is more specific as to law faculties themselves. Cairo University, the oldest of the Egyptian institutions, is regarded as having the best law faculty, while Ain Shams and Alexandria are considered to be good but second-tier schools. Damascus University and its law faculty are thought to be almost on a par with Cairo University. Baghdad University is seen as another middle-tier school, perhaps of slightly lower quality than Ain Shams and Alexandria.

Beirut Arab University is unanimously regarded among educated groups as providing the poorest legal education in the area, especially through its system of external education. BAU correspondence school graduates as a group are held in scarcely veiled contempt by "better educated" legal practitioners. "They are not lawyers—they simply purchase their degrees through the mail!" one eminent lawyer exclaimed in disgust. Such easy access to the profession is believed by the elite lawyers to degrade the profession as a whole.

There is more to this sense than the belief that BAU's training is inferior, however; comments of a number of informants hinted of an underlying class bias as well.

The program of study in Arab law faculties is strictly prescribed, with only a few opportunities for elective courses during the four years required for the B.A. degree. The typical first year of study includes introductory courses in the theory of law, legal history, political economy, constitutional law, and Islamic law (*shariʿa*). Students are frequently required to study either English or French. In the second, third, and fourth years, they are exposed to more specific areas of substantive and procedural law, including public and private international law, contracts, commercial law, administrative law, labor law, criminal law, civil and criminal procedure, as well as different aspects of Islamic law (succession, personal status, trusts). While foreign languages sometimes continue to be required for several years, the number of courses in social sciences tapers off rapidly following the first year.

Classes consist of lectures, which are consciously abstract and theoretical. Students are expected to be passive listeners, because the format and class size sometimes exceeding one thousand permit little or no discussion or student-teacher exchange. Learning about practical aspects of lawyering is reserved for the postgraduate apprenticeship normally required of law graduates who wish to enter practice in one of the Arab countries.

The vast majority of working lawyers in the West Bank at the time of my fieldwork had discontinued formal study after reaching the B.A. level. Five to 10 of the total of 165 working full, or master, lawyers had continued studies to obtain a Diploma or an M.A.; none had acquired a doctorate. Among striking lawyers, however, there is a significantly higher proportion of holders of higher degrees: of 250 master lawyers, 15 held Diplomas, 22 had obtained a master's degree, and 10 had achieved the doctorate.[21]

Whatever the degree earned outside the West Bank, return to the region generally marks the end of an individual's formal education.[22] A small but slowly growing fraction of the working contingent has recently begun to brave community and peer disapproval to learn Hebrew, however, mostly to facilitate practice in the military courts of the West Bank.[23] It is noteworthy that, irrespective of requirements for foreign language study in Arab law faculties, in reality very few West Bank lawyers ever acquire anything but rudimentary proficiency in a foreign language; for professional purposes, most are monolingual.[24]

Informal education through conversations with fellow lawyers is continuous, of course. For the working lawyers, the main sites for informal exchange of professional knowledge are the waiting rooms for lawyers found in most of the court buildings. Striking lawyers congregate either in the offices of individual lawyers, or in the West Bank office of the JLU, where, in addition to informal conversations, public examinations of apprentice lawyers provide a framework for academic discussions of legal topics.

Apprenticeship

An aspirant to the practice of law in the West Bank must spend two years in training (*tadrib*, or sometimes the French *estage*) under the auspices of a master lawyer (*muhami istaaz*) who has practiced five years in that status. In the scheme of Arab legal education, the apprenticeship phase is intended to complement the theoretical learning gained in the university and to acquaint prospective practitioners with the substantive and procedural laws of the particular jurisdiction in which they will practice.[25]

Apprenticeships are typically arranged between a recent law graduate and a master lawyer at the initiative of the former. Unless the aspiring apprentice has a close relative who is master lawyer, he or she might first seek out one who is a family acquaintance, or one with a reputation as a successful practitioner. *Estagiares* customarily are not paid by their master lawyers and, usually young and single, live with their parents. In addition, by law they are barred from seeking other employment during the period of their training. Therefore, apprentices usually endeavor to make arrangements with law offices in their towns of residence, if courts are located there, or in the closest adjacent court towns.

It is at this point, if not before, that the new law graduate must make a decision about whether to adhere to the terms of the strike. That decision will largely govern the selection of master lawyer to be approached for an apprenticeship and will determine the procedure through which the apprenticeship is sanctioned. If the apprentice decides to honor the strike, a striking master lawyer must be sought out and the apprenticeship arrangement approved by the West Bank regional office of the JLU. If the decision is to join the ranks of the working lawyers, an agreement must be reached with a working master lawyer and subsequently registered with the Israeli officer in charge of the judiciary.[26]

Jordanian law delineates few parameters for the conduct of apprenticeships, and in practice it appears that neither the West Bank office of the JLU nor the officer in charge of the judiciary exercises any effective oversight over them. In consequence, the character of the training of a *muhami mutadarrib,* or training lawyer, depends almost wholly on the whim and interests of his or her *istaaz.*[27] Hence the *istaaz* enjoys substantial latitude in regulating the manner of the *mutadarrib's* introduction to the local professional scene.

There is consensus within the profession that this introduction is the single most critical factor in determining the subsequent professional fate of a novice lawyer. The period of training is one in which litigation skills and local jurisprudence must be learned. An apprentice is introduced to the delicacies of handling clients, colleagues, and court personnel. Among the last, specific personalities must be measured and cultivated, as cordial personal relations with clerks, judges, and other judicial department employees can significantly facilitate such matters as expeditious case scheduling or frictionless interaction in court pleadings. While the development of these relationships depends ultimately on the apprentice's own conduct, he or she will enjoy an initial boost when a respected master has made the introductions.

The apprentice may also be introduced to the master's network of clients, among whom may be found the first toehold for the apprentice's independent practice at the termination of the training period. A successful mentor with a surplus of clients will not be threatened by the prospect that a share of them may eventually defect to an *estagiare.* A less successful master, on the other hand, may view the apprentice as a future competitor and will jealously guard his or her clientele, restricting interaction with them and refusing to entrust the trainee with any genuine responsibility.[28]

Potential antagonisms between the *istaaz* and the *mutadarrib* based on inequalities of power and sometimes conflicting interests are often tempered in practice by other interests of the *istaaz* that favor the acceptance of a trainee. Trainees may be used to perform onerous and menial tasks associated with legal practice. Regulations permit a master lawyer to open branch offices in other towns and to staff them with *estagiares,* thereby widening the net cast into the sea of potential clients.[29] In addition to these directly objective interests, supervision of *estagiares* is an accoutrement of a thriving legal practice and thus enhances the public and professional image of those lawyers most avidly pursued as mentors. For a number of master lawyers, diligently training the upcoming generation is an obligation that they feel they owe to the profession and to the public at large. Thus it makes their sense of corporate solidarity and adherence to the ethic of professional service real.[30]

A *muhami mutadarrib* training under a reasonably conscientious working *istaaz* spends much of his or her first year running court errands (standing in line to file cases, pay fees, copy documents, and so on), reading statutes and cases from local jurisdictions, attending court sessions with the *istaaz* or sitting in on meetings with clients as a passive listener, and occasionally conducting research related to the master lawyer's cases. The conscientiousness of *estagiares* varies as much as that of their masters, and the amount of time spent weekly in these pursuits ranges from nearly zero to twenty or twenty-five hours.

In the second year, the trainee is legally permitted to appear in magistrate courts as an agent of the supervising lawyer, and the pace of training usually picks up. In the beginning, the trainee's court appearances are limited to hearings involving simple issues in which financial or other stakes are low. Gradually, the *mutadarrib*'s responsibilities are increased, until at the end of the two-year period he or she may be functioning virtually as a master lawyer, managing cases (though still the less weighty) through all stages of litigation.[31]

Attainment of *istaaz* status for working lawyers is marked by no public or formal ceremony, although private parties are sometimes held. In fact, it is very common for administrative complications or delays in the confirmation of *estagiares* to compel them to remain in the office of their masters beyond the legally obligatory two years.

The training of new lawyers intending to observe the strike parallels that of apprentices under working lawyers insofar as their masters continue to be active in the profession, particularly in litigating cases in the Islamic or ecclesiastical courts. But very few striking lawyers actually engage in religious court litigation on anything but a limited part-time basis.[32] As little other legal work is done regularly by the majority of striking lawyers, there is commensurately little that they can offer to apprentices beyond intellectual guidance in theoretical reading and research. Indeed, a distinct sense of purposelessness and frustration afflicts many of the striking apprentices. In the words of one young *estagiare* who had started his training with a striking lawyer and subsequently enlisted with a working one:

> The strike? Well, I am one who can evaluate it on the basis of experience, because I observed it when I first returned to Jenin after graduating from the university. I enlisted as a *mutadarrib* with an eminent striking lawyer, a member of the local committee of the Lawyers' Union. But the atmosphere in the office was that of a *diwan* [the customary sitting room in which guests are received and served refreshments], not that of a proper law office. I got sick of sitting around drinking coffee

and gossiping with old men about general topics one could hear about in the streets. I felt like I had just come home and put my law degree on a shelf to gather dust.

Perhaps in the realization that it might suffer further defections by bored and discontented *estagiares*, several years ago the West Bank branch of the JLU instituted a requirement that an apprentice undertake a research project under the supervision of the master lawyer. The written product is then reviewed by a panel of three or four other master lawyers chosen by the local union office for their expertise in the relevant area of law. A public defense is then held in the office building housing the JLU.[33]

For the young *mutadarrib*, a close relative in the profession provides significant advantages. These include virtual exemption from competition for desirable apprenticeships, generally more caring and conscientious training, and inheritance of both the physical assets and the clientele of an established office.[34]

It is not uncommon for the *istaaz-mutadarrib* relationship to continue to have functional significance beyond the termination of the formally defined two-year period of training. Sometimes an *istaaz* will form a partnership with a former *mutadarrib*, saving his charge the tribulations of carving out an independent practice. More frequently, the *mutadarrib* receives referrals from a former *istaaz* with whom a cordial relationship has been maintained, often for many years after the period of *tadrib*.

Career Paths

The core of the contemporary West Bank legal profession is constituted by individuals who have never engaged in any other vocation. Among the senior lawyers who graduated from the Jerusalem Law Classes, a few remain who conform to the pattern established during the Mandate period of migration from the civil service (most frequently from the Judicial Department) into private law practice. In fact, this pattern has abated but never disappeared, either during the period of Jordanian administration or under Israeli occupation. A small number of lawyers, perhaps ten to fifteen of the working faction and slightly more of the striking faction, worked for a number of years in government departments. Again, most common were those who had held positions in the Judicial Department, as court reporters, clerks, and, less frequently, prosecutors.[35]

One of these had started as a court reporter during the Jordanian era, studied law by correspondence through Damascus University, and then had succeeded in winning a post as a lower court judge (*qadi sulh*). After several years which bridged the periods of Jordanian and Israeli administration, he was promoted to membership in the Nablus Court of First Instance. One year later, he had resigned from the judiciary to become one of the first of the community of Nablus lawyers to break the strike and resume an active practice. At the time, the strike had rendered the market for legal services wide open. With his credentials as a former judge, this lawyer established himself as one of the most successful private practitioners in Nablus, with a constant coterie of apprentices and a West Bank–wide reputation among practitioners as one of their luminaries.

Other former civil servants included a few teachers and several employees from the Land or the Tax Department. Those from the latter two departments, though few, were important. They constituted almost the entirety of the region's genuine specialists in particular areas of substantive law. They worked almost exclusively in land or tax law, in which they had developed both expertise and personal relationships with responsible officials. Judicial Department employees–turned-lawyers tend not to specialize, although one former criminal prosecutor left government service to become the most prominent criminal defense lawyer in the region.

Financial motives were invariably cited for moves from government employment to private law practice, although the prospect of independence lured some as well. Most of the subgroup of second careerists I interviewed had entered the civil service directly or shortly after having completed secondary school studies, although one of the more intriguing individuals I encountered during my research had not. His story, though exceptional, is instructive:

> I was born in 1941 in Salameh, a village in the Haifa area, to a very poor family. In the war of 1948, we were forced to flee, losing what little land we had, and ended up in an UNRWA camp in the vicinity of Tulkarm. I finished preparatory school in an UNRWA school in the camp, but as there was no work to be had, I started selling Eskimo ice cream bars, walking through neighborhoods with a can slung from my shoulder with ice to keep the bars cold, taking any other part-time jobs I could find. With rations from UNRWA and the earnings of the various family members, we barely scraped by. I managed to take a one-year course in land surveying in an UNRWA vocational school in Kalandia camp [near Jerusalem]. Then I went to Saudi Arabia, where I found a job with the Land Reclamation Authority. I worked there for five years, and then returned

to the West Bank in 1966 with five thousand dinars in my
pocket, at a time when people were very poor. After a while, I
got a job as the director of the Land Registry Office in the
Jenin-Tulkarm-Nablus area. By this time, I had gotten married
and had six kids. But I had the ambition to improve my status,
so I studied law by correspondence through BAU, from 1974
to 1978, finishing in four years without failing a course, despite family and job obligations. After finishing law studies, I
worked for two years as a court reporter, which was more like
working as a judge, since I actually wrote and made the decisions, while the judge simply signed them. Then I trained for
two years with a Nablus lawyer, but basically he taught me
nothing and I was working on my own. From the beginning
I've worked exclusively in cases related to land—people in this
area know that I know my business, so whatever problem they
have that involves land, they bring to me.

Another important category within the profession includes individuals who began independent practice, were recruited as judges or
prosecutors, and then after periods of service ranging from two to
ten years, returned to private law practice. Several had joined the Judicial Department very early in their careers, when the job security
and prestige of a civil service position was an attractive alternative
to a fledgling and uncertain law practice.[36] It is clear that these former judges and prosecutors, who number about twenty, have prof-
ited as lawyers from their associations with the judiciary, as they are
currently among the most active and successful in the legal profession. The reasons for this are several, and not all obvious. I asked one
practitioner if clients sought out lawyers who had been judges to represent them because of their presumed legal expertise. He scoffed,
and said:

You have to understand how people here think. They are
simple-minded, and neither know nor care about this thing we
call "legal expertise." When they look at a lawyer who has
worked for some time as a judge, they figure, first of all, that
his former colleagues, the currently sitting judges, will favor
him, maybe give him a little more weight or respect. Second,
they figure that he might know which among them is on the
take. And third, it might enter their minds to think that if he
hadn't been a more "clever" (*ashtar*) lawyer than most of his
fellows, he wouldn't have been appointed as a judge.

As we shall subsequently see, the popular calculation was not without a certain validity.

Most West Bank lawyers begin their practices in the same town in which they apprenticed and have some notoriety. Often this is also the young lawyer's town of origin, where family ties and acquaintances also help to provide a core clientele. Those who attain a modicum of success in a smaller town with only a magistrate court typically open a second office in the closest town with a district court (either Nablus, Ramallah, or, recently, Hebron). Some split their time between the two locales permanently, although most do so only temporarily, eventually shifting their practice to the larger urban center.

A small contingent of attorneys has spent some portion of their legal career outside the West Bank.[37] These individuals play a special role, however, for their experience in other legal environments affords them a comparative basis on which to evaluate the impact of occupation on the legal system of the West Bank. A number have refused to engage in practice in the West Bank, claiming disgust for the decrepitude of the local legal system. Those who have chosen to work regale West Bank lawyers with tales of what it is like to practice in a "real" legal system, confirming their colleagues' frustrations and honing their resentment against the occupation.

The large group of striking lawyers bears a separate discussion. Their career paths are not normal, but reflect individual responses to the limitations imposed by the strike. For the very few who continue to practice law full time, the strike has obliged them to shift their focus of activities from litigation in the civil courts to a varied practice that includes providing legal advice, drafting legal documents, and litigating religious court cases. Several of the most active striking lawyers are retained as legal advisers for municipal governments, religious sects or associations, hospitals, and schools. As mentioned above, a somewhat larger number supplement their strike stipend with practice in the religious courts, although they seldom work for more than ten hours per week.[38] Many striking lawyers have completely abandoned the law to work in journalism, currency exchanges, or to partake in business ventures of various kinds.[39] At least as many are more or less idle, supporting themselves from personal assets and their strike stipends, in a sense, making a career of the strike itself.

Movement from the legal profession into political office, common during the Jordanian era, has been mostly blocked because of the circumstances of occupation.[40] But municipal elections were held in the West Bank in 1972 and 1976. One lawyer, Karim Khalaf, was elected on a nationalist slate to the mayorship of Ramallah and went on to achieve international fame as a leader of the national movement in the Occupied Territories. Another prominent lawyer and former judge was elected to the municipal council of Tulkarm in 1976.

Conclusions

The social composition of the West Bank's legal profession has undergone significant changes since the Mandate period, when it was primarily the province of Palestinian society's social elite. Increasing access to legal education has led to the influx of members of more diverse social backgrounds. Vocation as an element of social identity in Palestinian society remains subordinate to such factors as family status and wealth and village or town origin. As a result, the entry of individuals of lower economic class and social status to the profession has done less to elevate their individual social positions than to lower the prestige of the profession as a whole. The diffusion of the profession's social identity is matched by a diminution in its internal cohesion, trends with parallels in a number of other societies.[41]

In general, the profession no longer attracts the most dynamic and capable members of society. With the exception of a few highly motivated individuals who affirmatively choose to practice law and the small group that steps immediately into the professional elite by virtue of kinship links to eminent practitioners, the legal profession has become a residual vocation into which some appear to drift because they are barred from more prestigious fields, like medicine and engineering. The actual and perceived power of West Bank lawyers is significantly conditioned by these facts.

Several other changes in the composition of the profession and within its working and striking factions are more directly linked to the Israeli occupation. Movement between the realms of law and nationalist politics, crucial to the high status of lawyers in the Mandate period, has been mostly blocked by the punitive policies of the military government. Those who attempted to assume leadership in opposition to the occupation were exiled, depriving the profession of a small but publicly visible segment of its elite. There is evidence, moreover, that many of the most talented legal professionals have been siphoned off by the brain drain described in chapter 1. Finally, the strike has immobilized a large proportion of the established profession. This is suggested by the age distribution of the older striking faction and the younger working faction. It thus appears that a number of forces associated with the occupation are working to deprive the profession of the talents of its most respected and able members. The negative impact of these forces on the group's fortunes, though difficult to weigh, cannot be questioned.

If access to the West Bank legal profession has gradually broadened, substantial advantages are bequeathed to aspiring lawyers of higher social class and status, especially those who have close relatives already involved in the profession. After they enter the profession, the obstacles and advantages experienced by individuals of different social background reappear even more strongly in the determination of who among them achieves professional success. Thus the stratification within the profession in many regards reproduces the social hierarchy characteristic of the general society, with individuals often occupying roughly comparable positions in the two systems of ranking. This topic will be explored more fully in the next chapter.

6. The Organization of the Legal Profession

The previous chapter examined who the individuals composing the West Bank legal profession are. It also attempted to explain the characteristics of the group as a function of the processes according to which membership in the profession is gained and maintained. This chapter will describe how lawyers in the West Bank conduct their work—in what form, within the framework of what kinds of relationships with their colleagues, with what resources, human and physical, at their disposal, and for what gain?

The Form of Legal Practice

The model or ideal type of practice to which most West Bank legal professionals aspire, and to which most, in fact, conform, is that of the solo practitioner. Vocational independence is regarded as an essential feature of law practice and a sign of a successful professional life. Most lawyers tend to view partnership arrangements as deviations to which individuals resort only under financial pressure. As such, partnerships are believed to communicate to potential clients that the attorneys are struggling and unsuccessful.

Among 165 working master lawyers in the West Bank at the time of my fieldwork, 150 were solo practitioners, 12 were engaged in partnerships with 1 other lawyer (that is to say, 6 partnerships in total), and the remaining 3 were joined in a single office. Among 250 striking master lawyers, I was able to ascertain the existence of only 1 partnership engaging 3 lawyers in Hebron. A substantially larger number of informants, although engaged in solo practice at the time of my research, had been involved in partnership arrangements at one point or another during their careers, however, usually at an early stage.[1] Once established in the profession, they had dissolved their partnerships and pursued their careers as independent professionals.

Lawyers referred in this connection as well to the alleged difficulty that Arabs have in cooperative effort, and to the problems of
establishing trust with others in business relationships. The latter
concern echoes general beliefs and values in West Bank society
about the public sphere and the world of commerce. Life beyond the
household or, at best, the extended family, is seen to be governed
only by the laws of self-interest, a constant game of wits and power
that rewards the assertive, clever, and sometimes devious. Parties
are expected to act unscrupulously and are even begrudgingly admired for doing so. In the words of one lawyer, "Why should I have a
partner? Every time a client walked through his door I'd be wonder-
ing if they're striking some side deal that would cut me out of my
share of the fee. Why do I need the headache? It's just simpler for me
to work on my own."

Under these circumstances, it is not surprising that of the seven
functioning partnerships involving working lawyers, three—including the only one that had been in existence for more than five
years—were formed by individuals who were related somehow. This
included one of two brothers, another of two brothers-in-law, and
the third of two brothers and the son of one, nephew of the other.
Four partnerships joined lawyers still in the first ten years of their
practices, while a fifth was formed by an older lawyer and his
younger former trainee. With one exception, these partnerships appeared at least modestly active and successful and, in some cases,
were among the leading offices in their respective locales.

Specialization, Stratification, and the
Professional Division of Labor

One of the implications of the preponderance of solo practitioners in
the West Bank's legal profession is that, with the exceptions of the
above-mentioned civil servants–turned-lawyers (and a few further
qualifications to be noted below), the great majority are generalists.
This phenomenon is conditioned on the low demand for legal services relative to the number of current practitioners, exacerbated by
a highly unequal distribution of work favoring the small professional elite. Low demand for their services obligates the majority of
legal practitioners to accept whatever type of case is brought to
them.

The number of elite lawyers whose services are in such demand
that they can select both the quantity and the type of cases to accept
probably does not exceed twenty for the entire region. Many, though
not all, of the members of the professional elite are forty-five years of

age or older and operate out of offices in the larger towns, which are the seats of district courts. Another thirty lawyers are comfortably busy but of necessity less discriminating in the cases they accept. The remainder are consigned to chronic work shortages and insecurity of varying degree. Many younger lawyers at the time of my research were scarcely earning enough to cover office expenses.

The share of the legal market captured by the professional elite is not entirely random. It typically encompasses the range of legal problems encountered by the well-to-do individuals, corporations, and other institutions that form the elite's clientele and excludes the kinds of cases that involve middle-class or poor clients. Hence cases involving issues of corporate law, trademarks, labor law, and similar matters often are handled by elite lawyers. In contrast, successful lawyers seldom appear in the Islamic courts, for example, which service mostly a poor clientele, or in criminal cases other than those involving serious offenses. The cases handled by the professional elite are invariably the most lucrative.

This results in a kind of specialization by area of law among elite practitioners, albeit of a limited degree. The thirty or so lawyers occupying the middle range probably have the greatest diversity in types of cases handled. The lowest—and largest—stratum, of young and less successful lawyers, is consigned to a sort of residual specialization in types of cases involving less affluent clients, in the lower civil courts, petty criminal cases or collection of small debts, and those held in the religious courts.

The impact of the small but very active professional elite on the organization of the market for legal services cannot be underestimated. A case in point is the above-mentioned three-person partnership formed by the two brothers and son-nephew. In many ways, their office is unique in the region, whereas in others, it embodies a number of features of the profession that I have attempted thus far to describe. For both its representative and exceptional characteristics, this office is worthy of further examination.

The office is located in Ramallah, currently the judicial center of the West Bank and the town to which the family moved from its home town of Jaffa in 1948. The uncle of the two brothers was an eminent judge during the period of the British Mandate and a leading member of the Christian Arab community in Palestine. Both brothers were educated in the Jerusalem Law Classes. The elder had worked for some time in the Judicial Department, and the younger one had just finished an apprenticeship at the end of British administration. Each practiced independently or in partnership with others for a while, then formed a partnership around 1970. In the late seventies, they were joined by a son of the elder brother, who had obtained a B.A. in English at the American University of Beirut (which has no law faculty), studied law at Lincoln's Inn in London, and then returned to the West Bank to train under his father and uncle.

In 1985, the office also contained the full complement of four *estagiares* (two each under the supervision of the brothers; the son-nephew had not yet practiced five years and thus did not qualify to accept trainees), one full-time and another part-time secretary-receptionist, and another part-time accountant–office manager. The office itself, though furnished in utilitarian style, had separate rooms for each of the senior lawyers, a third shared by the younger lawyer and the *estagiares,* a sizable workspace for clerical staff, a seating area for waiting clients, a small utility area with a stove to prepare hot drinks, and a bathroom. Separate phone lines served all of the lawyers' rooms, and clerical staff had the use of both English and Arabic typewriters. By local scale, this array of human and physical resources made the office a veritable juggernaut, capable of production far beyond that of any other law office in the region. Indeed, the office handled almost every important case in the region involving issues of corporate law and trademarks (usually facing one of the same four or five other elite lawyers representing the opposing party) and was on retainer for almost every foreign interest doing business in the West Bank, some 120 corporations. The partnership also dealt with many other types of cases, including those in the military courts, and also regularly cooperated with an Israeli lawyer based in Tel Aviv in taking West Bank cases to the Israeli High Court.

Another minimal form of specialization exists that is institutional, that is, by court system rather than by area of law as such. A majority of West Bank working lawyers confine themselves to practice solely in the civil courts of the region, with perhaps occasional appearances in the religious courts. A smaller group works in both civil and military court systems (including military objections committees and other avenues of adjudication). Still fewer specialize in either the military or the religious court systems. Of these, only one of which I was aware was not joined in a partnership with another lawyer who specialized in the civil court cases. Because of the different topical jurisdictions of the three primary court systems, institutional specialization tends to be translated into substantive law specialization, but, again, only at a very general level.

The concentration of the majority of West Bank working lawyers in civil court practice is the consequence of a variety of factors. Religious court cases simply are not sufficiently remunerative to support a full practice and are generally regarded as intellectually and professionally unfulfilling. In addition, working lawyers must face competition in this area from striking lawyers, for whom appearances in religious courts are permissible under the terms of the strike. A large number of West Bank lawyers at the time of my research had made limited forays into military court practice, but had returned to the civil courts. Many expressed distaste for the atmosphere in the military courts and for direct dealings with the Israeli authorities. Military courts were described by many as "not true," or farcical courts, in which the legal efforts and skills of an attorney were foiled by procedural laws disadvantageous to defendants and sentences in which were determined by Israeli military intelligence rather than by judges. For others, the law of the military courts was simply unfamiliar, and they felt awkward pleading in Arabic and having to rely on court interpreters to convey their arguments to the Hebrew-speaking Israeli judges.

The Role of Israeli Arab Lawyers

Perhaps a more important, though often unarticulated, reason for the West Bank lawyers' relatively low level of activity in the military court system is the competition they face in that arena from a group of fifteen to twenty Israeli lawyers. Most of these are Palestinians of Israeli citizenship who have trained in Israeli law faculties and are in the first ten years of practice, although two of the most prominent of this group are internationally renowned Jewish Israeli women associated with leftist Israeli political parties.[2] Several others are former military prosecutors who completed their service in the army and subsequently went into private law practice.

While this small circle of Israeli lawyers is not part of the group that is the focus of this study, namely, West Bank lawyers, their role in the legal scene in the Occupied Territories is too critical to ignore. From their offices in Jerusalem or such northern Israeli-Arab communities as Tireh, Tayyibeh, and Nazareth, these lawyers travel up and down the West Bank, handling fully 60 to 70 percent of the military court cases that arise there.

The major competitive advantages they possess over their West Bank counterparts are mastery of Hebrew, knowledge of Israeli law, and a better general familiarity with Israeli legal culture.[3] Israeli lawyers are also the beneficiaries of several contemporary folk beliefs prevalent in the West Bank Palestinian community. One of the most influential of these is that Israeli lawyers, especially Jewish ones, have better *wasta* with the military government than do others.[4] A closely related popular perception holds that Israeli lawyers are less intimidated by Israeli military bureaucracy and hence are more zealous advocates of their clients' interests. As one Israeli Arab lawyer expressed it to me, "It is a slave mentality. People simply refuse to believe that they can be helped by another slave in a conflict with the master."

This perception redounds principally to the benefit of Jewish Israeli lawyers, and secondarily to Israeli Arab lawyers, who are recognized at least as having the protection of Israeli citizenship (which residents of the Occupied Territories do not).[5] But the advantage to Jewish Israeli lawyers is somewhat offset by popular distrust of them, particularly in cases that have sensitive political dimensions. Israeli Arab lawyers do not suffer this liability and so, on balance, are the most strategically positioned of all.

It must be recalled that, between the military courts and the objections committees, substantial inroads have been made into the jurisdiction of the West Bank civil courts. As a result, many cases that formerly would have been treated in the West Bank civil courts are now handled in an institutional framework that favors Israeli lawyers. We have also seen that Israeli civil courts, in which Israeli lawyers have an effective monopoly, have displaced the West Bank civil courts in a variety of contexts: in Jerusalem, where the jurisdiction of Jordanian courts was extinguished on annexation of the city; in a number of civil cases arising in the West Bank involving insurance claims against companies based in Israel; and in appeals to the Israeli High Court. The market for legal services, once monopolized by West Bank lawyers, has thus been opened to nonreciprocal competition from Israeli lawyers under conditions distinctly favorable to the latter group.[6]

The role that Israeli Arab lawyers play in the West Bank's legal scene is not limited to the narrow functional task of providing legal services to the community in the contexts enumerated here. Interaction between them and West Bank practitioners has occurred not only in the courts but also in the framework of cooperative activities among the more politically inclined members of both groups.[7] As the handful of lawyers in the West Bank who have practiced elsewhere, Israeli Arab lawyers provide their West Bank colleagues with a benchmark for comparison between the practice of law under occupation and professional life in a normal situation. The comparison is all the more poignant for the West Bankers as it highlights the quality of the legal system Israel is capable of administering when committed to doing so. The image conveyed by Israeli Arab lawyers to their West Bank colleagues is that of a competent and conscientious Israeli judiciary supported by an efficient administrative apparatus.

While structural factors will continue to favor Israeli lawyers, both Jewish and Arab, in cases conducted in Israeli civil courts, the circumstances in the military courts appear to be changing. Increasing numbers of West Bank lawyers are building relatively prosperous practices in the military court system and are taking a larger share of the overall demand for legal services in political-security cases. The West Bank community, having seen that Arab lawyers from Israel can effectively represent Palestinian clients, may now be beginning to perceive that its native sons and daughters, who often charge lower fees than Israeli Arab lawyers, may be just as effective.

It is also possible that military court practice is serving as a basis for Israeli Arab lawyers to establish a professional reputation, after which they move on to other, more lucrative and professionally stimulating, areas of practice. Several well-known Israeli Arab lawyers who were very active in the military courts in the seventies and early eighties have begun to shift their focus to civil practice solely in the Israeli courts, which they claim brings them more income and greater job satisfaction.[8] West Bank lawyers are accordingly faring better in the field of military court practice than they had in the past.

Cooperation and Professional Networks

It seems that lawyers rarely cooperate with each other on cases. Even partners work individually on the cases of their own clientele (although consultations may occur between partners on difficult issues). Informal assistance in the form of advice may be given by practitioners who are friends or who sometimes cover each other's practice in the event that one travels outside the region or is incapacitated in some way. During the period of my research, one attorney from Hebron was arrested on charges of rendering assistance to a "hostile organization" and was detained for three months. His lawyer friends in the meantime serviced his clients, reserving the fees earned for his family, and volunteered their services toward his defense.

In cases involving multiple parties represented by several attorneys—for example, a number of young men charged in military court with participation in the same demonstration—lawyers may coordinate their arguments or offer tips on how to plea, but this is generally done casually, in the hallway on the way into the session or during recess, not through special strategy meetings.

West Bank lawyers cooperate with Israeli lawyers in one situation in which they are obliged to, that is, in handling an appeal to the Israeli High Court, before which, as we have seen, West Bank lawyers are not allowed to appear. A few West Bank lawyers maintain regular contact with Israeli lawyers for the purpose of bringing cases to the High Court.[9]

Given the simplicity of most cases and the comparatively minimal specialization by area of substantive law, lawyers tend to refer cases to others only when they are too busy to assume them personally. I once asked an extremely prominent practitioner if he received referrals from other lawyers. To my surprise, he responded icily, "I am the kind of lawyer who gives referrals, not the kind who receives them." As I eventually learned, master lawyers sometimes are focal points of informal professional networks that link them to former *estagiares* throughout the region. Referrals are often handed from the *istaaz* to former trainees. Referred cases are sometimes less remunerative, or less professionally stimulating. An *istaaz* may not relish traveling to handle a case arising in an outlying town, instead referring it to a former *estagiare* based in that town or nearby. There are also some lateral referrals, particularly between friends who tend to focus their work in different court systems.

Support Staff

Many West Bank lawyers hire at least part-time receptionists who may also do some secretarial work. Almost as many do not hire any support staff at all. The responsibilities of receptionists are typically limited to maintaining a physical presence in the office during the morning hours while the attorney goes to the court building, receiving clients and preparing and serving them and the lawyer hot or cold drinks, and answering the telephone (although the lawyer will often do this when in the office). Even those who perform some clerical tasks seldom know their employer's schedule, this being solely managed by the lawyer, and are almost never asked to perform tasks that involve discretion or judgment. Office accounts are also exclusively kept by the lawyers themselves.[10]

Thus with the exception of master lawyers supervising *estagiares*, West Bank lawyers maintain direct personal control over virtually all aspects of their practice. At the same time, they perform all of the tasks demanded by their work, frequently finding themselves caught between scheduling conflicts, frustrated by the need to be several places simultaneously.

Occasionally, lawyers contract the services of other independent professionals. This occurs most frequently in cases involving disputes over land (either between private parties, or a possessor of property and the military government), which routinely require maps prepared by licensed surveyors. The more active lawyers maintain standing relationships with surveyors in the towns in which they practice. Accountants are sometimes consulted in tax cases, and the expert testimony of others such as engineers and physicians is solicited if the complexity of the case and the interests at stake warrant it, although this is rare.[11]

From time to time, lawyers have need for specialized clerical services, such as translation of documents (most frequently from Hebrew to Arabic). Such tasks, if beyond the capabilities of the lawyer and the support staff, are farmed out to general services offices, found in most towns. One lawyer fluent in Hebrew augmented his income by translating documents from Hebrew to Arabic for his colleagues for a modest fee.

Physical Resources

The distribution of law offices in the West Bank represents a rough physical code of the local professional hierarchy. The offices of the older, more prominent lawyers are typically near court buildings or the commercial centers in the district court towns, on a major thoroughfare, and are seldom above the ground or second level of the building. The offices of younger and less successful lawyers, if in the district court towns, are progressively more distant from courts and the heart of town and are often either more obscurely located or are on the upper floors of buildings, much less accessible to clients. Otherwise, they are located in magistrate court towns, where rents are cheaper and competition for suitable space is less intense.

Ironically, choice office locations are often held by prominent practitioners under old lease agreements that fixed rent at levels appropriate twenty or more years ago. Under the landlord-tenant laws that govern such agreements, it is extremely difficult to raise rents. Given inflation and increases in real income in the West Bank, the monthly amount actually paid under these leases now equals the cost of a lunch in a moderately priced restaurant. Prospective tenants wishing to occupy particular premises are now forced to surrender a one-time payment to its current tenants, referred to as "key money," to induce them to vacate.[12] Landlords now demand much higher monthly rents of new tenants than they did in the noninflationary years of Jordanian administration. As a result, the costs of entry into the profession in a competitively advantageous location and subsequent maintenance expenses have multiplied, further securing the favored position of already established lawyers.

At the lowest rung of the professional ladder are the less fortunate lawyers who have been forced by the high costs of obtaining and keeping an office to operate their practices out of their homes. To visit one lawyer living in an older and generally poor section of Nablus, I wandered through back alleys and with the aid of neighborhood children eventually found a rickety wooden gate, which I was assured led to my prospective informant's home. I announced my arrival by yanking on a string attached to a bell located somewhere inside the house. The lawyer led me through a junk-strewn courtyard, up a flight of stairs, through the kitchen—common area of the house (where we briefly greeted his mother and wife, who were preparing lunch), across a precarious catwalk exposed to the elements to a room on the upper floor of an adjacent building. This room served as his office as well as a storage area for the house. There we sat talking, amidst crates of oranges and vegetables, interrupted occasionally by the shouts and arguments of several of his six children playing just outside in the street.

The size and quality of furnishings of offices vary considerably. Most consist of two rooms, the first containing a desk for a receptionist and four or five simple chairs lining the walls, and the second containing the attorney's desk, library, and a few chairs for clients. Many are scarcely larger than closets and were obviously not originally designed as office space, as, on occasion, they exhibit rather idiosyncratic configurations of space.

As a general rule, the quality of furnishings serves as no indication of the professional status of the occupant. Some of the most successful lawyers, who own palatial residences, operate out of tawdry premises. Some change is discernible among younger lawyers; among those who can afford it, there is a clear tendency to invest more in the appearance of one's office.

Many offices are equipped with manual Arabic typewriters, but nothing else in the way of office machines. Fully half of the offices lack telephones.[13] I entered only one office that contained a copy machine. Lawyers' libraries are usually limited to Jordanian statutes and a few treatises left over from university years.[14] Any extensive research must be conducted with borrowed materials or with those contained in the two legal libraries housed in the court buildings in Ramallah and Nablus.

Lawyers who can muster the cost of an automobile—which, due to Israeli taxes of almost 100 percent on some imported goods, can cost roughly double the cost in the United States or Europe—and can afford the gasoline to run it, enjoy a great competitive advantage over their less fortunate colleagues. One must recall the small scale of the West Bank; the main court and administrative centers of Nablus, Ramallah, Jerusalem, and Hebron are separated by a distance that may be driven in approximately two hours. For legal cases in which substantial interests are at stake, the West Bank functions essentially as a single market for legal services. While geography confers some advantage, especially on the centrally located lawyers from the Jerusalem and Ramallah areas, it does not confer anything approaching a monopoly. Lawyers with cars can and do frequently travel up and down the West Bank, handling cases in the courts along the way.[15]

Fee Arrangements

In Jordanian law, the defeated party in a civil suit bears the burden of court costs and attorney fees for himself or herself and the opposing party. The amount of attorney fees due is fixed by the judge in accordance with general standards established by law and is added to any award emerging out of the substance of the case. The fees determined by these standards, however, bear virtually no relation to those actually charged in practice, which are far greater than the formal standards specify. The legal maximum for cases in magistrate courts is ten Jordanian dinars, for example, whereas in some cases, actual fees run into thousands of dinars. In effect, then, victorious parties bear the brunt of their own attorney costs, receiving little more than symbolic compensation through the judgment of the court.

Limits are also imposed on the amount a lawyer can earn through contingency arrangements, from 5 percent to 10 percent of the amount in controversy. However, I encountered no lawyers who actually worked according to contingency arrangements even to the extent legally permitted. I received the distinct impression from some informants that the notion of investing the attorney with an economic stake in the outcome of a case was offensive and demeaning to a lawyer, who required no incentive other than his or her own sense of duty to perform conscientiously. Equally germane, I suspect, is that lawyers were probably no more anxious to gamble on the outcome of a case than were their clients, particularly given the unpredictability and long delays that afflicted the civil courts.

Attorneys' fees in criminal cases in the West Bank civil courts or in military court cases are borne by the defendant irrespective of acquittal or conviction and, to my knowledge, are not limited in any way. In practice, fees in these cases seem to be determined in the same manner as in civil cases. The most common form of fee arrangement for all types of cases is a fixed sum calculated for each stage in the litigation or for each court session.[16] As one informant described his custom to me:

> If you were to come to me wanting only a consultation or legal advice [*istishara qanuniya*], you would describe your problem, presenting me with all relevant documents, and then we would agree on a consultation fee. The amount would depend on the complexity of the case and the weight of the interests it involved. I would perform my study, opening a temporary file, and then render my opinion either orally or in writing. If that settled matters, then you would pay me the agreed consultation fee. If, on the other hand, you were being sued or wanted to file a suit against someone else, I would open a permanent file and we would then agree on a new fee that would incorporate the cost of the consultation in addition to covering my work to the termination of the case in the court of first instance [either magistrate or district], which would be due only at that point. If the case went to the appellate court, we would negotiate still another fee, but the amount of that would probably be less, since most of the legal work has really already been done. If your case succeeded at all levels and went to the Execution Department, we might even have to agree on another fee; execution is usually straightforward, but at times involves more work than any other stage of litigation.

Needless to say, different attorneys charge different fees for the same work, depending on their status in the professional hierarchy and on the wealth of their clients, which, as we have seen, can be closely related matters. The fees charged by lawyers in the larger and generally more prosperous towns such as Nablus and Ramallah are higher on average than those of lawyers in less prosperous towns such as Hebron or smaller towns like Jenin or Qalqilya.

It is difficult to state with confidence what fees constitute in actual sums, for standardization throughout the market for legal services appears to be emerging only gradually. One informant, a young
lawyer of modestly successful standing, told me that his normal
charge for a court appearance—requiring two to three hours of preparation and two to three hours in and around the court—was between 70 and 100 dinars ($3.30 U.S./dinar in 1984–1985). Fees in
military court cases of the most straightforward variety apparently
range anywhere from 150 to 250 dinars for less expensive lawyers to
500 dinars for top lawyers.[17] Land cases, whether in the civil or military courts, can involve significant financial interests and thus may
lead to much higher fees, sometimes exceeding 5,000 dinars.

A small number of lawyers hold general retainerships (*wakalat
ʿama*), which obligate them to perform all necessary legal tasks for a
particular client in return for a fixed monthly or annual payment.
While these arrangements can generate tensions between lawyers
and overly demanding clients, from the perspective of most lawyers,
they are highly desirable for the stable income they provide. General
retainerships seem to be arranged with three categories of clients:
(1) institutions of various kinds (nonprofit associations, churches,
hospitals, municipalities, and the like) that have a relatively steady
need for legal services; (2) business concerns (sometimes corporations, but more often owned by individuals or partners); and (3) individual migrants to places outside the West Bank.

The first two categories are serviced almost exclusively by the
members of the professional elite. The third category is frequently
serviced by lawyers who have kin relationships with the migrant.
Attorneys retained by migrants most commonly manage their real
property assets, collecting rents, paying taxes and other fees, and
so forth, vital interests that clients prefer to entrust to family
members.[18]

Income and Standard of Living

There was no category of information, including political, that I encountered greater difficulty in gathering than that pertaining to income or, indeed, anything from which income could be inferred
even vaguely. Few informants were willing to go farther than to
speculate about the amount a lawyer would charge in specific hypo-
thetical circumstances, or to volunteer estimates of the ranges of incomes within the profession. The simple and sometimes openly admitted reason for lawyers' reluctance to divulge data bearing on

personal finances was that many of them, like the majority of West Bank residents, evade taxes and fear that any disclosure of financial information might subject them to investigation by tax authorities.

Another difficulty in obtaining reliable information about lawyers' incomes was income fluctuation in response to the vagaries of the demand for legal services. Individual conditions aside, however, there was unanimity that the legal profession as a whole had seen much more prosperous days. According to some of the older lawyers, after the 1968–1973 boom in the West Bank, business in the region had steadily if slowly declined.[19]

Lawyers were acutely conscious of the dependence of their profession on the welfare of the business sector: "What is our work without business? Nothing! When the businessmen stay at home, we sit in our offices drinking coffee and playing backgammon!" Even during periods of relative prosperity, it was claimed, the type of economic growth in the region did not produce a stable demand for legal services, at any rate, for those offered by West Bank lawyers. Increased consumption alone led to increases in some kinds of cases; many more autos on the road meant more accidents and thus more insurance compensation cases, but these were usually handled in Israeli courts by Israeli lawyers.

Mainly, though, the low level of economic organizational complexity that characterized the West Bank during the Jordanian era has changed little under occupation. As such, demand for legal planning is light and there is a paucity of cases involving complex, technical legal issues, which occupy so much of the time of lawyers in more economically complex societies. Finally, as I was reminded, the specific kind of legal work generated by the conditions of occupation—political-security cases and other disputes between citizens and the occupation administration—also tend to benefit Israeli lawyers more than their counterparts in the West Bank.

Table 2 presents a general estimate of monthly incomes for working lawyers in the West Bank.[20] These figures, when translated into approximate qualitative terms, yield the following picture: the lawyers who cluster around the two hundred dinar monthly income mark represent the lowest end of middle class status; any dropping substantially below that, probably few in number, are genuinely poor. The cluster around the five hundred dinar monthly mark may be termed squarely middle-class, while those approaching one thousand are comfortably upper middle class. The 10 percent who earn more than one thousand dinars a month are truly wealthy by local standards, but probably no more than two or three are among the wealthiest members of West Bank Palestinian society, and these probably not solely by virtue of the income derived from legal work.[21]

Table 2. *Estimated Monthly Income of Working Lawyers, 1985*

Income Range (JD)	Percentage of Lawyers
0–200	40
200–500	25
500–1,000	25
More than 1,000	10

Note: In 1984–1985, the dinar was worth approximately $3.30 U.S.

Lawyers were no less reticent about divulging information regarding other personal assets, whether income-producing or not, for the same reasons. Surely some of them do hold other assets, most likely in real property, which is the most popular form of local investment after personal residential construction. And the most likely among them to have such assets are members of the notable families who have inherited shares of family holdings. An exceptional few have doubtless bought in to real property with earnings from law practice.[22]

Conclusions

West Bank lawyers are persons of relatively modest means, both in the human and physical resources they command in performing their work, and in the income they derive from it. As in many other societies, wealth and status are closely linked in Palestinian society, and the profession's mixed but mostly unspectacular economic performance has done nothing to enhance its power or prestige, especially when measured against its position during the Mandate period. In part, the economic difficulties currently facing lawyers are due to the substantial increase in the number of legal practitioners and to the simultaneous narrowing of the market for legal services caused by incursions into the jurisdiction of West Bank courts. Many cases that formerly would have been tried in these courts are now routed to tribunals in which Israeli lawyers enjoy substantial competitive advantages, if not an outright monopoly. In addition to the factors specifically affecting the welfare of the lawyers, as they themselves pointed out, their fortunes also depend greatly on the general prosperity of society, especially the business sector.

In chapter 5 we saw that one of the primary appeals of the legal profession is its promise of vocational independence. We now see that this promise is in fact fulfilled for most legal practitioners and that most succeed in achieving the goal of solo practice. Perhaps for the personalities it attracts as well as for the structure in which its individual members subsequently operate, the practice of law in the West Bank is highly individualistic. Colleagues are, in a very real sense, also competitors in a market that is ever more restricted and challenging. Collective professional interests are cross-cut and weakened by the contradictory interests of the profession's individual members. Group interaction is relatively infrequent. The structure of the profession, thus, is not strongly conducive to tight group solidarity and coordinated collective action.

Stratification within the profession mirrors the structure of the larger society of which it is an element. The professional elite services and interacts with the general social elite, as do members of the middle and lower strata of the profession with their social peers. The lateral relationships that link lawyers with nonlawyers of similar social background and status are probably stronger than the vertical associations between lawyers at different levels in the professional hierarchy, again militating in favor of relatively low internal social cohesion.

7. The Content of Legal Practice

Chapters 5 and 6 described the social identities of the lawyers of the West Bank and how or in what forms they went about their business. This chapter will delineate what the business of the West Bank lawyers actually is, beginning with the way in which legal work is conceived, and then turning to the daily routines followed by lawyers. It will also examine the types of cases, setting and atmosphere, and style of sessions in the civil and military court systems, which are the primary centers for the West Bank legal profession's major work activity: litigation. Practice in the religious courts forms a less significant part of the work of most West Bank practitioners and, accordingly, will receive briefer treatment. Finally, we will consider the activities of lawyers in several nonlitigation-related areas of practice.

The Conception of Legal Work

The essence of legal work, in the eyes of most West Bank lawyers, is litigation, more specifically, oral pleading (*murafaʿa*). The mark of a successful lawyer, according to a number of my informants, is that he or she "is always in court." Other professional activities are seen as mere preliminary steps leading toward the real business of court pleadings. Lawyers are sometimes disdainful of aspects of their work that, measured against the standard of the ideal conception, are felt to be nonlegal and thus unbefitting a legal professional.

When queried as to the amount of time he spent in conducting negotiations with administrative authorities on behalf of clients, one successful lawyer grimaced distastefully, saying, "*Good* lawyers don't get involved in these kinds of things." Informants were almost always happy to have me as an audience during their court appearances, but were befuddled by my curiosity about the broader range of their professional activities, most of which they dismissed as "just sitting around in the office."

Ironically, court pleadings occupy proportionally little of a lawyer's actual daily work time. Why then is the whole of legal practice understood to be exemplified by one of its small constituent parts? First, its monopoly over appearances in court most fully distinguishes the legal profession from any other sector or group in society. While others may act as informal arbitrators in disputes, or as intermediaries between citizens and administrative bodies, only lawyers are qualified to represent clients in court proceedings.

Second, of the array of possible services offered by legal professionals to laypeople, representation in court is the one most highly valued and most commonly sought. The prevalent pattern is for people to resort to lawyers if and only if they intend to initiate some court action or themselves have been drawn into litigation as defendants. In short, lawyers, both in their own and the popular perception, are for litigating. Hence, for a majority of West Bank professionals, court proceedings are, in fact, the focus of their work, toward which most other activities are oriented.

Finally, court appearances are the most public aspect of a lawyer's work and provide a forum for the display of his or her talents and value. This is of special significance in a society like the West Bank, which has a relatively low literacy rate and in which the principal medium for the publication of knowledge continues to be oral.[1]

Daily Routine

The West Bank lawyer's work time is loosely structured according to the schedules of the courts. Local civil courts operate six days per week (Friday is the Muslim Sabbath) from 8:00 A.M. to 1:00 P.M.[2] Court sessions are scheduled only by the day, not by the hour, so a lawyer must be present and ready to appear at any time after the opening of the courts.[3] Accordingly, few if any morning appointments are made by lawyers, and a great deal of their work time is spent in and around the courts.

Much of this time is consumed by the conduct of minor litigation-related errands—filing cases and procedural motions, scheduling court sessions, obtaining notarized signatures on documents, and similar tasks. But the greatest part of lawyers' time in the court buildings is spent waiting, in the foyers outside the courtrooms and in the special waiting rooms designated for lawyers, for their cases to be called.

Many lawyers chafe at the ostensible waste of their time caused by the inefficiency of the court bureaucracy and the need to spend half or more of their working day loitering in court buildings. In fact, many other social and professional functions are being fulfilled during these apparent lulls in work activity. Not the least of these are the exchanges between lawyers, which serve, on the one hand, to build whatever sense of corporate solidarity they feel and, on the other, to enact and demonstrate their respective positions within the internal professional hierarchy. Indeed, the courts provide virtually the only focal point for collective interaction and thus have come to function as the informal social centers for the working contingent of the profession.[4]

The nature of their work is such that lawyers almost always have something, even if only a minor errand, that takes them to the courts each day. Once there, much additional time is spent in the lounge discussing current cases, new court decisions, the personalities and competence of judges, current professional issues, and merely trading banter with colleagues. Maintaining a daily presence in the courts also plays a part in projecting an image of professional success and in gaining new clients.[5]

Most West Bankers, including lawyers, take a lunch-siesta period between 1:00 and 4:00 P.M. The midday meal, which is the main meal of the day in the region, is almost always eaten at home with the family. At 4:00 most lawyers go to their offices to receive clients, study case files, and perform other office tasks. They remain there until 6:00 or 7:00 P.M., after which they return to their residences. The workweek of a full-time practitioner, therefore, probably averages six to seven hours per day for six days, or roughly thirty-six to forty-two hours.

On a day-to-day basis, and within the broad parameters imposed by the schedules of the courts, the only seemingly consistent feature of lawyers' work routines is the absence of predictability. The typical workday involves a great deal of running around and the commitment of many small blocks of time to a multitude of tasks, mixed with a certain amount of nonprofessional business and errands. Events frequently disrupt the lawyer's schedule and force him or her to be somewhere other than promised, doing something other than planned.

The relatively unstructured and spontaneous quality of legal work in the West Bank is characteristic of the conduct of business there in general. A mixture of infrastructural and political factors contribute to this. Telephone service is limited, is susceptible to frequent outages, and is not trusted as a medium for the communication of important or confidential information.[6] Transportation is just as vulnerable to disruption: many vehicles are in poor repair and are prone to breakdown; buses and other forms of public transport are infrequent and irregular, especially in outlying areas; random military checkpoints can result in unexpected delays in reaching an appointment. Periodic political convulsions in the area lead to strikes, curfews, more checkpoints and more stringent searches at them, arrests, and an atmosphere of fear, which inhibits normal travel.

After more than twenty years of occupation, lawyers, like other residents of the West Bank, have adapted to a life of unpredictability. Appointments, if they are made, are understood more as general expressions of intent to be in a particular place at a particular time than as firm pacts and are as often broken as kept. Because it is accepted that circumstances frequently prevent one from being somewhere or doing something one has promised, little personal blame attaches to failure to follow through on a commitment.

The unpredictability of life in general is magnified for those whose work pace is wedded to the irregular rhythms of governmental bureaucracy. The bureaucracy figures in people's experience as a quasi-natural force over which they have no control. This was emphasized for me on one occasion when I had arisen at 5:00 A.M. to drive from my home in Jerusalem several hours to the northernmost court town of Jenin, where I was to attend several court sessions with a working lawyer based there. I arrived at the court on time, but was unable to locate my informant. After waiting for almost an hour, I was finally able to ascertain that he had come to the court and departed before I had arrived. I eventually located him in his office, drinking tea with a friend. My self-righteousness dissipated with my anger as he explained to me what had transpired:

Yesterday I had postponed a case here in the Jenin Magistrate Court in order to attend a court session in the Nablus District Court for a murder case in which I'm representing the defendant. In this sort of a case, the court must be composed of three judges. When I got there [the drive from Jenin to Nablus takes about one hour], the court reporter informed me that one of the judges was on vacation. He apologized, saying that the session would have to be postponed. They had even been in touch with the police to tell them not to bother to bring my client from the prison! But me? It didn't even occur to them to give me a call, even though both my home and office phone are listed at the court! Two days ago I appeared before the judge here in the Jenin court, and nothing was said to me about any

impending court recess. After preparing myself for the session
this morning, I came to the court building, only to discover
that the judge—and there is only one judge in Jenin, there are
no substitutes—has decided to take a vacation! It seems that
he won't be back for ten days, so all sessions have been moved
back for that length of time. They never bother to warn people
in advance of these things, even though they could if they
wanted. So lawyers come to court, only to have their time
wasted, and even worse, clients travel sometimes for hours
from their villages only to be told to go home. You see, with
Arabs there's not much value on time.

Of course, Arabs *do* value time, no less than do others. The ways
in which people treat their own time and the time of others, however, often subtly expresses the inequality of power between the two
parties. The powerful never wait, but are always waited for.

In this light, it would seem that for lawyers to surrender the task
of maintaining their schedules to clerical staffers or to commit
firmly to time-specific appointments not only would compromise
their flexibility in adapting to an authority greater than theirs (the
court system), but also would force them to relinquish a significant
symbolic and functional power over clients, the power to make them
wait. This power is occasionally manipulated to fortify the image of
the totally unencumbered, independent professional, an image that
lawyers both emulate and project.[7]

Some working lawyers make a special point of social rounds,
simply to be seen in public and to become readily recognizable. In
the midst of a whirlwind workday in the courts of Hebron with one
young lawyer, my informant, Ali, turned to me, saying "Let's go
snatch a cup of coffee." Rather than going to any of the several cof-
feehouses within walking distance of the court building, we traveled
some distance across town by car to an appliance store. The proprietor, an acquaintance of Ali, brought out seats and cups of Turkish coffee and then sat with us chatting about general matters. I was
a bit mystified that Ali would take this time out of his busy schedule and later queried him. "Look," he responded, "A lawyer in order
to be successful has to be sociable [*ijtimaʿi*]. The Prophet Muham-
mad said 'A mosque built in every town.'" He winked and chuckled
in self satisfaction, "I have built many mosques."

The routines of striking lawyers are as various as the pursuits and
vocations in which they are engaged. Those who practice in the religious courts follow a pattern similar to that of the working lawyers,

attending to court business in the morning and holding office hours in the late afternoon and early evening, but on a less intensive basis. The many idle striking lawyers form small local cliques and pass their time visiting each other, discussing union news and general political events, and simply exchanging professional and personal gossip.

Types of Civil Court Cases

The civil court system in the region is composed of three tiers. Eight magistrate courts (*mahakim as-sulh*) try criminal violations carrying fines up to 200 JD or prison sentences up to three years and hear civil claims involving up to 250 JD. In addition, the magistrate courts have special jurisdiction over certain kinds of controversies, regardless of the monetary values involved in them. These include disputes over rights in land and water, such as those involving rights of way, pasturage, and watering of animals, and including disputes between landlords and tenants.[8]

The three courts of first instance (*mahakim al-bidaya*), or district courts, have residual criminal and civil jurisdiction, that is to say, jurisdiction over all cases with sentences or amounts greater than those assigned to the magistrate courts, or over cases that do not fall in the latter courts' special jurisdiction. The district courts also hear appeals from the magistrate courts in a limited category. The highest civil court currently sitting in the West Bank is the court of appeals (*mahkamat al-ist'naaf*), located in Ramallah. It hears all appeals from the courts of first instance and the vast majority of appeals from the magistrate courts.[9]

A very large proportion of civil disputes relate in one way or another to land. Perhaps the most frequent are eviction cases and disputes arising from lease agreements. These are of sufficient import and frequency that they are regarded by local lawyers as constituting a category unto themselves, distinct from cases involving other interests in real property. Disputes over other interests, such as boundary disagreements, trespass, and damages to real property, also form a significant share of the cases heard by the civil courts.[10]

Another major category of civil court cases concerns collection of debts of various kinds, mostly involving small amounts and thus being transacted through the magistrate courts. Plaintiffs are frequently merchants who have received bad checks or who have extended credit to customers who subsequently default on installments.[11] The lawyer brings written proof of the existence of the debt to the court, which then issues an arrest order for the debtor. Apprehended debtors are brought before the court. The judge usually orchestrates the negotiation of a repayment schedule, which is then entered as the judgment of the court and is enforceable by the Execution Department.

The other main areas of civil practice include criminal cases, usually of a petty variety (such as small thefts or unarmed assaults), labor cases, simple contractual disputes, and what are referred to by local practitioners as "insurance cases," claims against insurance companies for damages to persons and property, most frequently arising out of traffic accidents, but occasionally from workplace mishaps as well. Claims for compensation for personal injuries inflicted on one individual by another or damages to another's property that occur outside of these two contexts are almost never brought to court, but instead are handled informally, often through the system of tribal adjucation.[12]

Disputes raising issues of corporate law, trademark infringement, intellectual property, and the like are a steady but small proportion of the cases brought before the West Bank civil courts. Prior to occupation, administrative law cases had been another mainstay of the profession. But military orders restricting suits against the occupation administration and its agents have caused this field to wither steadily since 1967.[13]

The West Bank civil courts also handle a considerable volume of cases in which litigants are unrepresented by lawyers. These cases, which call for only small fines, often involve traffic violations or citations for violations of municipal building or licensing codes. Plaintiffs and defendants occasionally do not seek representation in cases in which one party is pressing a petty civil claim or criminal complaint against the other. In such cases, it is not uncommon for the judge to act as an arbitrator, attempting to cajole the parties into a settlement, before invoking strictly legal procedures and issuing an authoritative judgment.

A large percentage of represented cases are also settled by negotiations between lawyers and parties. A standard blue form is sent by the plaintiff's lawyer to the defendant. This form notifies the defendant that if positive response to a claim is not received by a particular date, court action will be taken. These forms are sometimes sufficient to initiate negotiations leading to settlement, obviating the need for court proceedings. More frequently, settlements are negotiated between lawyers after a suit has been filed but prior to a final judgment.

Setting and Atmosphere in the Civil Courts

Civil courts are generally housed in buildings close to the commercial center of town, but never seem to be situated on main streets or town squares. Metal signs are hung over entrances to identify the courts, which are otherwise indistinguishable from other government or private buildings. Only some of the buildings were actually designed and constructed for use as courts, and the vestiges of prior usages are sometimes oddly apparent. The Ramallah court complex, for example, is housed in a building originally designed as the town market. In the magistrate court in Jenin, the room that serves as a visitation cell for prisoners was formerly a restroom. There is still a hole in the floor, presumably from removed plumbing fixtures, and the metal rack from which toilet paper was hung is still visible.

Court buildings generally contain offices for judges, prosecutors, and lower-level court personnel, storage rooms for court records, and a public courtroom. Lawyers are provided with a special lounge. The court buildings in Ramallah and Nablus contain law libraries of several thousand volumes, which are available for lawyers to use. Furniture is metal and wood and bears the scars of many years of heavy use. Office machines are scarce. The court buildings lack central heating, and can be uncomfortably cold in winter.

Typically, on entering the doors of a West Bank court building, one sees in the anteroom knots of men, standing together smoking; women are notably few, but are not segregated. Some converse earnestly and quietly, others argue loudly. Some simply sit silently on the hard benches ranged against the walls, fidgeting with prayer beads or key rings. Lawyers are easily distinguishable by their clothing—always Western-style jackets and ties, although of varying condition and quality—and trademark briefcases, and even more by their air of comfort and authority, almost a proprietary ease vis-à-vis their surroundings. In contrast, clients and other citizens often wear the *hatta* and *'agal* (the indigenous headdress consisting of a square of cloth secured to the head by a ropelike fastener) and, sometimes in the smaller towns, the ankle-length gowns still worn by many villagers. Their stances, gestures, and expressions reflect a bewilderment tinged with exasperation. A master lawyer wafts through the hall. In his wake trails an *estagiare* carrying an armful of papers and leading an anxious-faced client. Lower-level court personnel scuttle back and forth with trays of coffee and tea, which are delivered to lawyers in their waiting room or to the judges in their chambers. Boisterous laughter erupts into the hallway with a cloud of cigarette smoke as the door of the lawyers' waiting room is momentarily opened. The low buzz of conversation is periodically punctuated by the braying of the court bailiff as he calls out the names of cases to be heard and of the lawyers involved in them. Telephones ring in the various administrative offices. Several civilian policemen slouch around the door, armed with pistols, ostensibly there to guard the building and to escort the occasional criminal defendant to the courtroom.

Cases at all levels of the West Bank civil court system are tried before judges. The jury trial is alien to the region, as it is to the entire Arab world. Most cases are tried by a single judge. Criminal cases bearing a possible punishment of imprisonment for ten years or more and all cases in the court of appeals are heard by three judges, one of whom sits as president of the court.

In jury trial systems, the practical obstacles of convening a jury militate in favor of concentrating as much of the litigation as possible in a relatively discrete event, the trial. West Bank courts face no such pressures, and it is the norm for cases to be litigated through many brief sessions, each of which may be convened only to hear a single witness or to consider a single procedural motion.[14] Of the sessions I observed, the average length was perhaps five to ten minutes; this does not include cases of minor traffic or license infractions, which I witnessed being transacted at the rate of thirty per hour.

Proceedings in ordinary cases are usually heard in the judge's chambers rather than in the open courtroom, according to the discretion of the judge, and are rarely attended by persons not party to the litigation. Murder trials are held in open court and are often attended by relatives and friends of the victim and defendant. Trials implicating significant public interests, which attract curious citizens, members of the press, and other interested parties, may also be held in public sessions. Routine cases are also sometimes heard in open court, and the room may contain any number of parties to upcoming cases and lawyers, who wait in their respective positions in the audience or at the desk for lawyers, situated between the raised bench of the judge and the rows of seats occupied by the public.[15]

A typical magistrate court session commences with the entry of the judge to the bailiff's cry "*Mahkama!*" (court), upon which lawyers and audience stand until the judge takes his seat. The judge utters a few quiet words to the scribe or reporter, seated to his side and below him, who then calls the first case. A lawyer rises, and from his position at the desk announces to the judge, addressing him as "Siyadat al-qadi" (roughly translated, "Your Excellency the Judge") that he has brought a witness to testify. The witness is directed to the podium toward the front of the courtroom, where he is sworn in with the oath, "I swear before God that I will tell nothing but the complete truth," repeated after the judge. The judge solicits such standard data as name, age, place of residence, and occupation for the court record, then relinquishes questioning to the lawyer. The judge and lawyers speak to each other during the course of the session in classical Arabic, while witnesses and parties speak and are spoken to in colloquial Arabic. As the lawyer questions the witness, the judge simultaneously translates the questions and responses into formal Arabic, dictating slowly for the court reporter. The reporter scribbles furiously with pen and paper to keep pace. The response of the witness is unclear, obliging the judge to repeat or rephrase the lawyer's questions, his intonation reflecting mounting irritation. The witness is upbraided by the judge for shifting back and forth on his feet and gesticulating and is told to stand still, hands at sides. Testimony finished, the witness is dismissed. The judge confers briefly with the two attorneys and then announces the date of the next session for the case, two months hence. Lawyers and parties file out of the courtroom as the next case is called and the cycle recommences.

Sessions held in chambers are similar to those in open court, but are somewhat less ceremonious.[16] The tone is more conversational. Court employees sometimes enter after a cursory knock and move about the room slamming file cabinet drawers. Between proceedings, the judge calls home to tell his wife when he will be home for lunch and shares tea and conversation with lawyers waiting for the next case to be heard. Still, the behavior between judge and lawyer remains formal. The lawyer enters the chambers with a quick half-bow in the direction of the judge, whom he addresses as "Siyadat al-qadi," just as in open court. In turn, he is addressed by the judge as "Istaaz."[17]

Court arguments often revolve around procedural formalities. While lawyers regularly complain that the courts' approach is overly technical, reflecting the lack of self-confidence of poorly trained judges to go beyond the letter to the spirit of the law, it is equally clear that lawyers exploit technical arguments when it suits them. This was demonstrated in a hearing before the court of appeals that pitted perhaps the two preeminent practitioners in the entire West Bank against each other.

The case involved an internal struggle for control of the directorship and assets of a nonprofit association and raised a variety of complicated issues of corporate, employment, and property law. It had been filed in 1972, and for years had bounced back and forth between the district court and the court of appeals on a number of interlocutory appeals. Now the case was being appealed on its merits, and the court of appeals was readying itself to make a final judgment.

Sessions for the case were delayed twice for reasons unknown to me, until finally a session was scheduled not long before my departure from the region. I arrived early at the court building in Ramallah, meeting my informant in the lawyers' lounge. He escorted me upstairs to the chambers of the president of the court appeals, where I was introduced to the judges. When all had settled and the court was called into session, my informant stood to present his *murafaʿa*, or oral argument. Before he could start, the opposing attorney interjected, asking to raise a procedural point. It seemed that the original power of attorney held by my informant—the one given him by the party in 1972—did not explicitly authorize him to represent the party on appeal, nor to claim the relief that he was currently claiming, which was different from the relief first sought in the case.

My informant disgustedly requested a recess to "study this unexpected matter," and the session came to a close five minutes after it started. As my informant stormed off to his office, the opposing attorney, whom I also knew and had interviewed, approached me somewhat sheepishly, saying, "I don't like to have to resort to these technicalities, but with these stupid judges I'm forced to. They wouldn't understand a good argument anyway! After all, the Palestinian case [the claim for national independence placed before the United Nations in 1947] was lost on a technicality!" When I left the West Bank the case was still unresolved.[18]

Types of Military Court Cases

As we have seen, the military legal system in the West Bank is composed of two primary branches (fig. 3). The greatest volume of cases is processed by the military courts, constituted shortly after occupation by the military decree to enforce security regulations. They also exercise jurisdiction over violations of Jordanian traffic regulations and criminal law concurrently with the civil courts of the West Bank. A second branch is formed by the military objections committees, special administrative tribunals convened according to demand, which handle disputes of a generally civil flavor between citizens and governing authorities.

The majority of defendants charged with violations of security regulations are males between the ages of fourteen and thirty, many from the camps or villages. Because schools (both secondary schools and universities) are centers for agitation against the occupation, many defendants are students and face mostly minor charges of participating in demonstrations, throwing rocks at soldiers or Israeli civilian vehicles, or possessing banned material.[19] Students returning from abroad are frequently charged with "membership in hostile organizations"—groups alleged to be affiliated with the PLO—and occasionally with the more serious charge of weapons training. Other frequently encountered charges include recruitment to membership in hostile organizations, rendering assistance to members, and the illegal importation of currency.[20] Offenses such as possession of weapons and participation in military operations against Israeli army personnel or civilians are comparatively rare.

Although the military courts handle a large volume of traffic cases (in which most defendants, as in the civil courts, appear without counsel), their concurrent criminal jurisdiction is exercised selectively. In fact, my informants could only speculate about the procedure and criteria according to which cases falling within the jurisdictions of both court systems were routed to one or the other for prosecution, but they were convinced that military intelligence had a hand in these decisions. The only category of criminal case consistently brought before the military courts was those related to use and distribution of illegal narcotics. Otherwise, according to local lawyers, cases were referred to military courts only if, by virtue of surrounding circumstances or the identity of the parties involved, they had some political dimension.

The military objections committees were created by decree early in the occupation, ostensibly to expedite citizen claims against the authorities. The most frequent and important cases handled by the objections committees are those pertaining to land. Some of these cases begin with expropriations in the strict legal sense, others, with government assertions that a plot of land possessed by a Palestinian is actually public domain. Other areas falling within the purview of the objections committees include disputes over income tax and VAT assessments, pension rights of civil servants, and a host of others.

In a somewhat typical political or security case,[21] Rafiq, resident of the Kalandia refugee camp north of Jerusalem and a student at a local university, had not returned home at the expected hour. Knowing that there was to have been a strike at the university that day, and that strikes often spawned demonstrations that brought out the army and so devolved into confrontations, Rafiq's father anxiously inquired with friends as to his son's whereabouts. He learned that, indeed, Rafiq was seen at the forefront of the barricades of burning tires set up by the students on the road to the university. Another friend believed that he had seen Rafiq being dragged away by several soldiers in the direction of the vans brought to convey demonstrators to detention centers. On the advice of Rafiq's friend, several members of the family hurried to the office of a well-known Israeli Arab lawyer in Jerusalem. [Among students and other politically active segments of the population there is also an underground folk wisdom of sorts concerning the political leanings of individual lawyers who are perceived as being sympathetic to particular Palestinian political factions or organizations.]

Abed, the lawyer, began by placing phone calls to the office of the legal adviser of the military government and to administrators at the various prisons and detention centers throughout the region. By the next morning, he had ascertained that Rafiq was being held for investigation in the Fara'a detention center outside Nablus, thus far without charges. Military regulations permit persons arrested without warrants to be held incommunicado for up to four days, with extensions of up to eighteen days possible with the approval of police inspectors, and up to six months with the approval of a military judge. Abed filed a motion for a bail hearing, at which his client had to be in attendance; this was Abed's only means of seeing his client prior to trial. The subsequent stages of Rafiq's case will be described in the next section.

Setting and Atmosphere in the Military Courts

The setting of military courts and the atmosphere prevailing within them differ radically from those in the civil courts. Military courts are located within Israeli military compounds, most of which are on the outskirts of the towns of the West Bank.[22] Some occupy the facilities of former Jordanian army and police posts and still show the scars and pockmarks they received in the fighting of 1967. The compounds are entirely surrounded by high fences topped with concertina wire, except for the occasional breaks formed by gates. Moveable barriers, heavily guarded by green-bereted members of the Border Police (the wing of the Israeli army responsible for internal security), restricted entry of all but military vehicles.

I arrived in Nablus early one hot fall morning to attend Rafiq's trial, approximately three weeks after his detention. Ten days prior in a bail hearing, his lawyer's motion for release was denied. But lawyer Abed was able to whisper a few words of support and encouragement to the young prisoner, and the glimpse of him caught by his mother and other relatives allayed their most dire fears about his physical condition. Formal charges were subsequently filed against

Rafiq, alleging that he had thrown rocks at soldiers during the demonstration at the university.

Outside the Nablus compound, Palestinian men and women—mostly peasants and camp residents, judging by their dress—gathered at the gates, sometimes in clusters, sometimes in long lines, presenting their identity cards and submitting to pat searches before entering the compound to pursue their business. Periodic discharges from battered public buses replenished their numbers. A few bedraggled, dusty-leaved trees provided scant shelter from the sun. Arriving by car and parking on the shoulder of the road, Abed headed for the gate, briefcase and robe tucked under one arm, and was immediately besieged by a gaggle of clients. Shedding them with a few placating words, he presented his ID card with a greeting in Hebrew to a soldier and was admitted without search, as I was. A holding cell for defendants to be tried that day sat directly across the hall from the courtroom. Lawyers held whispered conferences with clients through a slit in the door. As there was no lounge, several lawyers waited in the short hallway connecting the courtroom and related offices for their cases to be called, sharing the area with four or five soldiers, armed and unarmed, who loitered about, smoking and joking in Hebrew. Inside the courtroom, the judge had not yet arrived. The look was familiar—the same drab and chipped paint, battered furniture arranged identically as in the civil courts, and lack of adornment—except for the plaques depicting the scales of justice and the emblem of the Israel Defense Forces hanging on the wall at the front of the room.

As the minutes dragged on, relatives of defendants began to filter into the room, silently assuming positions on the hard benches at the rear of the room. Unlike in the civil courts, many of them were women, worried mothers and sisters here to ascertain the physical condition of their incarcerated sons or brothers, and to provide them moral support. Toward the front, several more soldiers leaned against the wall, talking. At his desk, a West Bank lawyer leafed through his briefcase, absent-mindedly lighting a cigarette. A soldier straightened then strode over to the lawyer, speaking loudly and aggressively in Hebrew, then in broken Arabic. "Smoking is not permitted in the courtroom! Get out of here with that cigarette!" The lawyer retreated, visibly shaken, into the hallway.

As in the civil courts, cases in the military courts are tried by judges, who are appointed from among officers of the Israel Defense Forces. Many are army reservists who have attended law school and in civilian life are engaged in the practice of law or some law-related vocation in Israel.

In court proceedings, judges, military prosecutor, Israeli witnesses, and defense lawyers who are able, speak in Hebrew. Palestinian defendants and other witnesses, and non-Hebrew-speaking lawyers, must rely on Arabic. Simultaneous translation is offered by court interpreters, usually young soldiers either of Druze origins or of Jewish families from Arab countries. Court sessions are usually short, but in contrast to civil court cases, in all but those for the most serious offenses, military court cases are processed in one or two, and sometimes three sessions.

The court reporter and the interpreter entered, in rumpled military fatigues, and took seats on opposite sides of the table directly in front and below the judge's bench. Heads turned to the rear of the room as soldiers brought in Rafiq and five other defendants, all students, young men, and all facing similar charges arising out of the same incident. All had signed statements admitting guilt for the acts that they were alleged to have committed, including Rafiq. They cast furtive smiles of reassurance toward the anxious faces in the audience as they were brought to the podium toward the front of the room, where they were left standing.

"Mahkama!" All in the room leaped to their feet, startled by the bailiff's bellow. The judge entered, dressed in a neatly pressed officer's uniform, beret rolled and tucked under epaulet, and took his place behind the raised bench. All but the accused again sat down. The judge declared the session open, noting the names of the defendants, his words echoed in their Arabic equivalent after the briefest pause by the interpreter.

The floor was given to the military prosecutor, who read the charge sheet listing the defendants' alleged offenses. Each of the defendants was asked how he pleaded. In his turn, Rafiq shuffled forward, muttering in Arabic, "Guilty." He did so on Abed's instructions, as Abed had already negotiated a reduced charge in return for a guilty plea. The suspense thus revolved only around the severity of his sentence. Abed was concerned, since the military government had been under pressure from Jewish settlers in the region to crack down on stone throwers and had recently announced that it would impose stricter sentences.

Similar deals had been negotiated for all but one of the other five defendants, for whom the session was a "minitrial"—an evidentiary hearing on the admissibility of the statement the defendant gave during the period of detention. The defendant's lawyer claimed that his client was coerced into signing the statement, which was in Hebrew, through the use of force and trickery.

The lawyer stood, in wrinkled black robe, reciting in Arabic the abuses his client claimed to have suffered. As they were phrased in Hebrew by the interpreter, derisive guffaws exploded from the soldiers standing in the back of the room. The military prosecutor interjected, and a heated exchange followed between him and the lawyer. Their voices tangled over that of the interpreter, who now droned away without pause, producing a nearly unintelligible din.

Abed, also berobed, was the next to speak. Rafiq had not been arrested before. Yes, he participated in a demonstration in which stone throwing occurred, but none of the minor injuries inflicted had been specifically attributed to him. He had already spent ten days in prison, during which he missed classes at the university. Exams were upcoming. If treated with leniency by the court, he would surely remember this experience and next time refrain from such activities and keep to his studies. After similar recitations by lawyers representing the other defendants, the judge read their sentences one by one. Rafiq received a suspended sentence of six months and a fine of forty thousand Israeli shekels to be paid within twenty-one days. Abed smiled and nodded toward Rafiq's parents, pleased with the result. He left quietly from the rear of the court to rendezvous with the family outside. They were immensely relieved that Rafiq would be released later that day, although his father, a civil servant, rued the loss of half a month's pay to the fine.

Practice in the Religious Courts

The religious courts in the region exercise exclusive jurisdiction over cases arising among religious adherents that pertain to "personal status" (*ahwal shakhsiya*), or what would be roughly comprehended by the field of family law in the United States. In contrast to their policies toward the civil court system, Israeli military authorities have permitted the religious court system to function with relatively little intervention. The continued independence of the religious courts is highly touted by court personnel and lawyers as a source of their legitimacy.[23] Striking lawyers also rationalize their practice in the religious courts by referring to the absence of Israeli interference in them.

The most frequent subject giving rise to religious court action is succession, or inheritance, of real and moveable property. In both Muslim and canonical law in the region, a decedent's property is apportioned by law in fixed shares to relatives rather than by will or other instrument. Accordingly, the standard succession case involves little more than an application for a probation order from the court, which is forwarded to the Land Registry for execution. The most frequent claims leading to actual litigation in the religious courts are for "maintenance" (*nafaqa*), an amount that by Islamic law a man must regularly provide his wife for herself and any children during the period of their marriage. Divorces, disputes over custody and support of children, domestic obedience, and the like, all form smaller categories of cases treated in the religious courts. Claims pertaining to Islamic trusts (*waqf, awqaaf* pl.), which can be complex and interesting to lawyers, are comparatively rare. Islamic law permits nonlawyer relatives to represent litigants in court, and it is apparently not uncommon, particularly in *nafaqa* cases, for the father or brother of the wife-complainant to represent her, either directly in court, or in interactions with a lawyer. Litigation of these cases often requires little or no technical legal knowledge. Discussion centers on factual matters such as how much a husband can and should pay in maintenance. It is also not uncommon for *nafaqa* cases to be resolved through negotiations before formal court action has been taken, sometimes under the supervision of the *qadi*, with or without the participation of lawyers.

Religious courts differ little in appearance from their civil counterparts, except that they consistently seem to be closer to the centers of the towns in which they are located.[24] The style of architecture, quality and condition of furniture, arrangement of courtrooms, and the like, recall a magistrate court in one of the West Bank towns. Yet one need not spend much time in a religious court before its distinct ambience begins to be evident.

More of the men are wearing the *hatta* and *'agal;* this includes both litigants and court clerks. Lawyers are less easily distinguishable by their attire. While still usually in Western clothes, they dress somewhat more casually than in the civil courts, sometimes appearing without a tie or wearing a windbreaker instead of a jacket or suit, and occasionally even adopting the popular traditional headress.[25] More important, there is a more familial air to their interactions with clients and court personnel. Their voices are often hushed, more like those of wise and reassuring brothers than of brusque and impersonal authorities.

As in the civil courts, religious court cases are tried by a judge or, at the appellate level, by three judges. Sessions are typically brief, but unlike in the civil court system, the time lapse between them is short, usually no more than two weeks (compared to two or three months in the civil courts). Cases in the religious courts, therefore, are resolved relatively quickly, lasting an average of perhaps two months.

The majority of the routine cases in the *shari'a* courts are heard in the chamber of the *qadi*; only the few in which a number of witnesses must be heard are convened in open court. In either circumstance, the *qadi* is easily identifiable by his *jubba* and *ʿamama*, the long robe and hat (resembling a red fez with its base wrapped with a white cloth) of the Islamic holy man. His attire associates the *qadi* with an indigenous rather than an alien tradition. While his costume differentiates him from lay people, it contrasts more sharply with the Western garb of the lawyers than with the robes and *hattas* of the court's clientele.

Open court sessions in the Islamic courts are similar in almost all respects to civil court sessions. Sessions held in the chambers of the judge are also similar to their equivalents in the civil courts, although there are some subtle but telling differences as well. The *qadi*'s chamber is furnished simply with his desk and with chairs lining three walls, which seat lawyers and clients alike with no differentiating positions. Parties and witnesses are not always compelled to stand while offering testimony. Lawyers, on entering the *qadi*'s chamber, approach him and shake his hand before locating a seat. The *qadi*'s treatment of litigants is authoritative but familial, fatherly rather than distant.

Legal Research and Case Preparation

Having examined lawyers' work experience in the civil, military, and religious courts currently functioning in the West Bank, let us now turn to legal research and case preparation, activities that are subsidiary to litigation in all three legal systems. In fact, it seems that proportionately little of a lawyer's work time is spent performing legal research. While my data do not include precise figures in this regard, based on my observations and on the statements of informants, I estimate that the average lawyer spends no more than one hour per day conducting research. Although the reasons for this differ somewhat according to whether a case will be heard in the civil, military, or religious courts, most cases simply do not raise novel or complicated legal issues and can be handled fairly easily with the lawyer's fund of active knowledge.

In the civil courts especially, the partition of a case into many discrete sessions also means that for any given session little preparation is necessary. That courts are liberal in granting continuances means that few if any negative consequences result from lack of preparation. This has spawned the attitude among attorneys that there will always be another opportunity to raise an issue in the course of litigation. Many of my informants active in the civil courts claimed that the amount of time they and others spent doing legal research had declined since the advent of occupation. They alleged that dilatory, corrupt, and incompetent judges destroyed any incentive to invest time in research. On one visit to a conscientious lawyer, he held up a sheaf of paper to me, saying,

> You see this? This is a brief I've been working on for the last week or so for a case in the court of appeals. Now, I have the feeling—just a feeling, mind you—that when I go to court, the judges will not have read it. And even if they have, perhaps only one of the three will have understood it. And it so happens that the one who is sharpest legally is also the most corrupt, and since this case involves a fair amount of money, there's a good chance that he will have been bribed. So it's likely that I've wasted the time I spent putting this together.

Minimal time is also spent by lawyers in legal research or general preparation for cases in the military courts. A contributing factor in this is the rudimentary level of the reporting system for the military courts. The only published collection of decisions of the military courts is in Hebrew and runs only until 1976. According to lawyers active in the military courts, legal argumentation in political or security cases is based principally on their own direct experience and word-of-mouth knowledge gained from other practitioners; cases seldom demand research beyond this mentally retained jurisprudence.

In the eyes of local lawyers, however, the most important factor in this connection is that the overwhelming majority of cases in the military courts involve either confessions by the defendant or statements implicating him or her made by an alleged conspirator. Many more citizens are detained than are actually formally charged and tried. Informants claim that Israeli military authorities rarely prosecute unless and until a confession by or statement against the defendant has been obtained. Procedural and evidentiary rules leave defense lawyers little chance of successfully challenging the admissibility of these confessions and statements. Requirements for corroboration are almost always met by the prosecution, so conviction is virtually assured. One informant who had tried almost one hundred military cases in the last year claimed that he had won only three acquittals. Over and over, informants repeated the refrain, "There is no room for a lawyer's work in the military courts, no way to use his expertise."

Faced with this situation, lawyers generally have no viable option but to plea bargain with the military prosecutor for reduced charges and to appeal to the mercy of the court in sentencing by referring to mitigating circumstances surrounding the case.

Legal Planning, Counsel, and Administrative Transactions

Legal planning—the structuring of relations between parties through the drafting of contracts, partnership agreements, articles of incorporation, and the arrangement of other kinds of transactions—is practiced only by the few members of the West Bank professional elite who claim a significant number of businesses as clients. Most lawyers pointed out that to the community at large, the idea of resorting to a lawyer "before there is a need," in other words, in advance of a dispute, was totally foreign. Even among businesspeople, consciousness of the value of averting potential problems through proper legal planning was low, according to most lawyers.

One informant claimed that, because of the recent unpredictability of the civil court system, clients had begun to use "preventative law" (a phrase he had picked up from an American law review article), so as to avoid having to resort to the courts. Another tactic with an identical aim, which this lawyer alleged to be increasingly popular among businesses, was the inclusion of arbitration clauses in agreements. These clauses provided for arbitrators from the legal or business communities. I suspect, however, that these recent trends are confined to the minority of larger enterprises, which engage in more sophisticated kinds of business deals.

A similar situation prevails with the provision of legal counsel (*istishara qanuniya*). Lawyers most frequently offer legal guidance to organizational clients rather than to individuals, often under the terms of a general retainer. A municipality, for example, might seek the judgment of a retained legal adviser on the legality of cutting off electrical services to a resident who has violated building ordinances. A private corporation might consult its lawyer over a proposed logo closely resembling that of a competitor.

The scope of administrative transactions in which lawyers represent clients before government authorities is somewhat broader. Many of these transactions are relatively routine, including land conveyancing, registration of companies or of corporate trademarks, and applications for business licenses or zoning variances. Not infrequently, however, citizens have problems with the occupation administration that have a political or security dimension. To cite a common example, students planning to study abroad are often denied exit visas by the military authorities, especially if the applicant is suspected of political involvement or even has relatives abroad who are active in a member organization of the PLO.[26]

In such instances, lawyers raise the issue with the legal adviser of the military government and seek an explanation for the decision. While explanations are seldom forthcoming, persistent inquiries sometimes result in a reversal of the initial denial. If legal intervention fails to secure the desired result, the lawyer may appeal the case to the Israeli High Court. But in the typical exit visa denial, the costs and delays in High Court actions render it an ineffective remedy.

With respect to the realm of administrative transactions, it is important to recall that lawyers do not enjoy an exclusive monopoly, as they do in the courts. Citizens experiencing problems with government can and frequently do resort to intermediaries other than lawyers—*makhateer*, mayors, religious leaders, members of the Village Leagues, representatives of chambers of commerce, and others—to help them. Depending on an individual's resources, the intervention of several of these intermediaries may be solicited simultaneously.

Conclusions

Examination of the content of the practices of contemporary West Bank lawyers reveals several notable features. Litigation is in conception and in fact the essence of legal work. It is the function that distinguishes the legal profession and establishes its value. More specifically, it is litigation in the civil courts that is the real lifeblood of the profession. The West Bank civil courts are the principal domain of the working lawyers of the region. Civil court cases are the ones for which the lawyers' training is most directly suited, and among which are the highest percentage of more complex, challenging, and professionally rewarding cases (in both the intellectual and the financial sense).

One of the consequences of this nearly exclusive focus on litigation is to render the profession extraordinarily dependent on the proper functioning of the civil court system, for the quality of the services the lawyers offer depends greatly on the efficiency and integrity of the courts. We now shift our attention from the legal profession itself to the institutional framework in which it operates.

8. Deterioration of the Formal Court System

The condition of the West Bank's legal profession is closely tied to the current status of the institutions in which lawyers operate on a daily basis, namely, the formal court system. A number of problems have afflicted the civil courts of the West Bank since the advent of occupation, not the least of which is the competing military legal system, which has gradually cannibalized the jurisdiction of the West Bank courts. The judiciary, meanwhile, has suffered declining competence, challenges to its independence, lack of cooperation from police and other authorities, accusations of corruption, and a severe erosion of morale. Administrative maladies of various kinds blunt the efficacy and tarnish the reputation of the civil court system.

The military legal system, encompassing the military courts and the objections committees, is free of most of the administrative deficiencies plaguing the civil courts. But its laws are regarded as harsh and unjust. The conviction among Palestinians of the West Bank is that the military legal system is simply another instrument used by the occupation administration to suppress resistance and to enforce Israeli interests in the region. Only the naïve would expect justice from such a system.

The Effects of Changes in Court Structure and Jurisdiction

Note has been taken at various points of some of the changes in the structure of the West Bank's civil court system and of the impact these changes have had on the local legal profession. To review the most important of these, the annexation of Jerusalem and the attendant closure of Jordanian courts there have rendered a prime market for legal services inaccessible to West Bank practitioners. Occupation has barred recourse to Jordan's Court of Cassation, the highest appellate court in the country, thus eliminating an entire level of civil litigation.[1] Military decrees limiting the rights of citizens to file complaints against government authorities have blocked West Bank civil courts from hearing most administrative law cases. Military objections committees exercise jurisdiction over a wide range of issues, including land expropriations, disputes over income and value-added tax, retirement compensation for civil servants, customs levies, and others. Crimes against Jordanian law may now be tried in military courts.

It is difficult to ascertain precisely how these structural transformations have affected the volume of litigation arising in the West Bank. While certain areas of practice have been effectively eliminated, an entirely new realm has been opened with the creation of the military legal system. In fact, among the three primary legal systems functioning in the region (civil, military, and religious), the total number cases litigated annually has probably increased greatly since 1967, mostly due to the addition of the large number of cases tried in the military courts.

By now, however, it should be obvious that the structural transformations in the West Bank's legal system have occurred mostly at the expense of the institutional integrity of the civil courts. The interests of lawyers, whose welfare directly depends on the healthy functioning of those courts, have been compromised accordingly. Nor has the civil court system endured such buffeting without suffering a loss in the level of confidence the public, legal profession, and even court personnel have in it. "Courts for petty disputes among Arabs" was how many informants described the system. Such statistics as are available suggest that the rate of litigation in the West Bank courts is slowly but steadily declining.

The overall reduction in the number of cases handled by the West Bank civil courts is perhaps not dramatic. But it is revealing that the number of civil as opposed to criminal cases has dropped rather markedly, by nearly 50 percent in the magistrate and district courts in the years for which figures are available, while criminal prosecutions have remained relatively constant.[2] Of course, it is in civil cases, which are initiated mostly by private plaintiffs, where the level of trust or skepticism in a court system is most clearly visible.[3]

Lawyers' feelings of humiliation and helpless frustration at the erosion of their institutional base crystallized in a furor over the imposition of Military Order No. 1060. The order, decreed in June

1983, vested the jurisdiction of the West Bank civil courts over disputes concerning requests to register previously unregistered lands in a military objections committee.[4]

Great consternation developed in the West Bank legal profession over the effect Military Order No. 1060 would have in disputes over Israeli land purchases in the region—among the few categories of cases in which the West Bank civil courts still regularly exercised jurisdiction over Israelis. In recent years, many cases have been recorded in which Israelis or Israeli land development companies, often working through Palestinian middlemen (*samasira*), have attempted to establish ownership of land in the West Bank, especially in the north, where large tracts of land remain unregistered.

According to local lawyers, Israeli buyers and local agents have frequently engaged in a range of devices from forgery to physical coercion to acquire Palestinian lands. Palestinian *samasira* have attempted to sell land to Israeli speculators using forged documents that purport to grant them irrevocable powers of attorney from landowners for the sale of their lands. Genuine documents granting powers of attorney have been signed by illiterate peasant owners who are persuaded by one means or another to sign the papers, the true content of which is hidden from them, or threats of violence and actual physical abuse have been used to persuade people to sign. Forged maps, purporting to convey larger tracts than were truly the subject of the transaction, have been attached to legitimate documents of sale and purchase.[5]

Lawyers achieved a modicum of success in protecting Palestinian owners' rights by challenging illicit real estate transactions in the civil courts of the West Bank. It was feared that Military Order No. 1060 would prevent this protection by transferring disputes to a forum assumed to be more sympathetic to Israeli interests. Almost all of the local lawyers were convinced that the order represented collusion between the occupation administration and private Israeli entrepreneurs.[6]

Throughout the West Bank community, the struggle for control over the land, regarded as the national patrimony of the Palestinian people and the key to their *sumud*, or steadfastness, in the face of Zionist expansion, is a sacred responsibility. The incapacity of the West Bank civil courts and, through them, the legal profession to offer effective protection of the land from either private or government Israeli acquisition is a debility of the highest actual and symbolic order. Perhaps more than any other incursion into the jurisdiction of the West Bank courts, Military Order No. 1060 and other decrees pertaining to disputes over land have crippled the civil courts in the eyes of the public and the legal profession, rendering them peripheral and powerless vis-à-vis issues of the most vital community interest.

Competence of the Judiciary

Legal professionals were unanimous in the judgment that the local judiciary had declined greatly in quality beginning in the mid-seventies. Until that time, most of the judges in the West Bank's civil courts were appointees from the pre-occupation period and their integrity and competence were largely respected. As civil service salaries failed to keep pace with inflation, however, increasing numbers of judges resigned to enter the more lucrative field of private law practice.

Power to appoint judges has been exercised since 1967 by a committee composed of Israeli military officers, including the officer in charge of the judiciary, aided by several Israeli civilians. Despite apparently numerous and persistent efforts on the part of the committee to recruit judges from among the ranks of the more respected members of the local legal profession, its efforts have borne little fruit.

The simple reason for this failure, according to several lawyers who had been solicited for judicial posts, is the absence of any incentive to sacrifice their independence and substantial earnings for a minimal salary and employee status. Israeli authorities have been forced to tap younger and less-successful lawyers to fill judicial posts. Some have not even completed their apprenticeship; others have only a few years of listless performance in the profession.

Lawyers, therefore, refer contemptuously to judges. Some informants suspected judges of harboring feelings of inferiority and resentment toward their more successful former colleagues, feelings that were sometimes vented in vengeful behavior against lawyers in courtroom proceedings. Frequent mistakes by inexperienced or incompetent judges foul the normal progress of cases and destroy the lawyers' confidence in the judiciary.

The situation is claimed to have been vastly exacerbated in recent years by intervention of *wasta* and political considerations in the process of judicial appointments. Legal competence is subordinate to political approval from military intelligence, or the intermediation of politically favored personalities.[7] "*No one* obtains a judicial appointment without *wasta* these days" was the conviction echoed by many informants.

The Paucity of Judges and Prosecutors

Prior to 1967, the civil courts of the West Bank were staffed by some twenty-two judges and thirteen public prosecutors. A number fled to Jordan during or shortly after the June War; perhaps half of those remaining, or roughly eleven judges and prosecutors in total, agreed to resume their duties.[8] The occupation administration was thus faced with a severe depletion in the judicial ranks, a problem that has never been fully rectified.

By my count, there were eighteen civil court judges working in the region in early 1985. This situation obliged some judges to perform double duties. For example, the magistrate court judge in Hebron was also serving as the third member of the district court in that town. Only one magistrate court judge sits at present in Nablus, a large city with a constant and heavy demand for magistrate court services. Coverage is sufficiently thin that when a judge takes a vacation, or is ill, or, for some other reason, cannot fulfill his duties, other judges are forced to fill in, sometimes for months, while still performing their duties in their own court.[9]

While the loss of a mere four judges from pre-occupation days may seem insignificant, the implications are clearer when one considers the additional paucity of prosecutors, whose numbers appeared in 1985 not to exceed five, down considerably from the pre-occupation total of thirteen. As a result, magistrate court judges in Bethlehem, Jericho, Jenin, Qalqilya-Salfit, and Tulkarm all were serving simultaneously as the public prosecutors for their regions, under a provision in Jordanian law designed to meet temporary needs.[10] When circumstances demanded their immediate attention as prosecutors, as in the investigation of a crime, judges were sometimes forced to declare sudden recesses, creating unexpected disruptions in case proceedings.

All of the judges with whom I spoke complained of being overworked, with loads of an average of thirty-five cases per day, rising to hundreds on days designated for traffic cases. Insufficient time is left for case study and preparation. Many lawyers accused judges of not even opening case files until disputes approached final judgment and of searching for the flimsiest of pretexts to delay decisions, simply as a means to buy time to get through the docket for the day.

Challenges to the Independence of the Judiciary

The process and criteria of judicial appointments were seen by lawyers as being at the root of another malignancy afflicting the judiciary, its diminishing independence from the occupation authorities.[11] It seemed perfectly obvious to my informants that those appointed on the basis of their subservience to the military government could not be expected to contest its interests.

According to former judges, the occupation authorities had generally respected the integrity of the judiciary in the initial years of occupation. Gradually, intervention in the workings of the courts began to occur in the form of challenges to judges' decisions in cases by the officer in charge of the judiciary and, with respect to the president of the court of appeals, to his appointments of lower court personnel.[12] One judge sitting in 1985 hinted darkly of "ways" that the authorities had of retaliating for noncompliance with their more or less explicitly communicated directives. Others attested that retaliation included transfer to distant or undesirable seats and refusal to grant promotions or salary increases in a timely fashion.

Another form of intervention, the withdrawal of files of cases in progress before the West Bank civil courts and the termination or transfer of proceedings to the military courts, began to occur with increasing frequency after gaining specific sanction through military decree in 1980.[13] This practice has been particularly damaging to the image of the civil courts as it is widely viewed as a device used by the occupation authorities to recruit and shield collaborators.[14]

Most currently sitting or former judges with whom I spoke denied ever having had a case withdrawn from their jurisdictions. But when I questioned the frequency and so the gravity of the problem of case withdrawals, a practicing lawyer who had served as a district court judge responded:

> It's unimportant how *many* times this occurs in one's experience on the bench—it's the *way* that it's done—arbitrarily, with no explanation. You never know, sometimes even half an hour before it occurs, when a case will be withdrawn. You may be sitting in court, finish hearing a case, call the next one— only to find it has been withdrawn. The main thing is that the authorities do not provide an atmosphere in which you, as a judge, can make authoritative decisions. All of this led to a crisis of self-confidence among judges, in our very self-images as people. I could see it in the eyes of the common citizens that they regarded me as weak.

Another former judge, now practicing law, summed up the impact of intervention into the functioning of the civil courts on the feelings and perceptions of judges, lawyers, and the public: "Here a court may order the imprisonment of someone and the next day you'll see him walking free in the streets—and you know that it's because he cooperates in one way or another with the authorities. It doesn't take long for the message to sink in, that here there is a power *superior* to the judicial system—which is military intelligence [*mukhabarat*]."

Judicial Corruption

As we have seen, the problem of corruption in the West Bank is a general one and impinges on the functioning of a number of government departments. The community is populated with intermediaries referred to as "*mafateeh*" (keys, sing. *miftaah*), who convey cash bribes to officials and negotiate the dispensation of licenses, permits, or other goods at the officials' disposal.[15]

Rumors of widespread corruption within the civil court system were rife in 1984–1985. During the fourteen months of my fieldwork, hardly an interview passed in which the lawyer did not level accusations that judges were "on the take."[16] As one informant remarked cynically, "What we have here may look to you like courts, but don't be fooled—they're no different from the vegetable markets down the street. People buy cases like they buy a kilo of cucumbers."

The root of the problem, in the eyes of my informants, was the unwillingness of Israeli authorities to raise judicial salaries above minimal levels. Magistrate judges, for example, earned approximately 120 to 150 JD per month; the highest salaries, paid to the president and members of the court of appeals, were between 200 and 300 JD. No car allowances were provided, and other perquisites were few. This, of course, was scarcely more than a reasonably successful lawyer was capable of earning in a single day, a situation that was felt simply to invite bribery.[17] According to one lawyer who had recently resigned from his court of appeals judgeship, by the end of his term, his salary "was hardly enough for ten days' expenses, or to pay for the repair of the TV if it broke."

Originally, I was skeptical, at least insofar as the extent of the problem was concerned, having sensed that charges of judicial corruption were providing a convenient scapegoat for many of the lawyers' own failings. If true, the allegations would have important ramifications, and the difficulty of either verifying or discounting them concerned me. Just as I was departing from the field, local newspapers announced that three of the four members of the court of appeals, including its president, and two members of the district court of Nablus, had been detained and were under investigation on charges of accepting bribes. Several lawyers were also implicated, as was a former judge I had interviewed who had complained most vociferously about the problem of bribery. Only one of the three judges of the court of appeals was eventually absolved of wrongdoing; the remainder were convicted by a military court and received fines and prison sentences. The stiffest penalty was reserved for the president of the court of appeals, who was found to have accepted over one million dollars in bribes. He was sentenced to three years' imprisonment and payment of a substantial fine.

It is difficult to determine whether these efforts to stem corruption will deliver anything but a temporary boost to the credibility of the courts. What is certain, however, is that for the number of years in which rumors have flown unabated, that credibility has plunged to unprecedented depths. Lawyers, especially the more honest and proficient of them, are among the most jeopardized by this development, as bribery directly undermines the basis of their legitimacy, that is, their claims of technical expertise. No technical expertise is necessary to bribe a judge. Lawyers, however, interacting regularly with judges who are often their former colleagues, are natural targets for the suspicion that they are the *samasira,* or middlemen, who convey bribes. And some undoubtedly are.

One of the most damaging consequences of the proliferation of bribery, from the perspective of the lawyers, is the unpredictability it introduces into the court system. Reputable attorneys who could afford to forgo cases informed me that they had begun to encourage clients to avoid court actions at any cost. In the words of one informant:

> It used to be that a client would come to me with a problem, which I would study, and give my opinion according to the relevant law, recommending either settlement or raising a claim in court. If the latter, the next question was inevitably "Do you guarantee winning the case?" Before occupation, I would reply, "I can't give guarantees, I'm only a lawyer." But now it's absolutely impossible! If someone comes to me now with a claim for 1,000 JD, I might recommend that they settle for 600 or 700. How can I advise them to go to court, spending their money and wasting a couple of years, and with no idea what the outcome of the case will be? Lately, I've only been accepting very strong, clear cases, with full evidence.

The majority, however, can ill afford to decline cases or direct them away from the courts and thus only chafe at conditions that defy their control.

The Decline of the Civilian Police

The Jordanian civilian police force, staffed by local Palestinians, although under the close supervision of Israeli military officers, has continued to function in the occupied West Bank. Not surprisingly, the authority of the civilian police has suffered at least as severely as that of the court system, relegated as it is to handling petty offenses committed by Palestinians. Civilian police inspire little respect and almost no fear among citizens, and their emasculation at the hands of the Israeli military authorities has made them the butt of sarcastic jokes and sayings. Among them is one told to me by a lawyer: "Ash-shurta lil-mukhalafat, wa ʾl-mukhabarat lil-munazamat," or "The police for traffic tickets, the military intelligence for the [Palestinian political] organizations."

This, of course, is the same police force on which the civil courts must rely for the enforcement of their judgments. In a few fraudulent land purchase cases in which lawyers had succeeded in securing injunctions from the civil courts to halt work by Israeli speculators, civilian police simply took no action to enforce the court orders. Their unexplained lethargy only added to the convictions of the public and legal profession of the impotence of the local courts and the meaninglessness of their decisions.

The West Bank civilian police are often dilatory in performing other functions necessary for the smooth function of the courts. Attorneys are regularly frustrated by the failure of police to deliver imprisoned defendants or witnesses to the courts for hearings, resulting in delays. Explanations are rarely offered for these lapses.[18] Police are also said to act as "touts" for lawyers, keeping power of attorney forms for particular lawyers at hand in the police stations. Police officers refer arrested individuals to these lawyers in return for small kickbacks.

Other Administrative Problems

The problems of insufficient numbers, diminishing competence, and corruption also afflict the ranks of lower court personnel. *Wasta* and vetting by military intelligence are likewise claimed by lawyers to be necessary to gain employment as a court reporter, process server, or other minor court functionary. Employees are frequently pressed into service in multiple roles.[19] Many apparently do not find adequate motivation in low salaries, and so supplement them with small gifts and cash bribes from attorneys.

Particular obstacles to the normal progress of litigation were being encountered during my fieldwork in the area of service of process. According to Jordanian law, summonses to appear in court must be delivered in hand to witnesses and parties to a case by a process server, who is a court officer. In the Ramallah judicial district, only two process servers were provided. Their responsibilities extended to an area encompassing two large municipalities (Ramallah and el-Bireh), four refugee camps, and approximately ninety villages. With neither transportation nor allowances provided, a process server typically waits either for an accumulation of notices for a given village or area before traveling there, or for a lawyer's offer to transport him to a locale, sweetened with a promise of a bottle of whiskey or ten dinars. Many court sessions are delayed because parties or witnesses have not been served.

Another recurrent cause of delay is the necessity to obtain permission from the officer in charge of the judiciary to summon any Israeli citizen or any West Bank civil servant to appear in the civil courts. In a simple case for collection on a bad check, for example, Jordanian civil procedure requires the testimony of the bank manager to prove insufficient funds. Since 1967, all Arab banking facilities in the West Bank have been shut down, and the only services available have been provided by Israeli banks. All such cases thus require the summons of an Israeli citizen. Permission is apparently granted routinely, but often only after a delay of several months.

Lawyers I interviewed were particularly galled that the deterioration of services coincided with substantial increases in court fees. Their general sense was that the Israeli authorities aimed to milk as much revenue from the Occupied Territories as possible while returning the absolute minimum in services. They also accused the authorities of exploiting glitches caused by the steady devaluations of the Israeli shekel against the Jordanian dinar.[20]

Lawyers also complained of late and incomplete distribution of military orders that amended local laws. An official gazette has never been published regularly by the military government, which, instead, claims to distribute orders to all concerned parties. Copies for lawyers in Arabic are generally deposited in piles in their lounges in the civil courts. Some military orders have apparently never been made available to local practitioners, one of the most important of which is the military order that imposed the value-added tax on residents of the West Bank. Confusion and delays are the result, as one informant from Hebron testified:

> Last fall I filed a case for a local client in the District Court for the Southern District, with its seat in Ramallah. Unbeknownst to me, or to most of the rest of us, a military order had been passed two months before that revived the Hebron District Court, which then had begun to exercise jurisdiction in this area. As a result, the case was thrown out for lack of jurisdiction. Sure, I refiled in the Hebron Court—but my client lost time, his court fees, and I lost face! I'm sure my client thought me a complete fool, who didn't even know what court I was supposed to be in!

Court Security

Court buildings also suffer from poor maintenance and lack of security due to understaffing. The second of these problems stirs particular alarm among lawyers. Informants reported that in 1984 the Jenin court had been robbed twice and the Jericho court once and that case files had been destroyed or stolen on all three occasions. An attempt at arson had been recorded at the Nablus court, after which police apparently neglected to respond to requests by lawyers to step up surveillance. Finally, on December 20, 1984, a fire of suspicious origins broke out in the Nablus court complex and some thirteen thousand to fifteen thousand case files, some dating to the Mandate period, were destroyed.[21]

The West Bank lawyers were, not surprisingly, apoplectic. In press conferences and public statements, demands were made for the formation of a committee to investigate the fire and ways of coping with its aftermath. Lawyers insisted that they be included in the committee, as the authorities' foot-dragging in response to earlier requests for better safeguards represented strong evidence of official complicity in the act of arson.

Their suspicions, well-founded or not, are yet another measure of the distrust of Israeli intentions that prevails within the legal profession and the community at large. The civil courts had sustained all manner of abuse against their authority and institutional integrity, but that their very *physical* integrity was now vulnerable to attack almost breached comprehensible limits, adding, as it were, substantial injury to already deep insult.

Problems of Legislation

It will be recalled that on its establishment in the West Bank, the Israeli military government arrogated to itself all powers of legislation. Israel claims to have complied with the requirements of international law that govern belligerent occupation. International legal principles compel an occupying authority to apply preexisting law, with amendments or additions permitted only for reasons of military necessity or for the preservation of "public order."[22] Yet in practice, the military government has encountered no obstacles to the free exercise of its legislative authority.

Many military decrees obviously respond simply to Israeli interests. Even those that do not, seldom evolve out of close consultation and cooperation with the Palestinian community. At the root of this, of course, is the fact that the military government is not politically accountable to the Palestinian residents of the West Bank. The Palestinians are not Israeli citizens, do not vote in Israeli elections, and enjoy no institutional channels of communication to the military government. Thus the twenty or so years of occupation have witnessed great dynamism and extensive changes in some areas of substantive and procedural law; these have no relevance to the needs of the Palestinian community and combine with either stagnation or ineffective legislation in other areas of law in which amendments are desperately needed.

Hence, while a series of military orders promulgated in the early eighties required Palestinian landowners to count and register their fruit trees and eggplant and tomato plants and to secure licenses for the planting of any new ones—clearly a measure designed to protect the faltering Israeli agricultural sector—landlord-tenant law in the region remained frozen in its pre-occupation status. At the same time, radical economic changes in the West Bank created acute problems in tenancy relationships, which, as I have noted, resulted in a flood of eviction cases in the civil courts. At the very least, the lawyers I interviewed charged, the gravity of the problem and the financial stakes involved demanded the transfer of jurisdiction over eviction cases from the magistrate to the district courts, if not changes in the substantive law itself.

Initiatives of West Bank lawyers and the community at large to address the community's legislative needs have been mostly stymied by a political rhetorical paradox. Lawyers have repeatedly invoked international law in criticizing and protesting the alleged illegality of Israeli amendments to Jordanian law. They cleave to the position that the occupying authorities are bound to uphold the laws in force on the eve of occupation. The claim has become an addendum to practically every mention of military orders that lawyers make and is now echoed regularly in the popular press as well. Lawyers and others have been hard-pressed to rationalize appeals for amendments to laws when they must be directed to the same military authorities whose legislative powers they have refused to acknowledge as legitimate.

As the occupation has stretched on, the problem has become more acute but no more soluble. It is obvious that the semipermanence of the occupation makes it something of an anomaly, neither anticipated nor adequately addressed by current provisions of international law. But West Bank lawyers have been loath to raise this point, fearing to open a Pandora's box of rationales for the normalization and entrenchment of the occupation. Instead, they cling to the claim of their legal status as an occupied people, a status that bears consequences that, though onerous, are at least familiar and predictable.

The military administration has not been wholly neglectful of the interests of the West Bank Palestinians where it has been able to discern them and where legislation does not impinge on Israeli interests. Though formal consultative institutions do not exist, lawyers communicate informally with legal officers in the military government in small groups or as individuals on an ad hoc basis. The community articulates its concerns through such organs as the municipal councils, chambers of commerce, and professional associations.[23]

But military authorities are sometimes hampered by ignorance of and insensitivity toward local beliefs and customs even in good faith attempts to address community problems. This is exemplified in Military Order No. 1087, the military government's response to lawyers' complaints about problems of service of process. The order eliminates the requirement in Jordanian law that service of process be personal and permits notice to be sent by registered mail or delivered by lawyers themselves. As one lawyer told me in exasperation, "This sort of thing might be just fine for Israeli society, with reliable mail service and all of that. But it won't work for us. Anyway, we Arabs are an emotional people—we get angry, do irrational things. Can you imagine what would happen to me if I rode into Saʿir [a vil-

lage near Hebron whose residents have a reputation for fierceness]
and tried to serve somebody there? They'd thrash me the instant I
stepped out of my car!" By the time of my departure from the region,
the order had been in force for more than a year, and the problems of
service of process had not appreciably improved.

Problems in the Military Legal System

The military legal system suffers fewer of the administrative deficiencies that plague the civil courts. Judges are scrupulous, sometimes earning praise from West Bank lawyers for maintaining higher
levels of competence and professionalism than are found among
judges in the civil courts. A number of the lawyers I interviewed remarked, for example, that military court judges are more polite to
attorneys and do not harangue them to hasten their pleadings, as do
civil court judges.

Some administrative problems exist, however. To the extent that
military orders pertain to military legal system, their poor and late
distribution leads to confusion just as in the civil courts. The decisions of military courts and objections committees have not been
published since 1976; before then they were available only in Hebrew. Notice, especially in cases pertaining to land, has frequently
been haphazard.[24] But the primary complaints against the military
legal system almost all center around substantive and procedural
laws that narrow the scope of action that attorneys may take in defense of clients and that relegate them to peripheral roles in legal
proceedings.

In the minds of local practitioners, these laws are a reflection of
the very purpose of the military legal system, which is not to dispense justice, but to further the policy goals of suppressing Palestinian nationalism and facilitating Israeli settlement of the West
Bank. In this view, the underlying objective of the military courts is
less to affix guilt to specific individuals for violations of security
regulations than to exact a steady toll from the community in general for acts of resistance, in the hope that pressure will develop
within the community itself for the disciplining of its members.
This is felt to be the principal aim of policies of collective punishment, such as the imposition of curfews after rock-throwing incidents or demonstrations, or the demolition of the houses of families
with members who have violated security regulations, or the levy-
ing of high fines against young offenders, which can only be paid
through the pooling of family resources.[25]

From the lawyers' perspective, the most serious deficiency in the military legal regime is its failure to guarantee detainees the right to counsel in the pretrial period. Most detainees are held incommunicado until they are released or confess to the offenses with which they are charged. Only then are they referred to the court for trial. Lawyers, some of whom have themselves been imprisoned, maintain that Palestinians are systematically subjected to low-level physical abuse, intimidation, and trickery by military intelligence interrogators seeking to extract confessions or statements against others. More serious physical abuse is said to be less regular but not uncommon.

For many years, Israeli officials have vigorously denied such allegations; however, in November 1987, an Israeli government commission led by Supreme Court Justice Moshe Landau revealed that the Shin Bet (General Security Services) had been committing perjury in proceedings related to the admissibility of confessions since 1971. The commission found that "the service committed perjury to conceal its interrogation methods and to ensure that the accused are convicted since, in terrorism cases, the confession is the main instrument for conviction." These interrogation methods are described in the report as both psychological and physical "pressures." The commission condemned the Shin Bet's record of perjury, but rationalized "pressures" as necessary to the war against "terrorism" and promised to propose guidelines for their use.[26]

As we saw in Rafiq's case, the procedural law of the military courts requires that a confession or other admission is inadmissible as evidence if proved through a minitrial (or evidentiary hearing) to have been coerced. Lawyers and detainees claim that interrogators have adopted abusive practices that leave no physical marks, such as forcing prisoners to wag their heads back and forth for hours, depriving them of sleep for days, immersing them in cold water during winter, and placing a blood- and excrement-encrusted bag infested with vermin over their heads. Beatings with fists, feet, and clubs are alleged to occur. If obvious marks are left, laws permit the extension of detention to allow time for healing.

Psychological intimidation is said to take the form of threats to men that women in their families, who are claimed to be in detention, will be sexually assaulted by soldiers. Many lawyers related stories to me from clients concerning a room in each of the detention centers referred to as *"ghurfat al-ʿasafeer,"* the "room of the sparrows." The room is populated with *"ʿasafeer,"* or "sparrows," Palestinians said to be common criminals working as agents for the military intelligence. Their task is to gain the confidence of new detainees, who are placed alone in the room with the ʿasafeer, and then to elicit confessions from them. Information thus gleaned is passed on to military intelligence.

Laws of procedure and evidence leave little room to contest the admissibility of confessions, and requirements for corroboration are minimal.[27] By the time a lawyer enters a case, therefore, its fundamental outcome has already been determined. In the majority of cases, only the details of sentencing remain to be negotiated with the military prosecutor. Even the terms of negotiations are believed to be constrained, since sentences are often fixed by general policy decisions made by higher-level and nonjudicial officers in the military government.

Lawyers who are active in the military courts complain of the monotony of their work and their lack of a sense of professional and intellectual challenge. "When I go to court, I feel like a broken record," one remarked dispiritedly. Many express frustration over their feelings of helplessness genuinely to serve their clients. Another eventually abandoned a flourishing practice in the military courts, characterizing them as "theaters."

Military objections committees are considerably different in form and procedure than are military courts. Within very broad limits, committees are empowered to prescribe their own rules of procedure and evidence. According to Israeli legal specialists, procedural flexibility has permitted the streamlining of the operations of the objections committees, and lenient rules of evidence have allowed the committees to review evidence presented by petitioners that would not meet strict legal standards, thereby facilitating more just results than might be obtained in a formal court.[28]

Lawyers maintain that the absence of procedural guidelines has been exploited by the authorities to the detriment of Palestinian claimants. In support of their position, they refer to the large number of cases in recent years in which the military government has asserted state ownership of plots of land owned by Palestinians. Most of these lands fall within the 65 percent or so of the West Bank that had not yet been reached by the Jordanian cadastral survey, interrupted by the 1967 war. Palestinians are thus obligated to prove ownership without benefit of deeds. Most attempt to do this by presenting tax receipts for their respective plots. Yet military objections committees refuse to accept these as conclusive proof of ownership, and most appeals against declarations of state land, accordingly, fail. Lawyers I spoke to railed against the willingness of the authorities to acknowledge ownership for purposes of tax collection, but to dispute it in the context of an expropriation order.[29] In general, these lawyers viewed the military objections committees as inadequate substitutes for genuine courts and saw their function as merely the erection of a legal edifice for the usurpation of Palestinian lands.

Problems in the Religious Courts

The religious court system has continued to operate under occupation with relative efficiency and integrity. A few problems in enforcement have emerged, mostly where the operations of the religious courts and the civil courts intersect. Religious court judgments are executed through the Execution Department of the civil courts, and so suffer from the same inefficiencies and delays in implementation that civil courts suffer. Bribes are apparently the only means of ensuring expedient performance by a number of Execution Department employees.

Another occasional cause of complications is that decisions of the *shariʿa* courts of the West Bank are not recognized in Israel itself.[30] This becomes problematic in cases of marriage between Palestinians one of whom is a citizen of Israel and the other a resident of the West Bank. If a West Bank wife, for example, obtains a judgment from a West Bank *shariʿa* court against her husband in an Arab village in Israel, she will not be able to enforce the judgment against him within Israel and, instead, must register a new claim in a *shariʿa* court in Israel.

Efforts for Reform

By 1985, the problems of the administration of justice in the West Bank had reached crisis proportions. The legal profession was increasingly vocal in its protests against the professional environment. In meetings with the officer in charge of the judiciary and other responsible officials in the military government, and in numerous communiqués directed to the same quarters, practitioners repeatedly raised the issue of judicial corruption and general administrative inefficiency in the civil courts. Lawyers and journalists took the issues to the public in editorials and investigative articles published in the local Arabic press. Several lawyers published monographs and journal articles in English, which reached an international audience, that reported the problems faced by lawyers in the region. They spread their message on speaking tours in England, the United States, and in several UN-sponsored conferences.

Concern had been mounting within Israel as well. Knesset hearings delved into the question of corruption in the civil courts, entertaining testimony from several West Bank lawyers and other prominent personalities. The problems had been further probed in an Israeli television news special, which featured interviews with several prominent West Bank lawyer-crusaders against bribery.

Lawyers were keenly frustrated by the absence of effective response from the military administration. The problem was not, in their view, that the authorities were ignorant of the phenomenon of corruption.[31] Most had long since passed the point of despair and were steeped in cynicism. Echoing the sentiments of many lawyers, one ranted to me, "It's not because they don't understand the importance of judicial institutions—look at their own courts! They have clean, well-paid judges, decent administration. It's because they *want* the situation to be like this! They *want* us to be dependent on their institutions! They *don't* want us to have strong institutions of our own, which can protect our land and other interests!" A number of striking lawyers cited the deterioration of the civil courts, particularly the proliferation of corruption, as the principal consideration in their decision to observe the strike. I also encountered several lawyers who had chosen early retirement from lucrative practices, because, as one put it, "I have seen *ugly* things happen to this profession, things I thought I'd never see when I began to practice."

The military government eventually began to stir in the direction of reform in the fall of 1984. Its first move was to appoint the president of the court of appeals to the Judicial Appointments Committee, previously composed solely of Israelis.[32] Lawyers were little impressed, as the president of the court of appeals, while admired for legal acuity, was regarded as politically and ethically compromised.

Shortly thereafter, a second measure was taken with the filling of the office of the court inspector, which had, for all intents and purposes, remained vacant since 1967.[33] Lawyers were again only mildly encouraged. Opinions varied as to the honesty and competence of the individual nominated to the position, the brother of the president of the district court of Nablus and thus hardly expected to behave objectively.[34] More damning, however, was the fact that the office of the court inspector was established in Ramallah in a building owned by a well-known activist in the Village Leagues and was frequented by League sympathizers. In the words of one lawyer, "I actually have known the new court inspector since we were both kids and I respect him legally. But, by God, I'll never go visit him in his office! The people don't know anything about the court inspector's office, all they know is that Village League thugs hang out at that building. If I'm seen there they'll automatically assume that I have business with the Leagues!"

Despite the worst fears of the lawyers, however, a momentous action was taken with the above-mentioned arrests of the five judges, among whom were the president of the court of appeals and the brother of the court inspector. Some of the lawyers appointed to fill the vacated judicial positions were highly respected by their peers.

The purge of the judiciary almost surely has delivered a short-term boost to the image of the civil courts and thus, indirectly, to the legal profession as well. Whether the improvements are more than momentary will depend on efforts to address the numerous other problems afflicting the formal legal system.

Conclusions

The civil court system under occupation has been subjected to diminutions of its jurisdiction and challenges to its independence at the hands of the military government. Problems of numbers, competence, and personal integrity permeate all levels of the Judicial Department. Unpredictability and recurrent delays in litigation have spawned a crisis of confidence in judicial institutions among lawyers, the public, and even among court personnel themselves. Lack of cooperation from civilian police has hastened the erosion of public trust in the authority of the courts, particularly in the symbolically and functionally significant area of cases pertaining to land. Available statistics indicate that, in circumstances allowing choice, citizens are resorting to the civil courts with decreasing frequency.

The military legal system has developed at the expense of the authority and integrity of the civil courts. Neither lawyers nor the West Bank public view the military courts or objections committees as institutions modeled to dispense justice, but rather as ways of implementing policies directed at suppressing Palestinian national expression and the seizure of Palestinian land. Lawyers complain that their role in the military courts is minuscule.

Circumstances in both the civil and the military legal systems, hence, significantly limit the real and perceived value of the services offered by lawyers. Technical expertise has been nullified, as it is either lost on incompetent or corrupt judges or never finds an opportunity for expression in the military courts. This has produced a dual leveling effect: within the legal profession, between the competent and scrupulous and the incompetent and dishonest; and vis-à-vis the legal profession as a whole and other potential intermediaries between citizens and government, including *mafateeh* and brokers of *wasta*. Lawyers, while not necessarily understanding all of the roots of the crisis, are highly sensitive to its consequences. Experience has convinced them of their incapacity to better their situation, which has produced a deep and pervasive demoralization within the profession.

9. Disintegration of the Profession

Much of the foregoing discussion has centered around factors that are principally external to the contemporary West Bank legal profession, or, at least, that resist lawyers' conscious understanding and control. Yet the crisis of the profession is in part of its own making. The strike declared by the lawyers in 1967 and the rift within their ranks that subsequently emerged led to the fragmentation of the profession and the erosion of its corporate group status. In turn, these have undermined lawyers' capacity to defend their collective interests and have contributed to a decline in public prestige.

The general problems of indeterminacy and overcontrol are most strongly evident in the issues surrounding the strike. Against the backdrop of an indeterminate future, lawyers are forced to choose among courses of action each of which is fraught with particular perils. The capacity to dictate actions and policies within the profession has been lost to multiple external authorities, in whose hands the future of the lawyers and their society lie.

Genesis of the Strike

West Bank lawyers began the early months of occupation in the tradition of their counterparts in a number of colonial societies, as a vanguard of nationalist opposition to foreign rule. Prominent Jerusalem lawyers, for example, were among signatories to several proclamations protesting the annexation of Jerusalem.[1] Lawyers were also leading members of committees established to organize and coordinate community opposition to the occupation. In fact, they won the dubious distinction of being among the first in the community to suffer exile at the hands of the new military government.[2]

At the time of this early protest activity, the Jordanian civil departments in the West Bank, the civil courts among them, had suspended operation. The hiatus in the operations of the civil courts also caused a standstill in the practices of the fifty-odd lawyers who had remained in the West Bank after the fighting in 1967. Hence practitioners in the early months of occupation witnessed few of the major changes to which their legal system and profession would be subjected in the years to come. Still, it required little imagination for them to grasp the negative implications for their professional lives of Israel's annexation of Jerusalem.

Annexation, it will be recalled, entailed a number of changes in the structure of the legal system of the region that bore dire consequences for legal practitioners. The most significant included the imposition of Israeli law over Jerusalem, the displacement of the jurisdiction of the Jordanian civil courts formerly operating there in favor of Israeli civil courts, and the transfer of the courts thus displaced (including the West Bank Court of Appeals, and the Jerusalem District and Magistrate courts) from that city to Ramallah. Occupation further barred West Bank access to Jordan's Court of Cassation, the highest appellate court in the Jordanian legal system, which was seated in Amman.

Palestinian lawyers residing in Jerusalem who wished to continue practicing before its new courts were entitled to do so, but only after being admitted to the Israeli bar.[3] Moreover, they faced the prospect of competing in an alien legal system against more appropriately trained, Hebrew-speaking, and already-established Israeli lawyers. Their colleagues in the West Bank, meanwhile, were henceforth prohibited from appearing in Jerusalem's courts, thus losing access to a prime market for legal services.

Lawyers met in July of 1967 in Nablus and Ramallah and formalized the de facto state of professional inactivity as a "strike." The gesture was intended to protest the annexation of Jerusalem, the attendant changes in the structure of the civil court system in the West Bank, and the alleged illegality of the Israeli occupation as a whole. West Bank lawyers pledged themselves not to appear in either the civil courts of the region or the newly established military courts, which had begun to enforce a series of strict security regulations, or to engage in any other transactions with these institutions. The strike did not extend to any dealings with the Islamic or ecclesiastical courts of the region, which were relatively undisturbed by the occupation authorities.

Leaders of the profession declined either to limit the duration of the strike or to formulate any concrete conditions (short of total Israeli withdrawal from the Occupied Territories) for its suspension.

Nor did organizers make anything but short-term projections regarding the likely practical consequences of the strike. This clearly reflected the expectation of the professional leadership that the occupation would be of limited duration, a widely held view in the community at the time. Indeed, the strike was not consciously calculated to induce any specific tangible response from the Israeli authorities, but simply to give vent to the outrage of the lawyers over the annexation of Jerusalem and related actions, and to signal the profession's rejection of the entire scheme of occupation by strictly refusing to participate in it. Leaders of the strike fully expected theirs to be hailed as a vanguard position, to be greeted with wide community compliance and support, and even to be emulated by other occupational sectors.

Observance of the strike was initially almost unanimous, with no more than two West Bank lawyers violating its terms by resuming practice. Moreover, officials of the Jordanian Lawyers' Union in the East Bank acted quickly to affirm their solidarity with their West Bank colleagues. They blessed the strike with the status of an official union act and established a fund to pay stipends to striking lawyers, thereby softening the hardships caused by the loss of income.[4]

As part of a strategy to engineer a total community boycott of the civil court system, lawyers endeavored to convince the judges and prosecutors of the West Bank civil courts to join their abstention from work. In the meantime, criminal cases had begun to be routed by police to the new military courts, which tended to issue harsh sentences even for such non-political offenses as petty crimes or traffic violations. Public pressure soon began to mount for a resumption of regular civil court activities. Faced with entreaties for their services, and lacking definitive guidance from Jordanian administrators in Amman, approximately half of the twenty-two or so judges and prosecutors who had remained in the West Bank following the June war resumed normal duties.[5]

As the pace of activities in both the civil and the military courts gradually increased, so did the demand for legal services. Commitment to the strike was still strong among lawyers, however, and citizens were forced to submit to the authority of the courts without legal counsel. In response to this situation, the military governor issued Military Order No. 145, which authorized Israeli lawyers to appear in the military and civil courts of the West Bank.[6] The military governor also charged the officer in charge of the judiciary with the licensing powers and responsibilities normally exercised by the Jordanian Lawyers' Union.

Internal Dissension and the Split

As the occupation extended to several years, concerns among striking lawyers deepened over their increasing social and political isolation. Students, teachers, and other sectors of the population that had struck in the early months of occupation had long since returned to normal routines. Hopes for a total community boycott of the civil court system crumbled, in part as a result of the lawyers' own failure to offer viable alternatives for the resolution of disputes. Claimants' only options were recourse to the courts with the aid of Israeli lawyers, or informal alternatives.[7]

Lawyers intermittently reviewed the feasibility of establishing "popular tribunals" or arbitration boards based in form on *al-qada' al-ʿashaʾiri*, or tribal adjudication, but that would apply "modern" substantive law. Proposals always foundered on the problem of execution of judgments, it being assumed that losing parties to a dispute would simply flout unenforceable decisions. No genuine experiment was ever conducted to test this assumption. Instead, life in the civil court system was permitted to go on, with the lawyers of the West Bank voluntarily consigned to its margins.

Serious doubts about the value of the strike first surfaced publicly in the early seventies. In 1971, frustrated by the stubbornness of the local union leadership in persisting in what increasingly seemed an unrealistic and counterproductive position, approximately ten Ramallah lawyers opted to break ranks with the strikers and return to practice. One reflected on his decision in a later interview published in the local Arabic press:

> The basic issue we faced was: would we stand by our institutions or abandon them? Would we as a society shape and strengthen them or not? Our institutions—health, educational, judicial, municipal—are *basic* institutions, the products of long development and not gifts from anyone. And lawyers in *all* societies, even those of deep-rooted dictatorial traditions, represent the vanguard in the defense of right and of freedom. It is not acceptable for lawyers to assume a negative role, or to remain idle from work and spend their time in the coffeehouse or at home accepting charity; this is contradictory to the nature of things. . . . There are people in detention, pillage of our lands through forged documents, people in need of the services of a lawyer to represent them in their cases. The lawyer might win or he might lose, but it is incumbent upon him to *try*.[8]

News of the abandonment of the strike by some individuals led to swift censure by the JLU. In July 1971, West Bank newspapers reported that the JLU had permanently expelled ten lawyers from Ramallah, Jerusalem, and Bethlehem, accusing them of having appeared before "Zionist civil and military courts" in the Occupied Territories.[9]

Since the responsibility for accreditation of lawyers in the Occupied Territories formerly vested in the JLU had been assumed by the Israeli officer in charge of the judiciary, the sanction had no immediate effect on the working lawyers' capacity to practice in the West Bank. However, the expulsions deprived them of pension rights and other significant benefits gained through membership in the JLU. Working lawyers were also forced to weigh the odds of the reestablishment of Jordanian authority in the region and, with it, the authority of the JLU. At that point, the sanctions might become directly effective, resulting in the loss of livelihood. Moreover, as many informants hastened to assure me, this indictment by their peers and the public branding of them as outlaws and traitors inflicted deep personal wounds from which few fully recovered.

While severe, expulsion nonetheless failed to deter further defections from the strike. For the next several years, lawyers slowly filtered back into practice, periodically suffering the same penalty imposed on their predecessors. Most focused their practice in the civil court system, although a few dabbled, as well, in military court cases. By the early to mid-seventies, the number of lawyers who had returned to work in the region had reached approximately twenty-five, roughly half those who had first committed themselves to the strike.

Development of the Two Factions

The demographics of both working and striking contingents were gradually undergoing significant change due to the influx of new law graduates into the West Bank. Not having been privy to the original decision to strike, many of the young lawyers felt little bound by the strike decision. In light of this, it may seem paradoxical that through the seventies the majority of new law graduates opted for adherence to the strike.[10] In fact, the paradox is only apparent, for as time passed, general economic conditions as well as those prevailing within the legal profession created greater incentives for adherence to the strike than for entry to practice, at least for some.

Increasing numbers of working lawyers and decreasing demand for legal services associated with the post-1973 economic slump combined to create a highly competitive legal field. Many individuals found that the strike, with the certainty of its associated stipend, simply made the most financial sense. In the words of one informant, a striking lawyer and the single member of a poor family of thirteen to gain a university degree:

> I was fortunate to earn a scholarship through the Soviet Embassy to study law in Kiev. When I first came back in 1972, after having been away for five years, I was unfamiliar with life under occupation. I was originally confused about whether or not to strike; it seemed to me that there were legitimate arguments on both sides. In fact, I submitted a request to the military government to be registered as an apprentice, and I actually started working under one practicing lawyer. For a full year I didn't hear a word from the military government concerning my request. But in the meantime, I had decided to give up working and to join the strike. I did it for political reasons—as far as I could see, the military government had no respect for the law, anyway—but even more so for practical reasons. Who was going to support my family for two years (or more, at the rate things were going) while I did my *estage?* And who was going to pay for the expenses of opening my office? So I did it, and I have worked alternately as a teacher and journalist ever since.

While the amount of the stipend was not lavish and was no compensation for the income earned in a reasonably successful practice, at most points during the period of occupation, it exceeded the salaries of the majority of civil servants, including those of judges in the magistrate courts. Striking lawyers were permitted to engage in some other vocations while maintaining their status with the JLU; hence, as a supplement to another income, the stipend constituted quite an attractive financial inducement.[11]

The financial impact of the strike on those among its original members who persevere, and perhaps for some others, has been ruinous. But the composition of the striking faction has been qualitatively transformed since the early years of the occupation to include many whose motivations to strike are radically different from those of its charter members. The number of original strikers has been further depleted by deaths, voluntary emigrations from the region, and deportations, especially of the faction's leadership. These changes have had important ramifications for the chances of reconciliation between the two factions and the reunification of the profession.

With the exception of the slightly greater age of the strikers, the two factions are nearly indistinguishable by their social composition, signaling the complexity and idiosyncratic nature of personal decision making regarding the strike. Lawyers of virtually all social backgrounds and political tendencies can be found on both sides of the professional divide.[12] In Hebron, I encountered a working lawyer, a crusader for reform in the court system, whose brother was a leading member in the local branch of the JLU in the same city.

Efforts Toward Reconciliation and Reorganization

Periodic initiatives to resolve the strike and the rift it created in the profession have been hindered by the reluctance of some older striking lawyers to reenter practice in a changed and, in many respects, alien legal environment. Many have closed their offices, and would face substantial costs in reopening them. To regain accreditation through the Israeli officer in charge of judiciary, striking lawyers must undergo retraining as *estagiares* under working lawyers. The ignominy of first submitting meekly to the requirements of the enemy and then placing themselves at the mercy of upstarts for whom they have only professional disdain and political hostility is simply unthinkable to most.

One of the most serious proposals for reconciliation was aired in a three-part series of articles published in a local journal in 1980–1981. The author, a young working lawyer with a solid professional and political reputation, suggested the establishment of a committee of representatives of the nationalist institutions to mediate between the two factions. Striking lawyers would be offered the choice of immediate retirement with full union benefits, or resumption of practice with continuation of their stipends for a two-year period of readjustment. Despite their apparent merits, the suggestions went largely unheeded.[13]

Repeated unsuccessful attempts to arrive at a resolution of the strike have spawned a number of initiatives for the reorganization of the legal profession. Several informants related to me their involvement as early as 1972 in a move to establish an organization to represent the professional interests of working lawyers. A proposal to the military government met with initial enthusiasm, but subsequent concrete proposals reportedly evoked only guarded promises to "study the matter."

The first sustained organizing drive was mounted only in 1980, when a group of young working lawyers established the informal Committee of Arab Lawyers (Lajnat al-muhaamiin al-ʿarab; henceforth, CAL), with membership initially confined to the Jerusalem area.[14] Within several months, CAL organizers developed sufficient support to extend the group's range to the entire West Bank. A delegation was dispatched to Amman to discuss with union officials and others the founding of a "regional branch of the JLU" encompassing the West Bank, but was rebuffed. Organizing nonetheless continued.

The new group was violently castigated by the JLU leadership in Amman and union loyalists in the West Bank.[15] Noting that several working lawyers had in recent months met with Egyptian and American officials, the strikers charged CAL with complicity in the "Camp David scheme" to circumvent the political authority of the PLO and impose a settlement against the will of the Palestinian people, and with posing itself as an alternate local leadership compliant to Israeli and American interests.[16]

Public reactions to the controversy over CAL's establishment revealed a gradual drift away from trust in the continued efficacy of the strike and toward growth in respect for the working lawyers. A highly respected activist in the engineers' union confided to me a sentiment he asserted was shared privately by many, even among public supporters of the strike:

> What we're doing is paying lip service, nothing more. The strike has become a sacred cow and the strikers an order of monks—isolated, out of touch with the community, worshipping something that has no meaning to anyone else! All that holds them together is a kind of *taʿassub*, a primitive group solidarity. Nothing can be said to them; they're too defensive. Sure, we continue to endorse their strike—but more as a formality than out of genuine enthusiasm.

CAL's leaders were convinced that meaningful progress toward the group's goals could be achieved only if it gained the legal status of a lawyers' union. One of its paramount ambitions, for example, was to regain the profession's powers to discipline its errant members, lost since 1967 to the officer in charge of the judiciary. Given CAL's voluntary form, enforcement of disciplinary decisions relied solely on shaming and other forms of peer pressure and the withdrawal of the few small privileges that membership in the group afforded.

It was over the matter of the acquisition of formal legal status that CAL encountered obstacles that stymied its further institutional development. Spurned by the JLU, CAL had no other option than to seek licensing from the Israeli military government.[17] This simple requirement introduced knotty political problems into the movement for professional reorganization.

First, in the view of many, the request smacked of begging the enemy for a positive grant or benefit. But more challenging to the working lawyers was the legal and rhetorical conundrum resident in their call for the formation of a "branch" union in the West Bank. That specific demand was no accident; rather, it represented the attempt by CAL's supporters to maintain consistency with the position that international law limits Israel's powers of legislation in the Occupied Territories to matters affecting security and public order. This position, as we have seen, has been the bulwark for the West Bank legal profession and the community in opposing the numerous amendments to Jordanian law effected by the Israeli military government since 1967.

Seeking the establishment of an independent union, for which there existed no grounding in Jordanian law, was abhorrent to CAL organizers and, in any case, probably would have proved politically fatal. Yet the grounding which Jordanian law *did* provide them was decidedly infirm.[18] And against the backdrop of the JLU's fulminations against it from Amman, CAL's claim to legal standing appeared hardly compelling.

An equally intractable problem was posed by the group's insistence on the inclusion of Palestinian lawyers resident in Jerusalem. In itself this was not surprising, especially in light of the leading roles played by a number of Jerusalem lawyers in CAL's foundation. But the demand virtually doomed the group's quest for licensure. Acceptance of the group's composition as demanded would have involved violations of explicit Israeli laws concerning the legal profession in Jerusalem. At a symbolic level, such an act would have denied the validity of Israel's annexation of the city by reaffirming its unity with the West Bank.

Finally, it was clear that the organization was already on a collision course with the military government. For example, the one instance in which I was aware of CAL's use of its informal powers of discipline involved a local attorney who had acted in compliance with Military Order No. 1060 and in doing so, violated a CAL-orchestrated collective commitment to boycott the order.[19] A notice was posted in the lawyers' lounges in all of the civil court buildings announcing that CAL had struck the lawyer's name from its roster and calling on all practicing lawyers to refuse to cooperate or interact with him in any way. Although CAL had won a kind of de facto recognition from Israeli officials, it appeared unlikely that Israeli military authorities would hasten to lend legal authority to an organization encouraging defiance of the military government's own legislation.

Despite these difficulties, organizers of the group petitioned Israeli authorities for licensure as the union representing the active legal profession, with affiliation compulsory for all practicing lawyers in the region. Predictably, the petition was denied. An appeal was lodged with the Israeli High Court, based on the claim that Jordanian law both guaranteed the legal profession the right to organize itself and provided the legal means for it to do so.

In November 1987, the High Court issued a ruling, which, though ambiguous, seemed to affirm the right of West Bank lawyers to organize a union. Lawyers had barely begun to study the implications of the ruling and how to act on it when the *intifada*, or uprising, broke out. Further efforts to found a professional organization have been shelved at least temporarily in view of the unrest.

The Role of External Parties

It is obvious that the course of the internal conflict polarizing the West Bank's legal profession has been influenced significantly by the positions of several external parties. Those exercising the most direct impact on the situation include the JLU in Amman and the Israeli military government in the Occupied Territories. But the Jordanian government and the PLO, even if by indecision and inaction, have also contributed in important ways to the current standoff between the working and striking factions.

The JLU's initial support of the strike simply represented an expression of nationalist sentiment on the part of a group that had always regarded itself as a progressive nationalist force in Jordanian politics. But with individual deviations from the strike and CAL's efforts toward professional reorganization, the parent union was faced with movements that threatened its organizational authority and integrity. As time passed and the number of strikers in the West Bank increased, solicitation of their support became a practical necessity for any aspirant to JLU office in Amman. By the late seventies, the striking faction represented the largest single bloc of votes within the JLU, and support for the strike was piously proclaimed by every candidate for union office.[20] Some working lawyers in the West Bank also charged that East Bank members of the JLU were promoting a covert protectionism, out of fear that the demise of the strike would lead to a flooding of the market for legal services in the West Bank, which would eventually spill over into the East Bank.

There is little question that the JLU's unflagging support of the strike has been a fundamental condition of its prolongation. The organizational resources of the JLU office in Amman afford the striking lawyers a variety of advantages in rallying support for their position within the West Bank, Jordan, and further abroad. For example, through its affiliation with the Union of Arab Lawyers (the regional professional association joining the bars of the Arab states), in the early 1970s, the JLU secured the extension of the disbarment of the working lawyers of the West Bank throughout the Arab world. This was more than a symbolic sanction, as those in the West Bank pondering the value of breaking the strike had to weigh the loss of the option to emigrate and establish practices in other Arab countries— as a number of prominent West Bank lawyers and judges had chosen to do—as well as the potential danger of losing their right to engage in legal work in the surrounding Arab countries should the West Bank revert to either Jordanian or Palestinian control.

Striking lawyers wear the alleged hostility of the Israeli authorities toward them and their strike as a badge of pride. Strikers point, on the one hand, to the deportations, house arrests, imprisonments, and other forms of harassment visited on them and, on the other, to the emoluments (such as high judicial posts) claimed to have been dangled before them by Israeli authorities as proof of the latter's anxiety to end the strike and, hence, of its value to the nationalist cause. Indeed, as regards the early years of the occupation, when the Israeli military government was most concerned with the normalization of life in the Occupied Territories, the strikers' claims have a ring of truth. But as the court system has gradually returned to normal functioning *despite* the continuation of the strike, it is almost certain that the attitude of Israeli officials toward it has become increasingly indifferent.

Many working lawyers during 1984–1985 were convinced that the fragmentation of the legal profession was a windfall for Israeli interests, resulting, at it were, from a self-inflicted decapitation by a potentially powerful political force. Many suspected that Israeli administrators were secretly content with the continuation of the status quo, a conclusion bolstered by the temporizing of military officials over initiatives for the reorganization of the profession and eventual rejection of CAL's bid for licensure.

In fact, it appears that, while Israeli military officials are willing to contemplate minimal reforms within the profession, the reestablishment of a full-fledged professional association is regarded with apprehension. Several informants reported being asked by Israeli officials to participate in a "Disciplinary Committee," to be granted limited authority and with membership from the active profession appointed by the officer in charge of the judiciary. The committee was proposed to counter requests for the licensing of a union.[21] When pressed, Israeli official were said to have admitted to fears that a union would be manipulated for "political purposes."

The positions of both the Jordanian government and the PLO vis-à-vis the strike have been characterized above all by lack of clarity and indecision. The Jordanian government materially supported the strike by providing the funds for the strikers' stipends, but began to back away from its commitment in 1977 with its decision to freeze the number of stipends at then-current levels. In a technical legal sense, the strike was an internal union matter over which Jordanian government officials had no direct control. The government could not have intervened without tangling with the JLU, long a formidable and organized adversary of the regime. With the future of the West Bank shrouded in uncertainty, the more prudent course was to eschew a strong position that would alienate one of the two factions and to cultivate clients on both sides of the professional divide.[22]

A similar policy may well have been pursued by the PLO. During the period of my fieldwork, both striking and working factions claimed support for their positions from the nationalist leadership. The striking faction had the tangible evidence of their stipends, paid by the Joint Committee since 1978, to reinforce their claim. But there is evidence that disenchantment with the strike had spread to PLO representatives in Amman by the early to mid-1980s.

The PLO is perhaps the single party possessing the political legitimacy to call an end to the strike and to make its call effective. Its apparent reluctance to do so may be motivated by fear that termination would likely lead to the emigration of several hundred Palestinian professionals from the West Bank. The strategy of *sumud*, or steadfastness, pursued by the PLO since 1978, with the support of the Arab states, has been predicated on stemming the outflow of residents from the Occupied Territories and preserving the Palestinian human presence there in the greatest numbers possible. If the strike is not the most perfect form of resistance to occupation, its continuity has temporarily aided some in remaining steadfast against the pressures toward emigration.

The Stalemate

My arrival in the field coincided with the distribution of a booklet published by the West Bank office of the JLU and authored by its acting head. Among other things, it reiterated the rationale for the strike, described the ongoing activities of the union, documented the alleged accomplishments of its members, and renewed the vituperation against the working lawyers.[23] To the old charges against active practitioners, the author added several new ones: working lawyers were merely conduits for bribes between clients and judges; others were acting as *samasira* in land deals between Palestinian owners and Israeli buyers, so aiding in the alienation of the national patrimony; in all cases, working lawyers were besmirching their own and the national honor by their pursuit of material gain at the expense of the community interest.

So the hornets' nest was again abuzz. Everywhere I went in the region the merits and drawbacks of the strike were the first topic addressed by almost every informant I visited, whether working or striking lawyer, even long after I tired of it and often against my protestations that the ground was already more than familiar. Notwithstanding the bold posture taken by the striking lawyers in the just-published booklet, the tone of their rhetoric—alternately plaintive and shrill with desperation—was a clear index of their slippage in public opinion and their consciousness of their social and political marginality.[24] The intensity of group interaction among striking lawyers had also diminished to minimal levels.

In contrast, the Committee of Arab Lawyers was clearly gaining momentum. In September of 1983, the group issued its manifesto, also in the form of a small booklet, outlining its aims and structure and enumerating its many complaints against the military government. In October, CAL organized a two-day strike from court work of its own, to protest Military Order No. 1060. CAL was spearheading the campaign against judicial corruption, and its steering committee members were being interviewed by local Arabic journals and newspapers concerning the issue. Several of its leaders were prominent in the Committee for the Defense of Prisoners, established in 1984 by several Israeli Arab and Jewish lawyers in solidarity with the prison strike in Jneid prison. CAL also raised a clamor following the burning of the Nablus court building and called for the creation of an investigative body, including representatives of the legal profession, and suggested a variety of remedies for problems arising from loss of documents in the fire. But CAL, too, faced continuing skepticism on the part of working lawyers, a considerable number of whom regarded its aims as laudable but unrealistic. Hence, little in the situation I witnessed presaged either an impending resolution of the strike or the satisfaction of CAL's demands of certification.[25]

Cultural Dimensions of the Strike

A strike that by all appearances is perpetual is certainly an anomaly, although one perhaps perversely appropriate, given the indeterminacy that obscures the West Bank's political future. It is obvious that the strike was caused by the occupation, that is, that it would not have occurred but for the advent of Israeli rule. Yet the strike was only one of a number of possible actions that the legal profession might have taken. In this sense, it was not a *necessary* outcome of the occupation, but instead reflected a choice of action exercised by a specific group conditioned by the circumstances confronting it and by the dominant ideas and values of the wider society of which the group was a part.

Strong undercurrents of the ethos of honor are discernible in the lawyers' sophisticated legal and political rhetoric concerning the strike. Apart from the practical difficulties imposed on them by the annexation of Jerusalem, that measure in a variety of ways would have forced them to act out the reality of annexation through their daily professional routines. Each appearance of a Jerusalem lawyer in an Israeli civil court, or of a West Bank lawyer in the court of appeals newly seated in Ramallah, would have been a reminder and, in a sense, a validation of the annexation.

The strike seems to conform to the structure of traditional disputing, in which the appropriate first step of an offended party is to withdraw from interaction with the offender, awaiting the intervention of others to initiate reconciliation.[26] The notion that to deal with an offender while a dispute is outstanding is to sacrifice honor, and that interaction involves recognition of the social equality and legitimacy of the other, underlies the strike just as it does the stance of the Palestinian peasant who refuses to raise a civil claim against Israeli settlers vandalizing his orchards. In its initial spontaneity and failure to forecast practical consequences, and in the financial sacrifices it demanded of its first adherents, the strike created the opposition between material interests and the values of honor that constitutes the classic occasion for the latter's display.

In the Israeli military government, though, the lawyers were dealing with an alien authority operating according to a different cultural logic. Nor has any third party stepped into the breach between the profession and the Israeli military regime, perhaps, in this case, because no appropriate mediator exists to do so effectively.

The Impact of the Erosion of Corporate Group Status

The status of the legal profession as a corporate group has eroded significantly since the pre-occupation period. This erosion has substantially diminished the power that lawyers exercise in their work environment and in the wider social fields in which they operate.[27]

The periodic rounds of insults and invective exchanged between the two factions have probably edified neither in the eyes of the general public, but instead have sullied the reputations of both, particularly as some of the charges traded have contained a kernel of truth. Some working lawyers *have* acted as middlemen in covert and illegal land deals with Israelis, or been involved in bribery of judges and other officials.

As for the striking group, its collective lethargy and the hypocrisy of some of its members' commitments have given rise to snide references within the community to the "profession of the strike." Given the values of the surrounding society, the fact that some lawyers have developed an economic stake in the strike's maintenance has been particularly destructive of the profession's collective image. Whereas the gesture of the early strikers defied material interests and demonstrated their honor and integrity, the opportunism of later adherents has robbed the strike of its symbolic power.

The vain attempts of the working contingent to reorganize itself with formal recognition from the authorities have left it helpless to stem the proliferation of unethical practices on the part of working lawyers. Such practices taint the whole group, despite the small numbers who actually engage in them. Neither has the working group mustered strength to oppose military government policies regarded by Palestinians as illegal or inimical to their community interests.

The precarious economic conditions prevailing within the profession have also undermined its status. While these conditions were not in any sense caused by the erosion of the profession's corporate status, its capacity to defend individual members through collective action has been impaired, as I was passionately apprised by one young working lawyer: "What can the public possibly make of us when some lawyer tries to steal a case from another by undercutting his fee, asking five dinars for his work? If *we* don't place a higher value on our services, how can we expect our clients to? At the very least, a union could establish and enforce a schedule of minimum fees, and perhaps do something to distribute the work a little more fairly so that younger attorneys can pay their office rent and buy food!"

As his statements suggest, the crisis of public confidence in the profession is matched by severe demoralization and frustration within it. No one senses the profession's decline more acutely than its members, both striking and working, nor the futility of their efforts to resist the process:

> We desperately need a union, both to defend our collective in-terests—against the authorities, abusive judges, and the like—and to ensure that we indeed deserve our status as members of one of the sacred, noble professions. Now we're like a bunch of sheep without a shepherd, wandering every which way with-out guidance! But how can we possibly accept the concessions the military government will surely try to extract for recogni-tion of a new union? We simply can't. And so things go on, getting worse almost daily.

The decapitation suffered by the profession as a result of the strike was not simply organizational, but involved personnel as well. Much of the elite of the profession absented itself from active prac-tice in 1967, and although some eventually returned, many did not. What emerged as the working wing of the profession was to a con-siderable extent a *new* profession that developed without full bene-fit of the cultivation and grooming normally given a new generation within a profession by its older and established members. How much expertise and lore was not passed down, how many networks of clients, or even office space and libraries not inherited, cannot be known, nor can the effects of these things be calculated. But this dis-continuity in tradition has surely exacted some toll on the profes-sion's power and social standing.

The fragmentation of the legal profession and low level of cohe-sion within its respective antagonistic factions has diffused the very meaning of the term "lawyer" to the extent that it hardly refers any longer to a distinct social category. Whereas lawyers were quintes-sentially "those who worked in the courts," the strike has given rise to lawyers who *renounce* law and the courts, and to the spectacle of "lawyers-as-money-changers," "lawyer-as-journalists," and "lawyers-as" all the other vocations in which the strikers engage, including idle receipt of funds from an external source.

Conclusions

The disunity of the profession has contributed to the overall decline of its actual power and its status and to palpable frustration and demoralization among its members. The indeterminacy of the political future of the region impinges on the decisions of individuals in facing the issue of whether to strike and adds risks to courses of action that threaten to evoke sanctions from a potential future authority. It has also confined the working faction to a legal and rhetorical position that virtually ensures the failure of its program. The stage of development at which the Committee of Arab Lawyers has stalled expresses organizationally the limbo in which the profession and general society remain suspended. As is the case for the community at large, the power to address the lawyers' most pressing needs and problems escape them, remaining vested in the hands of higher or external authorities.

10. Conclusions

The point of departure for this study was the observation that the circumstances of occupation seemed to afford lawyers of the West Bank significant opportunities for the advancement and consolidation of their social position. Noting the deep crisis in which the Palestinian lawyers of the region founder, I posed the question: What accounts for the decline and social marginalization of the West Bank's legal profession during the twenty years of Israeli occupation? Let us now briefly review the principal factors contributing to the current crisis.

The Occupation Administration

The contemporary West Bank legal profession is the product of many factors. Among the most important are the indeterminacy of the political future of the West Bank and the nature and actions of the Israeli military government, which has introduced great unpredictability and insecurity into the life of the Palestinian community under occupation. Notwithstanding its outwardly legalistic orientation, the Israeli military government is perceived by Palestinians as arbitrary, despotic, and hostile to their collective interests and aspirations.

The military government's dual character—law-oriented, at one level, but capricious and unconstrained as viewed from the perspective of its subject population—is one of the distinctive features of what I have attempted to highlight by the reference to "Orientalist despotism." A syndrome analogous to the stereotypical Oriental despotism, but with distortions and even some exaggerations of the traditional model, has been created by a new and different conjuncture of circumstances.

The ability of the West Bank's legal profession to mediate effectively between citizens and formal authority has been critically impaired in this environment. Public trust in the efficacy and integrity of the institutions that establish the lawyers' raison d'être and that provide them their lifeblood of cases—the civil courts—has plummeted, as those courts are afflicted with problems of inefficiency and corruption. The outcomes of court actions have become highly unpredictable, which reduces the appeal of formal institutions as avenues for dispute processing. Political favoritism and patronage have flourished, thereby undermining the value of legal expertise. Tarnishing the image of the civil courts even further is their perceived impotence to resist the Israeli government in its execution of policies viewed as destructive to Palestinian interests. This is especially true of Israel's land acquisition policies and the settlement of Israeli civilians in the region.

Military tribunals, meanwhile, are seen as mere extensions of the power of the military government, as instruments for the seizure of Palestinian lands and the muzzling of nationalist opposition. In their own and the popular perception, lawyers are consigned by substantive and procedural laws in the military legal system to the role of beggars for the mercy of the military courts. The scope for the use of technical legal knowledge and thus for the validation of the distinctive expertise of the legal profession is exceedingly narrow. Lawyers are employed in the simple hope that they might succeed in winning lighter sentences or fines; negative verdicts are seen almost as foregone conclusions.

The West Bank's legal profession has also suffered considerably from its subjection to nonreciprocal competition from Israeli lawyers, both Arab and Jewish. Israeli lawyers, for example, are generally regarded as being more effective than their West Bank colleagues in softening the judgments of military tribunals. West Bank practitioners are barred from appearances in Israeli courts. The application of Israeli law to Jerusalem and the establishment of Israeli civil courts there constituted a major loss for the West Bank profession, as that city was the site of businesses and other institutions that formerly generated a fairly steady demand for legal services. The large number of military court cases handled by members of the Israeli bar also deprives West Bank professionals of numerous opportunities for tangible earnings and gain. Given the reduction in the number of cases in the civil courts, the Israeli lawyers' capture of the lion's share of cases in the military courts has been particularly felt.

West Bank lawyers' disadvantage in facing competition from Israeli lawyers is deepened by the latter's monopoly over appearances in the Israeli High Court, the sole legal institution that exercises any effective restraint over the military government. West Bank lawyers have lost to their competitors a potentially important symbolic resource—the capacity to pose as the embodiment of the normative regulation of government power,[1] and thus as the effective champions of the interests of the Palestinian community.

Indeterminacy and Overcontrol

As we have seen, for more than twenty years, the status of the Occupied Territories has remained unresolved, their residents hostage to the will of larger external political forces. This legal and political limbo is largely responsible for the general atmosphere of uncertainty that plagues the community and for the sense of insecurity and loss of control over the future that has come to characterize the individual experience of many Palestinians during the period of Israeli occupation.

The indeterminacy of the political future of the region has touched the legal profession in a variety of ways. In the first place, the continuing legal categorization of the West Bank as an "occupied territory" is a condition for Israel's administration of the region through the expedient of military government, with all the negatives for the legal profession that such a system implies. Unpredictability has chilled local entrepreneurial activity, thereby inhibiting development of the kind of complex enterprises that typically have fueled demand for legal services in other societies. Lawyers charting individual career paths—deciding whether to strike or to work, or whether to study Hebrew, for example—are forced to weigh the implications of short-term actions against the backdrop of an uncertain future.

Indeterminacy has also given rise to the phenomenon of "overcontrol," the subjection of the West Bank to multiple external authorities exerting contradictory pressures on the local community. Israel exercises direct power through the agency of the military government. Jordan exercises indirect influence through its control of the flow of people and goods between the East and West banks and through its network of client-notables. The PLO commands some quasi-governmental resources and enjoys the political loyalties of the majority of the Palestinian community. The result is a combination of suffocating control in matters that involve the interests of the three external authorities and a breakdown in the system of social accountability and near anarchy in realms implicating only or primarily local community interests.

In its response to these forces, the legal profession may be viewed as a microcosm of the society in which it is situated. Control over its present and future has been lost almost wholly to external authorities. Maintenance of the strike is largely contingent on the support of the JLU, but even more so on the Jordanian government and the PLO, joint custodians of the source of funds for the stipends paid to striking lawyers. Without these funds, the strike would surely collapse. Regulation of the working contingent is now vested in the hands of Israeli authorities. The latter have been lax in enforcing discipline within the legal profession, which has permitted the proliferation of unethical practices, a development that has been profoundly injurious to the lawyers' reputation and status. The lawyers' own efforts to bring their wayward colleagues to account through the revival of a professional organization with powers of discipline have been blocked by the Israeli military government, which has viewed the establishment of such an organization as politically problematic. The profession thus remains fractured, half-reorganized, yet paralyzed from further effective action by the various external forces that dictate its fate.

The psychological effects of this situation on the group have been devastating. My informants regularly expressed feelings of professional and personal suffocation, isolation, lethargy, and frustration. Visions of normally functioning legal systems in Israel and Jordan, of which the lawyers have only minimal direct knowledge, despite their geographical proximity, tend to be idealized, as are the memories of the bygone Mandate era. Virtually all debilities suffered by the profession are conceptualized as having been caused by the occupation, and Israeli withdrawal from the region is fantasized as a panacea.

I have argued that the circumstances of occupation *are* indeed at the root of the current crisis within the profession. But I have also suggested that *some* stresses currently faced by lawyers are largely unrelated to the occupation. The role of the Israeli military government vis-à-vis these stresses is merely that of the authority presiding at the time of their occurrence. Corruption, inefficient administration, arbitrary executive authorities, and the like, are also typical of many postcolonial governments in the Third World. The situation in the West Bank seems only a variation, with the peculiar twist given it by the presence of an alien military government.

Ironically, the West Bank lawyers' convictions about the occupation and its relationship to their dilemma have metamorphosed for some into a sort of license for collective inactivity and slack behavior. When the roots of local problems are located in forces above and beyond the community, its members are liberated from responsibility for seeking solutions, and justification for self-serving behavior is only a short step away. Presented with no course of action that is unambiguously legitimate and honorable, and generally frustrated in efforts to defend concerns of the larger community, a number of West Bank legal practitioners pursue individual and familial interests, attempting to wrest at least a modicum of benefit from what is perceived as an overwhelmingly negative situation.

Apparently genuine opportunities to improve their shared conditions have not been consistently exploited by lawyers. The prime example of this is the failure to repair the breach within the profession caused by the strike. For all the external influences contributing to its prolongation, the strike could easily be ended were some agreement concluded among lawyers of the region. The tendency within the profession has been to abdicate its responsibilities, however, and to look to external sources for salvation.

The Erosion of Internal Cohesion and Corporate Group Status

Several developments have contributed to the erosion of the profession's internal cohesion and corporate group status. As I have noted, the rapid influx of members of diverse social backgrounds, as in the legal profession in surrounding societies, has diminished the group's homogeneity. More important, however, is the fracture within the profession brought about by the strike and ensuing disagreements over its prolongation. It is clear that these circumstances have led to the weakening of the West Bank lawyers' sense of collective identity. Moreover, viewed from the perspective of the broader society, the fracture within the profession has blurred the very meaning of what it is to be a lawyer. That term now applies to a number of individuals who perform widely disparate functions, and even some (striking lawyers) who practice vocations totally unrelated to law, or simply live on the dole from stipends dispensed by the Jordanian-Palestinian Joint Committee.

The Legacy of Imposition

The Palestinian legal profession is one of relatively recent and exogenous origins; therefore it enjoys only tenuous grounding in local society. As in many other parts of the Third World, the modern legal profession in Palestine was an outgrowth of the broad historical movement of the nineteenth and twentieth centuries that attempted to impose Western-modeled law and legal institutions and of government efforts to promote national integration through the extension of centrally controlled legal and political institutions.

This global process has been widely resisted at the local level, if covertly and subtly, as it has typically implied surrender of local autonomy to distant authorities. The agenda of interests and ambitions of national governments have often conflicted fundamentally with those of the communities under their rule.

As members of an imposed profession, the Palestinian lawyers have faced special problems of collective self-legitimation. Indigenous attitudes toward the state and its law, concepts of honor and appropriate methods of protecting it, the existence of alternative modes of dispute processing sometimes more effective and satisfying than formal institutions, and other social and cultural factors have slowed the consolidation of the social position of the legal profession. Given the low level of general public knowledge of state law, formal legal institutions, and the nature and function of legal practitioners, lawyers' activities have narrowly circumscribed the context in which their services are most immediately and obviously necessary, namely, in litigation and other court-related activity.

Thus the profession has been structurally dependent on formal institutions of the state—the courts. Yet the lawyers cannot control the integrity and efficiency of the courts. As these institutions have deteriorated during the period of occupation, their appeal to citizens has waned, as has the value of legal services. Lawyers have been more conscious than anyone of the deleterious effects on the community of the malaise in the formal court system and have led the fight for its reform. In the final analysis, however, the legal profession is still inextricably entwined with state institutions. Although the lawyers of the West Bank have generally distanced themselves ideologically from the occupation regime by posing as defenders of Palestinian national interests, they attack the legitimacy of the formal system only at the risk of undermining their own legitimacy and status.

In a sense, this is precisely what has occurred with the striking faction, which *has* radically challenged the legitimacy of the formal system as it was transformed by the Israeli military government—and, by the same act, has consigned itself to the margins of social and political life in the West Bank. Meanwhile, the working faction has scored the military government for its policies, but in a general sense, still of necessity favors and promotes the "legal" way of doing things. It is, in short, ultimately reformist in orientation.

The acute dependence of West Bank lawyers on the formal court system is one of the factors contributing to their vulnerability to state authority. But the profession also lacks the insulation from negative state actions that might have been provided by an understanding and sympathetic surrounding society. The nature and value of legal services are not clearly established in the popular mind, however. Society's sense of loss at the crippling of the profession is not a strong one; no social allies have leaped to its defense.

The profession's vulnerability to the state is a function of the legacy of its imposition, and not simply of the situation of occupation. Hence, the eminence of lawyers in the Mandate period was a figment of British policy, a product of a specific aim of the administration to develop the profession and to groom it for social and political leadership in an independent Palestinian state. But by the same token, its position was easily subject to reversal by a strong state authority, such as the Israeli military government, which included among its principal policy goals the prevention of the emergence of a local nationalist leadership in the Occupied Territories. However, this should not be taken to imply that the subversion of the legal profession during the period of occupation has unfolded according to some conscious policy of the military government, even though many Palestinian lawyers suspect as much. But the military government's policies toward the profession to some extent appear to have been based on a conscious estimate of the profession's potential political strength. Decisions damaging to it—such as the refusal of requests for the licensing of a new professional association—have been grounded on political considerations.

Lawyers and National Resistance

It may be impossible to define precisely the West Bank legal profession's role with respect to the nationalist opposition to Israeli occupation. Both striking and working factions regard themselves as active participants, if not vanguards, in the struggle against Israeli power. This conviction is sometimes articulated frankly in nationalist terms, other times, more indirectly, through slogans concerning the defense and promotion of the general principles of the "rule of law." In a certain sense, the lawyers' self-image is accurate, for, indeed, lawyers have done much to heighten public consciousness of the more subtle workings of the legal system under occupation and of the multitude of ways in which that system has functioned to the detriment of the Palestinian residents of the West Bank.

While the legal regime of the occupation administration is much resented and engenders more cynicism among Palestinians than legitimacy for Israeli rule, however, it may still elicit less resistance or less violent resistance than other potential forms of domination. The legal profession, at least its working faction, denounces and contests Israeli actions in the West Bank, and yet is committed to doing so in legal terms. At the same time, it invites the broader community to invest tangible and intangible resources in a nonviolent form of struggle, which is relatively less threatening and more easily contained and deflected by Israeli authorities than forms of resistance to which Palestinians might otherwise be forced to resort. Quite unconsciously—in fact, in diametric opposition to its conscious and articulated purpose—the legal profession at some levels may actually aid in the deflation of nationalist resistance to Israeli occupation.

A Prognosis

Evaluating the future prospects of the West Bank's legal profession necessarily involves consideration of the likelihood of changes in the constellation of power and authority within which the lawyers live and practice, and so demands a brief foray into the international politics of the Middle East. Until the uprising that began in 1987, it appeared that the status quo of Israeli military occupation of the West Bank would extend into the future with few or no alterations in its structure, style, or policies. In other words, probability favored the perpetuation of the state of "permanent impermanence" in which residents of the Occupied Territories have lived since 1967.

No party with sufficient power to break the diplomatic logjam impeding efforts to reach a negotiated peace in the Middle East had sufficient interest in doing so before now. Israel, the party with most immediate control over the West Bank, has stood pat, its interests well protected by the state of indeterminacy. The United States, Israel's principal backer in the region, has appeared convinced that no gain would be derived by pressuring the Israeli leadership into concessions it was reluctant to make. And neither of the two other contenders for authority over the West Bank—Jordan and the PLO—has enough independent power to wrest concessions from Israel, particularly with their Arab supporters depleted economically and divided politically.

Maintenance of the status quo in the region is likely to produce a parallel stasis in the position of the legal profession, perhaps with minor oscillations in its short-term fortunes. As occupation extends, more lawyers are likely to base career decisions on the assumption of the relative permanence of the situation. They may overcome their reticence to study Hebrew, or, for East Jerusalem lawyers, may seek authorization to practice in Israeli courts. With West Bank lawyers performing adequately in the military courts and allaying community doubts of their competence, they are likely to handle a greater share of political or security cases, particularly as Israeli lawyers move on to more lucrative and professionally rewarding areas of practice. Thus professional opportunities will gradually broaden, although probably only marginally.[2]

Some reforms leading to the improvements of the lawyers' professional conditions seem not to be inconsistent with Israeli interests in the region. It is quite possible that continued agitation by West Bank practitioners will lead to further actions along the lines of the 1985 purge of the judiciary, which appears to have had salutary effects on the civil court system.[3] But firm limits on reforms would seem to be established by the apparent determination of the military government to retain maximal control over such resources as land and to ensure the greatest freedom for itself in shaping the political contours of the region. Hence it seems farfetched that Israeli authorities would repeal military orders usurping the jurisdiction of the civil courts, the institutional integrity of which have been so undermined.

While the impact of the Israeli High Court ruling that affirms the right of West Bank lawyers to have a union is still not clear, working lawyers will surely insist on the inclusion of the Jerusalem contingent, which has always led the struggle for professional reorganization. Their demand for a union thus will continue to be framed in terms that Israeli authorities are sure to reject. Moreover, the strike will doubtless continue as long as it receives external support. Hence the West Bank's legal profession may well founder in its current state of fragmentation and incomplete reconstitution, suspended in painful limbo for the indefinite future.

Appendix

This appendix situates this study of the Palestinian legal profession in the context of current issues in the field of legal anthropology and expands the discussion of some of the theoretical questions raised in the introduction.

Interests and Modes of Dispute Processing

Much recent literature dealing with the cross-cultural study of "dispute processing" has been concerned in one way or another with categorizing the various modes by which individuals may choose to handle their problems with others and with analyzing the factors that structure and determine their choices.[1]

Work by a number of anthropologists and other social scientists mostly in the seventies elaborated a typology of basic dispute procedures employed worldwide. This typology was seen as a continuum of the degree and quality of third-party intervention and the nature of outcome.[2] According to Nader and Todd, the evolving view of disputes as "social processes embedded in social relations" stimulated a shift in concern from formal rules and institutions to individual decision making in disputes to something the authors termed a "processual model":

> In any dispute (or grievance or conflict) situation, people are interacting. They are involved in the process of making decisions about how best to maximize their own advantages, how best to obtain the results they seek. The processual model, unlike the structural-functional model, focuses on people enmeshed in networks of social relations, on people making decisions that are based on a number of competing factors.[3]

Informed by this understanding, students of legal anthropology fanned out to a number of societies to scrutinize the process of "forum shopping" in which disputants engage while pursuing their interests during conflict. Many researchers focused on the considerations governing the choice between use of "informal," or non−state-sponsored, local-level modes of dispute processing and resort to "formal," or state-sponsored, institutions, especially courts, and sought to explain the often-observed preference for the former in the communities they studied.

Explanations tended to center on the distinction between the authoritative adjudication and zero-sum outcomes purportedly offered by formal courts, on one hand, and the negotiations, mediation, and compromise outcomes characteristic of informal dispute processing.[4] Formal courts and procedures were seen as alien and impervious to local community control,[5] more likely to be employed in disputes over scarce or tangible resources of value sufficient to risk termination of a relationship.[6] In contrast, informal procedures were generally favored when parties had strong interests in the continuity of their relationships,[7] or where an intangible resource, such as honor, was at stake.[8] Formal courts were depicted as promoting conflict, while informal procedures were thought to be "therapeutic."[9]

These works and others of like bent surely broadened social scientific understanding of the complex of factors that direct an individual's choice among available modes of dispute processing in the course of conflicts with others; one may recognize this even while quarreling with some of the particular formulations their authors generated.[10] Indeed, I hope in part to add to the "choice of forum" literature by confirming some of its ideas and adding others.[11]

But beyond this, it seems to me that the considerable elaboration on the question of individual strategizing has not been matched by a similarly nuanced view of the many other vectors that condition whether and how a dispute is processed, of which volition of the immediate parties to dispute is only one.[12] In the first place, disputes are often not simply dyadic, but involve several, sometimes many, parties whose interests may be diverse and contradictory. These parties may be members of groups that have interests as collectivities distinct from and possibly conflicting with those of an individual constituent in a particular circumstance.[13]

But even a complex reading of the interests of parties to a dispute may not comprehend the major forces that structure its course. A wide variety of nonparties may be intensely interested in this course as well, as there are both tangible and intangible "goods" to be had through performance of the function of dispute processing. Some researchers have gone as far as to investigate the interests of local-level remedy agents or other "third parties" and the roles they play in determining the direction of disputes.[14] One has suggested that, "besides forum-shopping disputants, there are also 'shopping forums' engaged in trying to acquire and manipulate disputes from which they expect to gain political advantage, or to fend off disputes which they fear will threaten their interests."[15]

Here it is appropriate to observe that the "choice of forum" studies, especially insofar as they evaluated the relative advantage of non–state-sponsored disputing procedures as opposed to those of formal courts, were essentially studying particular local manifestations of a general phenomenon—the nineteenth- and twentieth-century movement of many non-Western states to centralize authority through the extension of unified systems of law and courts, often structured after European models—from the perspective of the local, often rural, communities that were the sites of most anthropological fieldwork. It is not surprising, therefore, that our more detailed understanding concerns the tactical maneuverings by members of these communities in their attempts to resist the penetration of state law and widening authority of formal legal institutions and to preserve local autonomy.

This is not to suggest that other researchers have been unaware of the larger context of their research; on the contrary, it has been explicitly recognized by many, even the majority of authors on these topics. Discussions of state authority are, in fact, ubiquitous in the literature. But few have viewed the general phenomenon of the extension of state law from anything but the vantage point of the local community or have systematically attempted to understand the issues surrounding it from the perspectives either of central authorities themselves or of allied or dependent private groups with interests in the extension of state power. There is a tendency, instead, to view the state as an abstract entity with a general stake in affirming its legitimacy and an inclination to monopolize dispute processing for its own institutions.[16]

By all means, the state's "legitimacy interest" in dispute processing is of decided significance and may lead to the interposition of state remedy agents between private parties to a dispute, irrespective of their wishes.[17] State authorities may have reason to politically empower specific nonstate actors by deputizing them as remedy agents or by granting them monopoly over rights of intermediation between citizens and formal agencies in other realms.[18] The state may also have direct, tangible interests in the outcomes of particular classes of private disputes, which cause it to direct parties

to institutions under its control, thereby ensuring the results it de-
sires. And, of course, the state itself is often a party to disputes, typically as a prosecuting agent (increasingly so with the extension and
intensification of state regulation), in which case, its "choice of
forum" will almost always be dispositive.

But the "state" is more than a mere abstraction; it is a complex set
of institutions staffed by real individuals whose tangible economic
interests and social authority and prestige turn, in large part, on the
reach and strength of these institutions. This is as true of courts and
other institutions of dispute processing, and of the personnel who
occupy them, as of any others.[19] The sustenance of formal courts
and, by extension, those whose economic and prestige interests are
lodged in them, is the body of cases and other transactions that the
courts judge or otherwise manage. As Moore states about the national courts in Tanzania, "Such a system of courts is a bureaucratic
animal whose only food is cases."[20]

Although this study may shed some light on the various interests
of the "state" and its real functionaries in the processing of disputes,
my primary focus is, rather, on another group, which stands outside
the legal institutions of the state but is dependently linked to them:
the legal profession. My aim is not to formulate a newer, more complex recipe for the prediction of the course of disputes. I intend
simply to suggest that lawyers are not disinterested bystanders to
the general process of the extension of state law in Third World societies (or elsewhere), but tend, on the contrary, to support it. I have
tried to examine the implications of this reality among a particular
group, the Palestinian lawyers of the West Bank. In doing so, I have
attempted to demonstrate that viewing matters from the vantage
point of an occupational group closely associated with state power,
instead of from the perspective of communities doing their utmost
to fend off formal authority, may be a modest aid in rounding out our
vision and understanding of the continuing struggle between central
and local authorities in many societies.

The Concept of an "Imposed" Profession

The nineteenth and twentieth centuries witnessed the extension of
Western law and legal institutions throughout Latin America, Africa, and Asia, either through the medium of direct colonial rule or
the "voluntary" adoption of Western legal forms by still independent non-Western states, which were often motivated to eliminate
extraterritorial rights conferred on European merchants by unequal
treaties.[21] A number of social scientists have conceptualized this

process as the "imposition of law,"[22] and have referred to "imposed law," "imposed courts,"[23] and the like. One by-product of this broad process was the establishment in many of the subject countries of a Western-style legal profession.[24]

I would propose that there is some value in viewing lawyers in societies that have undergone this process, including lawyers of the West Bank, as members of an "imposed" legal profession.[25] The underlying justification for this concept is the recognition that societies may have relatively distinct and coherent systems of ideas and values about disputation and the laws, institutions, and social actors engaged in it, which together form what some have termed "legal cultures."[26] Laws and legal institutions that develop within the particular social and cultural matrix of one society are likely to have a different and somewhat more complicated life when implanted in an alien society, the values and structures of which may differ radically from the original. Professions that grow around institutions so imposed may bear only formal resemblances to their counterparts in the source society.[27]

If this seems intuitively correct, the matter is less straightforward than it appears at first blush. A number of scholars have raised legitimate questions about the validity of the notion of "imposed" law and legal institutions, at least insofar as they refer to foreign transplants. They note that *all* law is in a sense "imposed":

> In complex societies, the relationship between moral and legal
> norms or rules may be no closer than it is when an alien law
> is imposed on another society, and the behavior of individuals
> in each case is as striking for its similarities as for its differences. In both situations people obey the law out of fear of sanctions, find its definitions alien and its solutions "unfair," are
> confused and baffled by it, use it to manipulate and gain power,
> and often prefer alternative ways of settling their disputes.[28]

At the root of this is the fact that the law and legal institutions in many societies may derive their very authority and legitimacy from the "deliberately" induced sense of their distinctiveness from other modes of discourse and social institutions. Kidder completely rejects questions about "imposition" as misguided; he favors "externality," the notion that "outsiders—people with less direct involvement in the conflictual context—will find externally grounded reasons for becoming interested in a conflict's outcome."[29] Law is more or less "external" according to the number of intervening "layers" of interested nonparties who are involved.

The genuine difficulties in defining "imposed law" and differentiating it from any other law do not render the concept useless. It is true that social organizational complexity of the kind Kidder describes can produce one form of social distance between disputants and the other actors and institutions with which they become entangled. But an important dimension of cultural distance may intervene as well.[30] Kidder's notion of "externality" would capture little of the distinctiveness, for example, of the experiences of West Bank Palestinians in the Israeli military tribunals, the Western-style civil courts, and the Islamic religious courts that function in the region and in which roughly equivalent "layers" of outsiders are involved. Of these, only the Islamic courts have any true moral legitimacy to complement the de facto recognition of their power. In dress, speech, and other behavior, the Islamic *qadi* partakes of symbols that are part of the tradition and thus the intelligible universe of those whom he judges, and his decisions, while authoritative, are more likely to be understood. This comprehensibility complements and reinforces the institutional legitimacy with which the *qadi*'s decisions are invested.

In contrast, the secular civil courts possess little moral legitimacy and the Israeli military courts none. In both, court functionaries perform with reference to symbols drawn from their own distinctive traditions and training. They enact a drama that may have internal meaning, but whose subtleties are largely lost on their audience. Hence their decisions are more likely to be experienced as the exercise of naked and unfathomable power.

Likewise, an imposed legal profession may face special problems of collective self-legitimation. Its existence and growth reflect conscious policies of the state, but not generalization of knowledge about state law and legal institutions, or of appreciation of the nature and value of lawyers' services. In these conditions, lawyers' activities may tend initially to remain narrowly circumscribed to contexts in which their services are most immediately and obviously necessary, namely, in litigation and other court-related activity.[31]

To enlarge the domain of their practice, the members of an imposed legal profession must proselytize, that is, educate other members of their society and induct them into the ways of the law and courts and validate their claim of monopoly over intermediation with formal legal institutions. The ideology instilled in them by their Western-modeled training and sustained by their sense of professional corporate identity predisposes them to go about the task of self-legitimation in their native society by appealing to the same ideals that classically rationalized professions in the West: technical expertise, the "service" ethic, collective self-regulation, and others. In the West, these ideals were supported by the distinctive dominant social ideology of secular and scientific rationality.[32] In many other societies in which a Western-style legal profession was imposed, the ideals have not been so supported, and other, sometimes contradictory, ideals and values have often prevailed.

The ways of the laws and courts, at least those that enfranchise lawyers, are also the ways of the state, and in their pedagogic function lawyers thus serve to extend state power. This may be done wittingly or unwittingly (if the former, perhaps under sincerely believed slogans of promoting "modern" and "rational" ways, or by helping disenfranchised groups to "know" and assert their "rights").[33] In either case, lawyers are inextricably linked in a dependent relationship to institutions that may be regarded by many with suspicion and hostility, and the power of which, as other anthropologists have demonstrated, may be resisted and evaded with great energy and ingenuity. Even solicitude for the interests of clients and ideological hostility to the reigning regime do not alter the lawyers' relations of structural dependence on formal legal institutions.

This does not imply that imposed court systems and the legal profession must always remain weak or removed from community life. A number of studies have demonstrated that imposed courts have been enthusiastically embraced in some societies, with the set of options they provide quickly entered into the calculus of disputants acting at the local level.[34] The legal profession has likewise flourished in some environments, especially where it has been able to forge strong ties with other powerful social groups.[35] On the other hand, the foregoing discussion suggests that an imposed legal profession, with relatively shallow roots in civil society and interests closely tied to the state, may be particularly dependent on the good will of state authorities. This dependency may not be so compromising if the state itself is weak, or if it elects to promote or appease the profession as a matter of policy. But lawyers of a transplanted profession may be highly vulnerable to a strong state, which neither needs nor chooses to respect their interests.

Notes

1. Introduction

1. Readers with greater interest in the relationship of this study to current issues and discussions in legal anthropology may wish to consult the Appendix, which explores some of the questions raised in this introduction more fully.

2. This incident is described in greater detail in chapter 3, where fragments of the conversation between Riad, the agency worker, and Abu Munif, the peasant, are reproduced. Unless otherwise noted, all names are pseudonyms.

3. Donald Reid, *Lawyers and Politics in the Arab World, 1880–1960.*

4. Farhat Ziadeh, *Lawyers, the Rule of Law, and Liberalism in Modern Egypt.*

5. On India, see Marc Galanter, "The Study of the Indian Legal Profession," *Law and Society Review* 3, no. 2 (1968): 201–217; T. G. Bastedo, "Law Colleges and Law Students in Bihar," *Law and Society Review* 3, no. 2 (1968): 269–294; and Samuel Schmitthener, "A Sketch of the Development of the Legal Profession in India," *Law and Society Review* 3, no. 2 (1968): 337–382. On Ghana, see Robin Luckham, "Imperialism, Law, and Structural Dependence: The Ghana Legal Profession," and, on Kenya, Amos Odenyo, "Professionalism and Change: The Emergent Kenyan Lawyer," both in *Lawyers in the Third World: Comparative and Developmental Perspectives*, ed. C. J. Dias, et al. The same volume has articles tracing similar themes in Tanzania, the Sudan, Malaysia, and a number of countries in Latin America.

6. Reid, *Lawyers and Politics*, pp. 395–396.

7. See Adnan Abu-Ghazaleh, *Arab Cultural Nationalism in Palestine during the British Mandate;* Ann Mosely Lesch, *Arab Politics in Palestine, 1917–1939;* Taysir Nashif, *The Palestine Arab and Jewish Political Leaderships: A Comparative Study.*

8. See, for example, Amnon Cohen, "The Changing Pattern of West Bank Politics," *Jerusalem Quarterly* no. 5 (Fall 1977): 105–113; Victor Cygielman "Voices from the West Bank," *New Outlook* 17 (August–September, 1974): 45–48; Rafik Halabi, *The West Bank Story;* Moshe Ma'oz, *Palesti-*

nian Leadership on the West Bank; and Joel Migdal, *Palestinian Society and Politics.*

9. Moshe Shemesh, "The West Bank: Rise and Decline of the Traditional Leadership, June, 1967 to October, 1973," *Middle East Studies* 20, no. 3 (July 1984): 292, refers to the intelligentsia as composed of "doctors, lawyers, writers, engineers, pharmacists," and others.

10. Peter Beaumont, Gerald Blake, and J. Malcolm Wagstaff, *The Middle East: A Geographical Study.*

11. No census has been conducted in the West Bank since 1967, and estimates by Israeli agencies differ. The various figures are reviewed in Meron Benvenisti, *The West Bank Data Project,* p. 1.

12. Sarah Graham-Brown, "The Economic Consequences of Occupation," in *Occupation: Israel over Palestine,* ed. Naseer Aruri. This figure is derived from UNRWA's own reports. The agency, with a middle- and lower-level staff almost exclusively Palestinian, continues to provide aid and primary education to camp residents to the present day.

13. *Laji'* also refers to townspeople of refugee background, although socially they have merged more with original residents of the towns than have camp dwellers.

14. There is a broad distinction between urban and village Palestinian dialects and identifiable local styles of speech and intonation.

15. Sarah Graham-Brown, "Impact on the Social Structure of Palestinian Society," in *Occupation: Israel over Palestine,* ed. Naseer Aruri. The extended family was and continues to be an important unit in the urban milieu as well, although the term *"hamula"* is seldom used there. A notable family, for example, is usually referred to as a "house" (*daar*). In the area of Hebron and the South in general, larger groups of related lineages, some numbering in the thousands, also form *'asha'ir,* or tribes (singular, *'ashira*).

16. This sense has sharpened over time, and in urban areas there is a general consciousness of three broad classes: *at-tabaqa al-adna,* the lower class; *at-tabaqa al-wusta,* the middle class, and *at-tabaqa al-'ulya,* the upper class.

17. The Israeli military government and its defenders have often pointed to economic growth and increasing consumption in the region as evidence of a newfound prosperity. See, for example, State of Israel, Ministry of Defense, Coordinator of Government Operations in Judea-Samaria and the Gaza District, *Judea-Samaria and the Gaza District: A Sixteen-Year Survey (1967–1983).* Others have emphasized the dangers of the West Bank's structural dependence on the Israeli economy. See Graham-Brown, "The Economic Consequences of Occupation"; and Brian Van Arkadie, *Benefits and Burdens.*

18. Both the Jordanian dinar (JD) and the Israeli shekel (IS) are legal tender in the West Bank. The dinar, a relatively stable currency, was equal roughly to $3.30 US during my research period. The shekel, highly unstable, was exchanged at a rate of 147 IS to the dollar at the time of my arrival in the field, and about 1,000 IS to the dollar on my departure fourteen months later.

19. Increasing reliance on local wage labor and growing international migration represent trends begun in the Mandate and Jordanian periods, re-

spectively, but that have intensified during the period of occupation. See Rachelle Taqqu, "Peasants into Workmen: Internal Labor Migration and the Arab Village Community under the Mandate," in *Palestinian Society and Politics*, ed. Joel Migdal. Migdal himself presents an analysis of the differential impact of labor migration on regions within the West Bank in the Jordanian period. Both trends are part of a general structural shift; since the 1930s, the percentage of the population that gains its livelihood from agriculture has dropped, from 70 to 50 in 1968, and to less than 30 at present. (Graham-Brown, "The Economic Consequences of Occupation").

20. This excepts some major Israeli enterprises in the West Bank, which interact very little with the local economy. Some industrial cooperation has emerged between Israeli and West Bank entrepreneurs, usually in the form of subcontracting arrangements whereby West Bank workshops perform one or several stages in the production process. The product is then finished in Israel. Israeli-produced textiles, for example, are cut and sewn in the West Bank and then shipped back to Israel for packaging and distribution.

21. For example, Benvenisti, *The West Bank Data Project*; and Janet Abu-Lughod "The Demographic Consequences of Occupation," in *Occupation: Israel over Palestine*, ed. Naseer Aruri.

22. Benvenisti provides the 40 percent expropriation figure in *The West Bank Data Project*. He provided the settler population estimate in a symposium at Tufts University held February 28–March 1, 1987. One of the best studies on Israeli settlement policies to date is William W. Harris, *Taking Root*. Essays by Ibrahim Dakkak, Ibrahim Matar, and Phillip Demant in *Occupation: Israel over Palestine*, ed. Naseer Aruri, also examine settlement in Jerusalem and the West Bank.

23. With the oil glut of the early to mid-eighties, defaults on commitments to the fund became more frequent, and the amounts reaching the West Bank slowed to a trickle.

24. In fact, Israel ruled predominantly Arab areas within its own borders through military government from 1948 to 1966, but this was more easily justified domestically and abroad as a necessity demanded by the early stage of state building in a hostile surrounding environment. See Ian Lustick, *Arabs in a Jewish State*.

25. A condition for the maintenance of some of these powers is the Israeli military government's "Open Bridges" policy, which was adopted shortly after the 1967 war and permitted the continued traffic of people and goods between the East and West banks.

26. This has been indicated by a number of studies and polls conducted in the West Bank. As one observer (an Israeli Arab) remarks, residents of the region by the mid-1970s fell into two camps, "PLO supporters and PLO members" (Halabi, *The West Bank Story*, p. 171). See also Ann Mosely Lesch, *Political Perceptions of the Palestinians on the West Bank and the Gaza Strip*; and Emile Nakhleh, *The West Bank and Gaza: Toward the Making of a Palestinian State*.

27. Although the PLO has organized support within the Occupied Territories, its principal base of power has always been among the Palestinians

in exile, from whom its leadership has mainly been drawn. The occupied and exiled communities have not always seen eye to eye, but still have managed to maintain a fairly unified political front. See Helena Cobban, *The Palestine Liberation Organization: People, Politics, and Power.*

2. Imposition of the Modern Legal Profession

1. See Reid, *Lawyers and Politics;* and Dias et al. (eds.), *Lawyers in the Third World.*

2. A concise review of the history of the *shariʿa* courts in Palestine is given by Beshara Doumani, "Palestinian Islamic Court Records: A Source for Socioeconomic History," *Middle East Studies Association Bulletin* 19, no. 2 (1985): 155–172. He provides a list of matters falling within their jurisdiction: cases of personal status; criminal and civil cases, with empowerment to impose the death penalty; approval of the construction or renovation of buildings, or the establishment of new businesses; endorsement of the heads of guilds and sheikhs of villages; supervision of the minting of coins and currency exchange; supervision of weights and measures and fixing of food and commodity prices and transport costs; supervision of religious trusts (*awqaaf*); the approval of transactions in real property; and others. Christians and Jews enjoy limited communal autonomy in the regulation of matters of personal status.

3. In virtually no place under Islamic rule and at no point in their history has the jurisdiction of the *shariʿa* courts been absolute. Islamic law posits the existence of a type of extraordinary justice termed *mazalim,* which stems from the absolute authority of the sovereign and his fundamental competence to deal with all litigations and to right all wrongs and his obligation to defend the public interest in accord with religious precepts. No text defines the categories of *mazalim* jurisdiction, but it was normally exercised directly by the sovereign himself, or by his deputies. The inexpedient procedural strictures of the *shariʿa* courts often served as justification for the vesting of criminal jurisdiction in the *shurta,* or police, who were responsible for investigations, arrests, trials, and punishment. Commercial matters were also often deemed too critical to the public welfare to be subject to the authority of the *shariʿa* courts. The apportionment of jurisdictions between *shariʿa* courts and other authorities varied in place and time, most importantly, perhaps, in accordance with the ebb and flow of power between central and local authority. The extensive jurisdiction of the *shariʿa* courts in Palestine from the sixteenth to the eighteenth centuries may be indicative of the slow weakening of Istanbul's grip over local affairs. See Emile Tyan, "Judicial Organization," in *Law in the Middle East,* ed. H. Liebesny and M. Khadduri, pp. 236–278; N. J. Coulson, *A History of Islamic Law;* Doumani, "Palestinian Islamic Court Records"; and Amnon Cohen, *Palestine in the 18th Century.*

4. Tribal adjudication is discussed in chapter 3.

5. Doumani, "Palestinian Islamic Court Records." For a survey of the Tanzimat, see Bernard Lewis, *The Emergence of Modern Turkey.*

6. The history of these laws is traced in Francis Goadby and Moses Doukhan, *The Land Law of Palestine.*

7. Reid, *Lawyers and Politics,* p. 2. In other parts of the world, as well, commercialization of agriculture frequently led to new kinds of economic relations and disputes and to new kinds of encounters with law and administrative bodies. Dias et al. (eds.), *Lawyers in the Third World,* p. 17.

8. Herbert Liebesny, "The Development of Western Judicial Privileges," in *Law in the Middle East,* by Liebesny and M. Khadduri, pp. 309–333; and Lewis, *The Emergence of Modern Turkey.* As Lewis notes, the Ottomans' efforts were in vain, and the abolition of the capitulations was only accomplished with the establishment of the Turkish Republic by Kemal Ataturk and the conclusion of the Treaty of Lausanne in 1923. Similar motives led to Western-style legal reforms in other parts of Asia (Barry Metzger, "Legal Services Programs in Asia," in *Legal Aid and World Poverty,* by Committee on Legal Services to the Poor in Developing Nations).

9. Herbert Liebesny, *The Law of the Near and Middle East.* A particular aim of the Land Law of 1858 was to dissolve various customary forms of communal tenure widely practiced in Palestine and in other parts of the empire.

10. Students of Islamic law seem to have taken little interest in this group. Tyan, "Judicial Organization," is one of the few exceptions, and even his discussion is limited to a few paragraphs.

11. At the same time in Egypt, for example, *wakils* and an often indistinguishable group of *'ardhaljis,* or petition writers, were frequently referred to as *muzawwirun,* forgers (Ziadeh, *Lawyers*). Lawyers in Russia at this time were tagged with similar unflattering names (Samuel Kucherov, *Courts, Lawyers, and Trials under the Last Three Tsars*).

12. Reid, *Lawyers and Politics,* pp. 84–85.

13. A *sanjaq* was an administrative unit between a *qaza* and a *vilayet,* or province. The *sanjaq* of Acre was part of the *vilayet* of Beirut, and the *sanjaq* of Nablus was part of the *vilayet* of Damascus. The *sanjaq* of Jerusalem, however, was "autonomous," i.e., not part of any *vilayet* but subject directly to Istanbul.

14. The final terms of the Mandate were not approved by the Council of the League until 1922, and the agreement came into legal force only in September 1923 (Walter Laqueur and Barry Rubin [eds.], *The Israel-Arab Reader,* p. 34).

15. Norman Bentwich, "The Legal System of Palestine under the Mandate," *Middle East Journal* 2 (1948): 33–46. The District Court of Jerusalem periodically visited the tribal courts to hear appeals and to try more serious criminal cases. The Palestine Order in Council of 1922, which lay the foundation of the Mandate legal system, also granted residents the right of appeal of decisions of the Supreme Court to the Judicial Committee of the Privy Council in London.

16. Bentwich, "The Legal System of Palestine."

17. See, for example, R. S. Khare, "Indigenous Culture and Lawyers' Law in India," *Comparative Studies in Society and History* 14 (1972): 71–96.

18. In the 1930s, district and magistrate court judges received annual salaries equivalent to six thousand and four thousand dollars, respectively, astronomical sums, given the cost of living at the time. Palestinian judges were regularly recruited from among the most eminent local practitioners (William Burdick, *The Bench and Bar of Other Lands*). Magistrate judges' salaries in the West Bank today are approximately forty-two hundred dollars per year, commanding a value perhaps no more than a tenth of the same amount during the Mandate years.

19. Similarly positive memories of British legal institutions are apparently also held by Indian lawyers. See Marc Galanter, "The Aborted Restoration of 'Indigenous' Law in India," *Comparative Studies in Society and History* 14 (1972): 53–70.

20. See Articles 2, 3, and 9 of the Mandate (Laqueur and Rubin, *The Israel-Arab Reader*). Article 9 specifically states, "The Mandatory shall be responsible for seeing that the judicial system established in Palestine shall assure to foreigners, as well as to natives, a complete guarantee of their rights." The Mandate obligation probably only reinforced a British colonial propensity, reflected in the establishment of schools of law and public administration elsewhere in the empire, such as in India and several places in East Africa. See Sidney Abrahams, "The Colonial Legal Service and the Administration of Justice in Colonial Dependencies," *Journal of Comparative Legislation* 30 (1948): 1–11.

21. The following information on the Jerusalem Law Classes and the legal profession during the Mandate is derived principally from Reid, *Lawyers and Politics*, and from my own survey of relevant files in the Israel State Archives (ISA), housed in the offices of the prime minister in Jerusalem. Materials in the archives are recorded by content, file number, record number, and box number, e.g., "Licensing of Advocates," File AG 14/4, 3-709 ("3" represents the record number, and "709" the box number).

22. Lectures on general legal topics were delivered in English and were attended jointly by Arab and Jewish students; religious law courses were taught separately to the two groups in Arabic or Hebrew.

23. Reid, *Lawyers and Politics*, p. 298. No other institutions of higher learning were established for Palestinian Arab students during the Mandate. For a review of the subject, see A. L. Tibawi, *Arab Education in Mandate Palestine*.

24. Reid, *Lawyers and Politics*, p. 298, gives the total number of graduates of the Law Classes for the entire period of the Mandate as one thousand, of whom roughly half were Arabs, and the other half Jews.

25. The same Advocates Ordinance authorized the Supreme Muslim Council to certify mastery of Islamic law, on the basis of which the chief justice of the civil Supreme Court would issue licenses to *shariʿa* court advocates (ISA, "Law Classes," File LS 194/23, 3-756).

26. Most admitted through the Foreign Advocates Examination were Jewish immigrants from Europe, although a few were Palestinian Arabs who had studied abroad, usually in England. Applicants were also required to be residents of Palestine and at least twenty-five years of age, and to present a

certificate of "good character" from the police (ISA, "Law Classes—Miscellaneous," File AG 83/34, 3-746).

27. Reid, *Lawyers and Politics*. The Arab Higher Committee was established by the nationalist leadership to coordinate political activities throughout the country. In 1936, it directed an uprising of the Palestinian Arab population to protest the British administration's support of Zionist objectives in Palestine. What is termed colloquially Thawrat sitti wa tlaateen, the Revolution of '36, began with a general strike and other forms of public protest and in some areas developed into sustained armed resistance. Unrest only diminished in 1939, with the British government's issuance of a White Paper, that retracted some of its promises to the Zionist movement. See Yehoshua Porath, *The Palestinian Arab National Movement: From Riots to Rebellion*.

28. Of thirty-two members of the committee from 1936 to 1948, sixteen were holders of higher degrees, nine of them lawyers and two others with a law degree and one other degree (Nashif, *The Palestine Arab*, p. 33). Accounts of the political involvements of lawyers are also given in Lesch, *Arab Politics in Palestine*.

29. Nashif, *The Palestine Arab*, p. 34.

30. The information on the PJBA is derived from ISA, "Societies: Jewish Bar Association," File AG 27/5, 3-736.

31. The twelfth General Congress of the Jewish Bar Association in Palestine, held in Tel Aviv in 1947, issued resolutions protesting the Emergency Regulations, "which run counter to the principles of law and justice . . . and which deny the fundamental rights of man, thus constituting a grave danger to the life, liberty, and property of the individual. These regulations deliver the citizen to the mercy of the Executive Authority, the Police and the Army, and set up an arbitrary rule of lawlessness, not amenable to effective judicial control" (in ibid.). Ironically, these are the same regulations that the military government currently enforces in the Occupied Territories.

32. Information on the ABA comes from ISA, "Societies: Arab Bar Association," File AG 27/9, 3-736. Reid, *Lawyers and Politics*, refers to the possibility that an Arab professional association existed as early as 1928, but I found no evidence to confirm this.

33. This impression was confirmed in my interview of the sole surviving member of its Executive Committee still residing in the Occupied Territories.

34. In the case of the Arab Bar Association draft ordinance, for example, British officers raised questions about its use of a linguistic definition of an "Arab," pointing out the presence in Palestine of Arabic-speaking Jews (ISA, "Ordinances: Arab Bar Ordinance, 1946," File AG 19/361, 3-729).

35. Reid, *Lawyers and Politics*, p. 313, offers the following distribution of Arab lawyers in Palestine in 1937: Jerusalem, 39; Jaffa, 21; Haifa, 20. Together these constituted approximately two-thirds of the total of 117. Gaza had 9 lawyers, Nablus 8, and Acre 7, while no other locale had more than 3. On the same page, Reid cites Bentwich as having reported 1,000 as the total

number of advocates practicing in Palestine in 1948, of whom half were Arab. In light of the more specific figures given by Reid from ten years earlier, Bentwich's estimate of some 500 Arab lawyers would seem to be high.

36. Although Jordan had been included in the original Palestine Mandate, the British almost immediately segregated it from Palestine west of the Jordan River and left its administration substantially in the hands of then Amir (Prince) Abdullah. The latter declared himself king when Jordan gained its independence in 1946.

37. Migdal provides the figure of 450,000 for the population of the West Bank and 450,000 for the number of refugees dispersed to camps on both sides of the Jordan River (*Palestinian Society and Politics*, p. 38). Menahem Milson cites "reliable estimates" that claim that in 1980, more than two-thirds of all Jordanian nationals, including 80 percent of the population of the capital city of Amman, were Palestinians. ("How to Make Peace with the Palestinians," *Commentary* 71, no. 5 [May 1981]: 25–35).

38. The national movement during the Mandate was divided between two rival factions formed around the Husseini and the Nashashibi families, both of Jerusalem. See Lesch, *Arab Politics in Palestine*. On the Jordanian period, see Mark A. Heller, "Foreign Occupation and Political Elites: A Study of the Palestinians," Ph.D. Dissertation, Harvard University, 1976.

39. Jordan ruled the West Bank through a military administration until 1949, at which point civilian governors were appointed in Jerusalem, Hebron, and Ramallah. In 1953, the Jordanian government passed an anti-Communist law, which permitted it to imprison members of the Communist party and disseminators of its propaganda. A political parties law dissolved all political parties and required all prospective political groupings to seek a license from the government. The Defense Emergency Regulations, though never formally repealed, fell into disuse after the first few years of Jordanian rule. See Shaul Mishal, *West Bank/East Bank: The Palestinians in Jordan, 1949–1967*.

40. Ibid.

41. A coup was narrowly averted when a personal appeal by the young King Hussein secured the wavering allegiance of the armed forces.

42. The term *"muhami"* (advocate) had already been borrowed from Egypt, and the lawyers looked again to Egypt in grouping themselves in a *niqaba*, which I have translated here and throughout as "union." It is probable that the term *"niqaba"* comes from *naqib*, the nineteenth-century word for the deputy to the sheikh, or the head of a guild. Reid translates *niqaba* as "syndicate," but I prefer "union," as the term is the same for workers' and other trade unions. See Donald Reid, "The Rise of Professions and Professional Organization in Modern Egypt," *Comparative Studies in Society and History* 16, no. 1 (1974): 24–57.

43. This was Shafiq al-Rashidat, in 1952–1953. Yahya Hammoudeh, later head of the PLO, held the office the next year, and Fuad 'Abd al-Hadi won consecutive terms until 1960. (Reid, *Lawyers and Politics*, p. 316).

44. E. T. Mogannam, "Developments in the Legal System of Jordan," *Middle East Journal* 2 (1952): 194–206.

45. Mogannam, a Palestinian lawyer from Jerusalem, clearly looked askance at a number of Jordan's "innovations" (ibid.).

3. The Social and Cultural Context

1. I do not mean to imply, however, that there is a uniform or "typical" developmental course for the legal profession in Western societies, let alone globally. See Dietrich Reuschemeyer, *Lawyers and Their Society;* and Terence Johnson, "Imperialism and the Professions," in *The Sociological Review Monograph*, no. 20, ed. Paul Halmos.

2. By "collective self-legitimation" I mean the affirmation of the social value and importance of the lawyers as a group within the society as a whole.

3. Joel Migdal, "State and Society in a Society without a State," in *The Palestinians and the Middle East Conflict*, ed. Gabriel Ben-Dor. As Mishal, *West Bank/East Bank*, has noted, Jordan gained "conditional legitimacy" with some sectors of the West Bank community during its rule. In recent years, of course, the closest substitute for a political entity incarnating the Palestinian nation and expressing its will has been the quasi-state PLO.

4. In the period of the Tanzimat, for example, when, to facilitate conscription and tax collection, the Ottoman government simultaneously undertook a population census and a cadastral survey, Palestinian *fellahin* (peasants) faded into the orchards and fields, leaving only the clan sheikh or village notable to register the collective landholdings in his name. Patrons are most typically seen in anthropological literature as making the interests of their clients known to state authorities. Here we see that they may also serve to preserve the anonymity of their clients vis-à-vis government, that is, to keep them unknown as individual persons.

5. There is, of course, a plethora of anthropological studies that document the venerated status of mediators (often religiously sanctioned) in Middle Eastern societies. See Ernest Gellner, *Saints of the Atlas* (Morocco); E. E. Evans-Pritchard, *The Sanussi of Cyrenaica* (Libya); and Abdullah Bujra, *The Politics of Stratification* (Hadhramaut, now part of South Yemen). The same pattern is observable in many societies outside the Middle East.

6. Most West Bank businesses, for example, are either owned by individuals or are small partnerships, often of kin; very few genuine corporations exist in the region. This reflects both the restricted development opportunities afforded by the economy and the strong individualist bent in West Bank society in respect of economic pursuits.

7. This is the exchange to which I alluded in the Introduction.

8. Part of Abu Munif's reticence clearly stemmed from the inconvenience of travel to the lawyer's office in Jerusalem, which would have amounted to a full-day expedition, given distances and intermittent public transportation. Despite the small scale of the West Bank, many of its villages are remote, few of its residents can afford cars, and most rely on poor public transportation to travel to and from the larger towns. This practical difficulty is doubtless a deterrent to villagers weighing the merits of filing a claim in the courts. Similar phenomena have been observed in other "un-

derdeveloped" societies (Laura Nader and Harry Todd, Jr. [eds.], *The Disputing Process—Law in Ten Societies*, p. 26).

9. M. G. Smith, "Historical and Cultural Conditions of Political Corruption among the Hausa," *Comparative Studies in Society and History 6*, no. 2 (1964): 164–194; Simon Ottenberg, "Local Government and the Law in Southern Nigeria," in *Traditional and Modern Legal Institutions in Asia and Africa*, ed. D. C. Buxbaum. The topic of corruption during the period of occupation will be taken up more specifically in chapter 8, especially as it pertains to the civil courts.

10. Since the days of Ottoman rule, if not before, the emolument offered to local functionaries of the central government was not a salary, but the right to retain a portion of taxes and other dues collected from citizens. This practice continued in some cases into the period of Jordanian administration, so citizens have long been accustomed to paying officials directly for the services they render. From the citizen's perspective, therefore, the distinction between "office" and the "personal interest" of its occupant, necessary to constitute the phenomenon of corruption, has never been clear.

11. Abdulla Lutfiyya, *Baytin: A Jordanian Village*, p. 90.

12. *"Wasta"* literally means "intermediary" and is used to refer alternately to the practice of mediation and to the one who engages in it. The French *"piston"* or the American "pull" capture the same general sense. *Wasta* is, of course, regularly discussed in the anthropological literature on the Arab world. A few examples from adjacent societies are Catherine Witty, *Mediation and Society: Conflict Management in Lebanon*; Amina Farrag, "The Wastah among Jordanian Villagers," in *Patrons and Clients*, ed. Ernest Gellner, and John Waterbury; and Victor Ayoub, "Conflict Resolution and Social Reorganization in a Lebanese Village," *Human Organization* 24, no. 1 (Spring 1965): 11–17.

13. The difficulty is compounded by the fact that, despite the spread of formal education within the population, a majority still has very little appreciation of just what constitutes the craft of the legal profession.

14. A frequent complaint about clients voiced by West Bank lawyers and an alleged index of clients' naïveté about the nature of law and the legal system was that "they always want me to guarantee that I'll win the case," or "they always say 'I'll hire you to take my case if you promise me a victory.'"

15. I do not imagine this trait to be unique to Palestinian society; it is characteristic of Arab society in general and perhaps of others as well. See, for example, Clifford Geertz, Hildred Geertz, and Lawrence Rosen, *Meaning and Order in Moroccan Society*; and Dale Eickelman, *Moroccan Islam: Tradition and Society in a Pilgrimage Center*. Ottenberg, "Local Government," also contrasts the "universalist" and rule-oriented ethos of British administrators to the "particularist" tendencies of Nigerians. Lloyd Rudolph and Susanne H. Rudolph, "Barristers and Brahmans in India: Legal Cultures and Social Change," *Comparative Studies in Society and History* 8, no. 1 (1965): 24–49, discuss the same contrast in slightly different terms in the context of India.

16. It should be clear from this example that transactions are not simply

chaotic, for underlying principles clearly contribute to their structuring. A butcher is far less likely to attempt to cheat a regular customer, for example. The principles that come into play in *particular* transactions, however, vary according to the relationship of the parties and are not fixed from the outset by a standard (a price-quality ratio, in this example) that runs with the transaction, irrespective of who engages in it.

17. One informant who had been caught red-handed for tax evasion described how his accountant approached the official, a Palestinian employee of the Tax Department: "Come on, Abu Mahmoud! Aren't we old friends from school? Don't our children go to school together today? Do this for me, Abu Mahmoud, come on now . . . for my beard, won't you?" and the like. What is critical here is not the mere fact of negotiability, but the quality of discourse, which is completely personalistic.

18. Stewart Macaulay, "Non-contractual Relations in Business: A Preliminary Study," *American Sociological Review* 28 (1963): 55–67, has demonstrated that relationships between businesses in the United States are far less rigidly structured by the terms of contracts than is commonly believed, so the West Bank case may be distinguished only by degree. I also saw some indications that this fluidity has recently increased. One businessman stated that the *force majeure* ("supervening cause") defense for breaches of contract had proliferated in the uncertain climate of the region. Laxity in business is apparently widespread; jobs and deliveries are always late and pretexts are always at hand. Damaged parties often accept their losses either out of resignation to the absence of effective legal remedy or out of expectation of greater leeway for themselves in the future course of the transaction.

19. I have personally witnessed merchants laughingly tear up tax assessments received in the mail. In a major case with which I became familiar, the Israeli military government had ordered the eviction of several hundred families of tenant-farmers in the area of Jiftlik in the Jordan Valley. A compromise agreement was reached through negotiations conducted between the military government and a lawyer hired by the affected landowners. The military government agreed to tolerate concentration of the farmers' seasonal shelters in a limited area on the condition that licenses were sought from the agency responsible for regional planning. When I learned about the case, one year had elapsed, and the owners—several of whom were highly educated members of a prominent Nablus family—had blithely neglected to apply for the required licenses, thus prejudicing their legal position. The military government threatened to proceed with complete eviction, and the landowners and their tenants appeared powerless to resist. No explanation was offered for the landowners' self-damaging lapse, and their lawyer was fuming.

20. See J. G. Peristiany (ed.), *Honour and Shame;* and Julian Pitt-Rivers, *Mediterranean Countrymen: Essays in the Social Anthropology of the Mediterranean.*

21. See M. J. L. Hardy, *Blood Feuds and Blood Money in the Middle East.*

22. The dispute I am about to describe is the one that Riad had originally taken me to discuss with Abu Munif. We learned of the military order re-

cently served on Abu Munif only after he had related to us the details of his prior problems.

23. This is very reminiscent of Kabyle society, about which Pierre Bourdieu, "The Sentiment of Honour in Kabyle Society," in *Honour and Shame,* ed. J. G. Peristiany, p. 200, writes: " . . . only a challenge issued (or an offense caused) by one's equal in honor deserves to be taken up; in other words, one only accepts a challenge if one considers the challenger worthy of making it."

24. A number of lawyers suggested to me that people hesitate to hire them for fear of projecting a sense that their claim or case is weak.

25. Similar observations have been made in India, where legal fighting is frowned on as a "display of economic pride" (Khare, "Indigenous Culture").

26. My treatment of this fascinating and colorful institution must be confined to a general outline and a discussion of its interaction with the formal court system. Two works in English on tribal adjudication in Palestinian society are ʿAref el-ʿAref, *Bedouin Love Law and Legend,* an amended translation of an earlier work in Arabic by the same author; and Omar Effendi el-Barguthy, "Judicial Courts among the Bedouin of Palestine," *Journal of the Palestine Oriental Society* 2 (1922): 35–65. Abner Cohen, *Arab Border Villages,* describes dispute processing, as does Lutfiyya, *Baytin.* A series of articles on the topic was published in Arabic by lawyer Jamil Salhout in the *al-Fajr al-Adabi* (a Jerusalem monthly) editions of November and December 1980, and January and February 1981. These dealt with the history of tribal adjudication as well as its current practice. Similar institutions have been studied elsewhere in the region; see, for example, Austin Kennett, *Bedouin Justice: Law and Custom among the Egyptian Bedouin.*

For some of the modes of dispute processing, "informal" is something of a misnomer, insofar as it implies the absence of regular and explicit rules and differentiated institutions. Some of them will be seen to be highly formal when judged by these criteria, while others are less so. A more accurate distinction would be between state-sponsored and non–state-sponsored institutions, and it is only with this gloss that I continue to use the less awkward and more conventional terms "formal" and "informal."

27. ʿAshaʾiri, "tribal," is derived from ʿashira, "tribe" in the singular. Qadaʾ, "adjudication," is distinguished from tahkim, arbitration.

28. El-ʿAref, *Bedouin Love Law and Legend,* describes a far more variegated system than I am about to describe, with "courts" both hierarchically ordered and of highly specialized jurisdiction. Lutfiyya, *Baytin,* refers to "al-hukm al-ʿahsaʾiri" instead of "al-qadaʾ al-ʿashaʾiri" and describes as well a process of arbitration (tahkim). The spottiness of data on the issue prevents one from judging whether these differences are regional or represent changes through time or a combination (as I would suspect).

29. Tribal adjudication is a male-dominated phenomenon. Women appear almost solely as victims (in which event, their case is prosecuted by male members of the family), and less frequently as witnesses. Research is warranted into the manner in which Palestinian women handle disputes among themselves.

30. Literally, *manqaᶜ* signifies a "swamp" or point to which water drains then turns stagnant; *damm* means "blood."

31. This is true even when the parties are Christian. Although most of the Christian communities in the West Bank are town-based and Western in orientation, Christian peasants in the Beit Jala-Beit Sahour areas apparently participate actively in *al-qada' al-ᶜashaʾiri*. I interviewed the only Christian *qadi* currently operating in the region, who also happens to be the vice-mayor of the town of Beit Jala.

32. The jurisprudence of the tribal judges is a study in itself. It distinguishes between a range of categories running from "intentional" offenses (*ᶜamdi*) to purely accidental wrongs (*khataʾa*). The greatest elaboration is reserved for the principles determining the amount of compensation for various injuries and offenses. A minor wound to the face is more serious than a major injury that less noticeably mars appearance. In *ᶜarad* cases, the amount varies according to the distance between the site of the offense against the woman and her home, whether the violation was merely verbal or involved physical contact, whether she was fondled through her clothing or her dress actually lifted, and a multitude of other factors. Little of this, it should be mentioned, has anything to do with the *shariᶜa*.

33. The "position" of *manqaᶜal-damm* or *manshad* tends to be handed down within a single family, from father to an interested and promising son, or from uncle to nephew. In some cases, these "judgeships" are reputed to have been retained by certain families, such as the Maraqas of Hebron, for centuries.

34. The payment is for 333.33 J.D. (about $1,000). I never received a satisfactory explanation for this sum. One informant referred to this as the "*diya Muhammadiya*," the blood money fixed by Muhammad "500 years ago" [*sic*].

35. Many "customary" legal systems appear to have attempted to repel the power of juxtaposed state-sponsored Western courts and to preserve autonomy by adopting some of the features of the alien system. This was the case, for example, of Native American legal systems in the twentieth century (Linda Medcalf, *Law and Identity: Lawyers, Native Americans, and Legal Practice*). See also Jane Collier, "Political Leadership and Legal Change in Zinacantan," *Law and Society Review* 11, no. 1 (Fall 1976): 131–163; and Francis G. Snyder, "Land Law and Economic Change in Rural Senegal: Diola Predge Transactions and Disputes," in *Social Anthropology and Law*, ed. Ian Hamnett. Among other things, the permeability of the informal systems to influences from state-sponsored legal institutions illustrates the fallibility of labeling the former "traditional" or "customary."

36. In fact, it is rare for middle- or upper-class disputants to appear before the Islamic courts, according to informants. The reason offered was that "all of these personal status cases involve differences over material things, mostly of petty value—for example, a poor woman who isn't getting maintenance [*nafaqa*] from her husband. Rich people can afford to settle their private disputes like this out of court." A like pattern of very active use of formal courts by members of the popular class and little use by members of

the middle and upper classes was noted in Egypt by Enid Hill, *Mahkama!* One result of the low level of economic stakes in Islamic court cases is that they provide little sustenance to the legal profession, and few lawyers are very enthusiastic about assuming them. I was not able to ascertain whether the situation is the same in the ecclesiastical courts that serve the Christian Palestinians, but my impression is that it is generally similar.

37. Aharon Layish, *Women and Islamic Law in a Non-Muslim State,* p. 331, finds that Palestinian Muslims in Israel, where civil and Islamic courts have concurrent jurisdiction over family law, prefer the latter over the former, despite less favorable procedural conditions. They apparently "prefer the more intimate atmosphere of the shari'a court (the proceedings of which are conducted in Arabic) and the qadi, who is close to them in his religious and social outlook and firmly rooted in the day-to-day life of his community to an alien, impersonal civil court, which is identified with government authority, and a judge removed from the Muslim environment."

38. The role of the mayors and of the Village Leagues will be treated in much greater depth in the next chapter.

39. In one respect, this simply expresses trends prevalent in the postcolonial Arab world as a whole, as burgeoning bureaucracies fuel demand for university graduates. Fahim Qubain, *Education and Science in the Arab World;* and Byron Massialas and Samir Jarrar, *Education in the Arab World.* But others see the Palestinians' heavy investment in the mobile asset of higher education as an adaptation to their experience of statelessness and loss of material sources of economic livelihood such as land. Palestinians of the West Bank and elsewhere have achieved a ratio of graduates per thousand higher than that of any other Arab group and on a par with a number of developed Western countries (Nabil Badran, "The Means of Survival: Education and the Palestinian Community, 1948–1967," *Journal of Palestine Studies* 9, no. 4 [1980]: 44–74).

40. University teaching is also a highly esteemed vocation. In the words of one specialist involved in educational development in the West Bank, "Everyone wants their sons (they don't care about their daughters) to be a doctor or an engineer. If they can't do that, they want them to get a doctorate in any subject and teach at the university."

41. Why this particular hierarchy has emerged in the Arab world is an intriguing question about which I can only speculate. It may reflect the mystique of modern science and technology in a society that views itself as having been outstripped and overpowered by other societies possessing those "goods." It may also emanate from the values of the military-technocratic elites that swept to power in the postwar period and that set educational policies and priorities for their countries. See Qubain, *Education and Science in the Arab World;* and Massialas and Jarrar, *Education in the Arab World.* The attitudes of Palestinians, who since 1948 have been mostly forced to seek higher education in the surrounding Arab countries, simply reflect the values predominant in the societies that host them. But it is significant that none of the institutions of higher learning in the West Bank

(which are of recent vintage) have made any concerted effort to found a faculty of secular law.

42. This process is almost certainly common to other professions in other places. Gary Nash, "The Philadelphia Bench and Bar, 1800–1861," *Comparative Studies in Society and History* 7, no. 2 (1965): 203–220, describes similar developments following the breaking of the upper-class monopoly over the early nineteenth century legal profession in Philadelphia. See also Reuschemeyer, *Lawyers and Their Society.* One might anticipate this effect particularly in societies in which vocation as an element of social identity is subordinate to such factors as family status and wealth, as it is in Palestinian society. Individuals are Jaradats, al-Tamimis, and ʿAbd al-Hadis before they are farmers, mechanics, or lawyers.

43. In postrevolutionary Iran, for example, the secular legal system has been abolished and the legal profession, which had flourished around it, sent packing. There are Islamic tendencies in the West Bank, which, as in a number of Middle Eastern societies, took great inspiration from the Iranian revolution. Strengthening of these tendencies within Palestinian society is a possibility, and one that would bode ill for secular lawyers.

4. Orientalist Despotism

1. The concept of "Oriental despotism" itself is not thoroughly scientific; in some ways, it represents only an academic formulation of European prejudices against Eastern societies, and my play on it is not advanced as a rigorous scientific construct. But neither is it simply a joke; I mean it as a didactic device to focus attention on the gap between the *image* of the Israeli military administration as rational-bureaucratic and legalistic, and Palestinians' experience of it as something entirely different. There is, it should be added, an effort by modern scholars to come to theoretical grips with the specific nature and role of the state in Middle Eastern societies. They have attempted to winnow the weightier theoretical kernels of the concept of Oriental despotism from the lighter chaff of traditional European fantasies on the matter. Anouar Abdel-Malik, *Egypt: Military Society,* for example, analyzes Nasser's Egypt with reference to Wittfogel's notion of a "hydraulic society." Some of the more recent works borrow on such theorists as Milliband, Laclau, and Poulantzas, in their discussions of the "autonomy of the state." For reviews of the current state of theory, see Elia Zureik, "Theoretical Considerations for a Sociological Study of the Arab State," *Arab Studies Quarterly* 3, no. 3 (1981): 229–257; and, more recently, Kirk James Beattie, "Egypt: The Struggle for Hegemony, 1952–1981." Ph.D. dissertation, University of Michigan, 1985.

2. These were held by Weber to be some of the classical attributes of a "patrimonial system," his particular version of the concept of Oriental despotism (see Bryan Turner, *Weber and Islam*).

3. According to theorists, the autonomy of traditional states in the region provided political rulers with the freedom to act without restraint from

forces in civil society, that is, to act despotically. See Beattie, "Egypt"; and Zureik, "Theoretical Considerations."

4. On neopatrimonialism, see James Bill, *The Politics of Iran: Groups, Classes, and Modernization.*

5. A number of Israeli Orientalists (students of Middle East and Asian culture and history), such as Menahem Milson, Amnon Cohen, and Moshe Ma'oz, have served as advisers to the military government or as administrators in it. Milson's tenure as head of the civil administration is described briefly in note 48 and in Chapter 4, "Village Leagues." Of course, this would not be the first time that an alien regime has attempted to manage a society under its control by manipulating putatively "traditional" structures and beliefs; this was the essence of colonial indirect rule. Nor for that matter would it even be the first time that Israel has employed such an approach, for its policies toward the Palestinian minority within Israel have also been guided by it. See Shukri Abed, *Israeli Arabism: The Latest Incarnation of Orientalism;* Talal Asad, "Anthropological Texts and Ideological Problems: An Analysis of Cohen on Arab Villages in Israel," *Review of Middle East Studies,* no. 1 (1975): 1–40; and Lustick, *Arabs in a Jewish State.*

6. The population of the West Bank immediately prior to the war was approximately 900,000, of whom some 200,000 fled to the East Bank to escape the fighting. Roughly 18,000 were repatriated under a program sponsored by the International Red Cross, but for months following the cessation of hostilities, residents of the Occupied Territories continued to emigrate to the East Bank in far greater numbers than were allowed to return. The net outflux between June 1967 and December 1968 has been estimated at 250,000 (Abu-Lughod, "The Demographic Consequences of Occupation"). A small number of Palestinians residing outside the Occupied Territories but having close kin within them continue annually to be granted residency permits under a "family reunification" program.

7. Shabtai Teveth, *The Cursed Blessing,* pp. 10–11. By 1963, according to Teveth, a regional administrative command intended for the West Bank was set up with Haim Herzog as its head.

8. Meir Shamgar (ed.), *Military Government in the Territories Administered by Israel, 1967–1980: The Legal Aspects,* p. 25. Shamgar continues to play a major role in crafting the legal and organizational form of the military government since his elevation to the bench of the Israeli Supreme Court of which he is currently chief justice.

9. Proclamation No. 1, June 7, 1967; quoted in Ma'oz, *Palestinian Leadership.*

10. A simultaneous government order expanded city boundaries to include a large peripheral area never before within the municipality and that contained a number of satellite villages as well as open areas. See Ibrahim Dakkak, "The Transformation of Jerusalem: Juridical Status and Physical Change," in *Occupation: Israel over Palestine,* ed. Naseer Aruri, p. 67.

11. Nimrod Raphaeli, "Military Government in the Occupied Territories: An Israeli View," *Middle East Journal* 23, no. 2 (1969): 177–190.

12. Quoted in ibid., pp. 28–29.

13. Armed resistance in the West Bank is almost always organized from without and executed by infiltrators, although sometimes with assistance from local Palestinians.

14. The establishment of military rule was greatly eased by the Jordanian practice of maintaining vertical administrative links between Amman and the districts of the West Bank, such that "it was merely necessary to rub out 'Amman' from the administrative chart and substitute Zahal [IDF] Command" (Teveth, *The Cursed Blessing*, p. 287).

15. Proclamation No. 2, quoted in Benvenisti, *The West Bank Data Project*, p. 37.

16. Ma'oz, *Palestinian Leadership*, pp. 64–65.

17. Halabi, *The West Bank Story*, p. 61.

18. One of the important structural changes was the creation of the Higher Planning Council, staffed by Israeli military and civilian administrators. It assumed responsibility for the supervision of land use in the region. Many Palestinians have encountered problems with the council's requirements for licensing of all construction activities.

19. Halabi, *The West Bank Story*, p. 54. The ratio of Israeli to Palestinian personnel in West Bank administration has always been relatively low. In 1980, the civil service in the West Bank was staffed by 600 Israelis and 11,500 Arabs, the school system by 19 Israelis and 10,803 Arabs (Shamgar, *Military Government*, p. 46). Sheer numbers, of course, say nothing of the distribution of power between low-level Palestinian civil servants and Israeli overseers.

20. The personalities and considerations involved in this decision are treated in detail in Teveth, *The Cursed Blessing*. It is highly significant that the bridges have been open not only to goods, but, to some extent, to people as well, permitting the outflow of Palestinians, especially young professionals, seeking jobs in the East Bank and farther abroad. The importance of their remittances to the home economy has already been mentioned.

21. Residents of the Occupied Territories are technically permitted only day travel into Israel and are required to return to their homes at night. Reciprocal provisions do not exist for Israelis venturing to the West Bank or the Gaza Strip.

22. In 1980, 88 percent of the West Bank's imports and 59 percent of its exports were with Israel (Graham-Brown, "The Economic Consequences of Occupation," p. 204). Israel has consistently regulated the influx of West Bank agricultural goods to protect its own agricultural sector. See Van Arkadie, *Benefits and Burdens*. Indeed, the motivation to protect the Israeli economy had led the military government to promulgate many economic regulations in the Occupied Territories. This is true, for example, of a series of military orders passed in the early 1980s that require West Bank farmers to register orchards and vegetable crops and to seek licenses for new plantings.

23. During the period of my research, for example, Jordan announced a ban on travel to the East Bank by West Bank university graduates. Although couched as a means of encouraging the "steadfastness" of the people of the

Occupied Territories, many saw it as a protectionist measure to reduce competition in the East Bank labor market, then being flooded with Jordanian emigrés returning from work in the flagging Gulf economies. On the other side, when an Israeli settler was murdered in Ramallah in the spring of 1985, all of that town's residents were barred by the military government from travel to the East Bank for about a month.

24. The restoration of services was hampered by the depletion of Jordanian employees, many of whom had fled during the war or had emigrated in the following few months. See Avraham Lavine, "Social Services in the Administered Areas," in *Judea, Samaria, and Gaza: Views on the Present and Future*, ed. Daniel Elazar.

25. The Jordanian office of *mutasarrif*, or district commissioner, was abolished by the military government (ibid.).

26. The most in-depth exploration of this topic is by Ma'oz, *Palestinian Leadership*, whose monograph is subtitled "The Changing Role of the Mayors under Jordan and Israel." See also Mordechai Nisan, *Israel and the Territories: A Study in Control*; and Sasson Levi, "Local Government in the Administered Territories," in *Judea, Samaria, and Gaza: Views of the Present and Future*, ed. Daniel Elazar.

27. For a history of the office of *mukhtar* in Palestine, see Gabriel Baer, "The Office and Functions of the Village Mukhtar," in *Palestinian Society and Politics*, ed. Joel Migdal. A *mukhtar* was nominated by his *hamula* and confirmed by the Jordanian district commissioner. By Military Order No. 366, *makhateer* are now appointed by the military government. As of the early 1980s, some 826 *makhateer* were maintained with small stipends from the military government and with the fees they charged for affixing their seals to documents (Moshe Drori, "Local Government in Judea and Samaria," in *Military Government in the Territories Administered by Israel, 1967–1980: The Legal Aspects*, ed. Meir Shamgar).

28. The text of the Camp David Accords may be found in Laqueur and Rubin, *The Israel-Arab Reader*, pp. 609–616.

29. See Benvenisti, *The West Bank Data Project*, pp. 43–47; and Raja Shehadeh and Jonathan Kuttab, *Civilian Administration in the Occupied West Bank*.

30. Al-Masri's assassination was widely condemned in the West Bank, his funeral procession joined by thousands, even though his acceptance of the appointment was generally disapproved of by politically articulate segments of the population.

31. See Zvi Hadar, "The Military Courts," in *Military Government in the Territories Administered by Israel: The Legal Aspects*, ed. Meir Shamgar. In 1980, numerous amendments to the original proclamation were consolidated in Military Order No. 378, excerpts of which are printed as an appendix in Shamgar, *Military Government*, pp. 476–488.

32. Raja Shehadeh and Jonathan Kuttab, *The West Bank and the Rule of Law*, argue that these legal relics of British administration had been repealed by implication in a number of laws passed by the Jordanian govern-

ment after the unification of the two banks in 1950. Similar contentions have been rejected by Israeli courts. See Hadar, "The Military Courts," p. 176.

33. These powers are extrajudicial in the sense that they can be executed summarily by the military governor, with no right of review in any military court. Palestinians have been able to contest these measures before the Israeli High Court, though with limited success.

34. Technically speaking, military court decisions may be appealed to the Israeli High Court, but would be overturned only in the case of an extreme and obvious error and miscarriage of justice. See Israeli National Branch, International Commission of Jurists, *The Rule of Law in the Areas Administered by Israel*, p. 39.

35. An earlier decree had exempted both the military government and its employees or agents from the jurisdiction of the Jordanian civil courts functioning in the West Bank.

36. See Israeli National Branch, International Commission of Jurists, *The Rule of Law;* and Raja Shehadeh, *Occupier's Law*, pp. 88–89. An administrative claims procedure for individuals suffering damage to person or property was established through Military Order No. 271. A variety of other specialized objections committees have been constituted by separate decrees.

37. Shehadeh and Kuttab, *The West Bank*, p. 29.

38. In the legal system of the area, the function of a High Court is to review citizens' complaints of unjust treatment by governing authority. As little functioning governmental authority that had not been immunized from local court jurisdiction survived in the Occupied Territories, this measure had little practical effect. It was a full year into my research that I even learned from an informant that the court of appeals was empowered to sit as a "high court."

39. This number was consistently provided to me by informants, and although I never came across corroborating documentary evidence, I have no reason to doubt its approximate accuracy. Perhaps another ten to fifteen had either been caught in Amman at the outbreak of war and remained there or had left the region during or shortly after the war.

40. The strike and its consequences are examined in detail in chapter 9.

41. The single significant change in the *shariʿa* court system following the annexation of Jerusalem was the closure of the court of first instance in Jerusalem and the vesting of its former jurisdiction in the court of Jaffa (which is part of the Islamic court system in Israel). The *shariʿa* court of appeals in Jerusalem continues to review cases appealed from the courts of first instance in the West Bank. The various ecclesiastical courts, all of which are still based in Jerusalem, continue to exercise both original and appellate jurisdiction over cases of personal status arising among Christian Arab residents of Jerusalem and the West Bank. Israeli authorities have intervened minimally to change the substantive law enforced in the religious courts.

42. Teveth, *The Cursed Blessing*, discusses this policy as it relates to

Israel's interactions with Muslim authorities in Jerusalem over control of the holy shrines in the Old City in the direct aftermath of the 1967 war.

43. Moshe Negbi, "The Israeli Supreme Court and the Occupied Territories," *Jerusalem Quarterly*, no. 27 (Spring 1983): 33–47 suggests a mixture of moral and pragmatic considerations underlying this policy.

44. The local court case, as it happened, involved a challenge to the legality of the military order granting Israeli lawyers the right to appear in West Bank courts. On this and the general matter of the Israeli High Court and the Occupied Territories, see Eli Nathan, "The Power of Supervision of the High Court of Justice over the Military Government," in *Military Government in the Territories Administered by Israel: The Legal Aspects*, ed. Meir Shamgar.

45. This convoluted provision has played a role in permitting Israeli settlers in the Occupied Territories to evade the criminal jurisdiction of West Bank civil courts. It and other laws pertaining to the personal status of Israelis in the Occupied Territories are discussed by Moshe Drori, "The Israeli Settlements in Judea and Samaria: Legal Aspects," in *Judea, Samaria, and Gaza: Views of the Present and Future*, ed. Daniel Elazar.

46. Nisan, *Israel and the Territories*, p. 70.

47. Mark Heller, "Politics and Social Change in the West Bank since 1967," in *Palestinian Society and Politics*, ed. Joel Migdal.

48. In a May 1981 *Commentary* article, Israeli Orientalist Menachem Milson argued that Dayan's "non-interventionist" approach in the administration of the West Bank ignored the local political culture of patronage, in which bureaucratic services were exchanged for loyalty through notable-intermediaries, and, by leaving daily administration to locals, had permitted the PLO to gain influence in the region through a combination of "terror" and traditional patronage. He advocated that the military government directly condition the extension of services, employment opportunities, licenses, and other goods within its control on compliance with its aims and policies. Shortly after the article's publication, Milson was appointed as the first civil administrator in the West Bank, and served in that capacity until 1982.

49. I refer principally to the Village Leagues, which are discussed later in this chapter.

50. The military government, on occasion, has addressed this problem by fielding immigrants from Arab countries in contact positions in the civil administration, but with mixed results. The head of the Tax Department, an immigrant from Morocco, was, by my informants' accounts, an "uneducated, ignorant fool" whose single qualification for the position appeared to be mastery of Arabic.

51. As Benvenisti, *The West Bank Data Project*, points out, the division owes more to political than to administrative considerations. In the Jiftlik lands case described in chapter 3 (note 19), the several large landowners and many sharecroppers had been given contradictory instructions by the custodian of absentee property and the Higher Planning Council.

52. It is possible that the aim of Military Order No. 854 from the outset was merely to provide the military government with the legal discretion to intervene when and where it saw the need, and was never intended to be strictly and universally enforced.

53. This pattern was guided by the "Allon Plan," the unofficial policy of the Labor governments, which projected a settlement with the Arab states based on a territorial compromise. Israel would return to Jordan the most heavily populated areas of the West Bank while retaining portions close to the coast and in the Jordan Valley sufficient to secure its strategic position. The Palestinian enclave would be linked to the East Bank by a corridor at Jericho. World Zionist Organization figures show that by 1976, fourteen *nahals* had been established in the Jordan Valley, along with ten civilian settlements elsewhere in the West Bank (Ibrahim Matar, "Israeli Settlements and Palestinian Rights").

54. Gush Emunim, or Block of the Faithful, was a group of Israeli civilians who saw the Zionist return to Eretz Israel (the whole of historical Palestine) as the beginning of a messianic redemption of the Jewish people. Colonization to them was no mere historical right but a religious duty. In the mid-seventies, the Gush embarked on a confrontational campaign of "direct action," unilaterally establishing settlements in the Occupied Territories in defiance of government policy. The Labor party's vacillation in the face of this challenge to its authority was a contributing factor in its electoral defeat in 1977. See Harris, *Taking Root*, pp. 131–138.

55. The Drobles Plan took its name from its mastermind, Mattityahu Drobles, an official of the World Zionist Organization. At the time of its adoption, settlers in the West Bank (excluding Jerusalem) numbered roughly twenty thousand. Peter Demant, "Israeli Settlement Policy Today," also discusses some of the electioneering aspects of the Begin government's position on settlements.

56. Under Ottoman land law, *miri* was one of several categories of state land. Its holder enjoyed an inheritable right of usufruct. Legal reforms of the late Ottoman period were gradually eliminating distinctions between freehold and *miri* lands. See Goadby and Doukhan, *The Land Law of Palestine*. The best discussion of the Elon Moreh case and its aftermath is by Ian Lustick, "Israel and the West Bank after Elon Moreh: The Mechanics of De Facto Annexation," *Middle East Journal* 35, no. 4 (1981): 557–577.

57. The Begin government was also concerned with consolidating the somewhat anomalous legal status of the already-existing settlements. A series of military orders in 1980–1981 assigned the settlements to "regional councils" and established "local councils" in those with larger populations. Modeled after the administrations of Israeli kibbutzes, the local councils had authority to issue ordinances and were equipped with courts to enforce them. This was a further step in exempting Israeli citizens in the West Bank from the jurisdiction of the civil courts (Raja Shehadeh, "The Legal System of the Israeli Settlements," *International Commission of Jurists Review*, no. 27 (1981): 59–74.

58. In fact, the Israeli occupation of southern Lebanon has never fully ended, although a pullout of the majority of IDF personnel was effected by late 1985.

59. See Matar, "Israeli Settlements"; and Benvenisti, *The West Bank Data Project*. Benvenisti provided the population figure in a symposium at Tufts University held February 28–March 1, 1987. None of these figures include settlement within the portions of Jerusalem annexed in 1967.

60. In the Dheisheh refugee camp south of Bethlehem, armed settlers from nearby settlements conducted searches of refugee shanties, often destroying personal property in the process.

61. On rarer occasions, settlers were the victims of more lethal violence. In May 1980, a group of settlers walking at night in the streets of Hebron were ambushed by hidden gunmen, and six were killed and many others wounded. The military government immediately dynamited the buildings from which the attackers were determined to have fired and exiled the mayor and Muslim *qadi* of Hebron and the mayor of neighboring Halhoul to Jordan, on charges of having "incited an atmosphere of violence." The killers were eventually apprehended and were discovered to have infiltrated from Jordan.

62. This was reported in the April 25, 1980, editions of the Hebrew dailies *al-Hamishmar* (Tel Aviv) and *Ha'aretz* (Tel Aviv) and the Arabic daily *al-Quds* (Jerusalem).

63. Shehadeh, "The Legal System."

64. The theoretical possibilities were three: the Israeli courts martial, which try soldiers for offenses committed in the line of duty; Israeli civil courts, which can try Israelis in the Occupied Territories as if they were in Israel; and the military and civil courts of the West Bank, which share concurrent jurisdiction over criminal offenses in the region.

65. A letter decrying settler vigilantism signed by fourteen academics at Israeli universities, including the heads of their law faculties, appears to have made a particularly strong impression on the government (*Jerusalem Post*, April 22, 1981).

66. The Karp Report took its name from Judith Karp, deputy attorney general who headed the commission. The report was not released to the public until February 7, 1984.

67. Salim Tamari, "In League with Zion: Israel's Search for a Native Pillar," *Journal of Palestine Studies* 12, no. 4 (Summer 1983): 41–56, provides much detail that I cannot include here.

68. These accusations were in some cases grounded in fact.

69. Tamari, in ibid., lists the vocations of a Hebron-area league: a bus driver, a former Jordanian soldier, a construction worker and guard, a part-time hotel worker, a shepherd, and others. The leaders of several leagues were acknowledged illiterates. In Ramallah, the local league hangout was a pool hall, where the members consumed liquor and indulged in other socially disapproved behavior. Other townspeople referred to the patrons of this establishment as *"zabaleh,"* "trash."

70. This plan was mentioned to me by several local lawyers, one of whom

had authored a newspaper editorial condemning it. Shehadeh, *Occupier's Law*, mentions a murder case in Tulkaram in 1984 in which the league there formed a "tribal court" and attempted to impose its judgment on the civil court trying the case, allegedly with the acquiescence of the military government.

71. In the summer of 1982 in the southern village of Saʿir, several hundred angry residents put two armed Village Leaguers to flight from a checkpoint they had set up on the village's main road. Under a hail of stones, the leaguers beat a hasty retreat to their homes, with the townspeople in hot pursuit, only to have their houses burned by the mob.

5. The Social Composition of and Entry into the Profession

1. Perhaps ten to fifteen lawyers had been stranded in the East Bank during the 1967 war, or took refuge there during the fighting or in the few months following the war. As I have noted, several others—all members of the profession's elite—were deported in the early months of the occupation for participation in political organizing.

2. The number of working master and apprentice lawyers was determined from the roster published by the Committee of Arab Lawyers in the appointment book/calendar it issues to its membership. The number of striking master and apprentice lawyers was given to me by Mursi Hajir, acting head of the West Bank office of the Jordanian Lawyers' Union in an interview at the union office. Other numerical data for this section are derived from my own observations and further discussions with leaders of the striking and working factions who were well acquainted with their constituencies.

3. The terms for classes are actually more diverse and flexible and are not limited to the urban milieu. People also refer to "*fellahin*" (peasants). The lower class is composed of agricultural and industrial laborers, crafts- and tradespeople, petty clerks, drivers, small landholders, and others of similar means; the middle class includes white-collar workers, teachers, shop proprietors, small businesspeople, money changers, and modestly successful professions; the upper class is formed of large landowners, bigger businesspeople and merchants, and members of the various professional elites.

4. In Qalqilya, for example, the only two lawyers in practice were members of that town's two major lineages, or *hamayil*.

5. Whereas most West Bank children study in Jordanian public schools in the region, refugee children study in schools administered by the UNRWA. Many administrators and teachers of the UNRWA schools are themselves Palestinian refugees and bring to their jobs an uncommon missionary zeal, which surely rubs off on their students. On education in the West Bank, see Leslie Schmida (ed.), *Education in the Middle East*.

6. I do not know if the paucity of women in legal practice is matched by similar levels in other professions, although I suspect that it is. Obviously, this reflects dominant attitudes in Palestinian society toward sex roles and the perceivedly different aptitudes of men and women.

7. These figures are approximate and are based on my observations and information conveyed orally to me by informants.

8. A separate law governs practice before the religious courts, and licensure of advocates appearing in them is administered by the hierarchies of the various religious communities.

9. Lawyers are also barred from a number of pursuits deemed to be inconsistent with the independence and honor of the profession, including salaried employment in any public or private corporation or body, working in "commerce," and heading any legislative authority or ministry. Lawyers are permitted to retain their status as practitioners while working in the legal or "cultural" press, to hold lower-level elected office, and to teach law in recognized institutions.

10. This excludes the Islamic and ecclesiastical courts, which continue to operate relatively freely of Israeli interference in all aspects, among them licensure of advocates.

11. For example, Arab residents of the parts of Jerusalem occupied in 1967 carry special identity cards, distinct from those issued to residents of the West Bank.

12. By "recruitment" I mean the process an individual undergoes that results in a decision to enter a profession. This may or may not involve active solicitation by those who are already members. It may also include responses to familial and peer pressures, financial considerations, and a multitude of other factors.

13. I saw no direct evidence that extended families actually plan occupational diversification, as may occur in other societies, although appearances suggest that possibility. Almost all of the major West Bank families were represented in the legal profession by at least one member, who thus provided his or her kin with a relatively trustworthy person to seek out for legal counsel.

14. A "diploma" may be granted after an additional year of specialized coursework, the M.A. following a second additional year of original research and submission of the M.A. thesis, and the Ph.D. after a minimum of two years of research beyond the Master's level and submission of a doctoral dissertation.

15. While, in theory, prospective students might apply for study at one of several Israeli law faculties, none do, for linguistic and political reasons. There is also a strong belief that discrimination against Palestinians would result in the summary rejection of their applications to Israeli universities.

16. The *intisab*, or external student system, was initiated in Egypt in the fifties to alleviate the pressure of massive enrollments in universities. It permitted nonresident students to study course materials at home and to come only once yearly to the campus to sit for final examinations. At the end of four years, external students were granted the same degrees as resident students. The system was restricted to fields that did not require laboratory or other on-site training. So while law, commerce, and social sciences could be studied by external students, medicine, sciences, and engineering could not.

See Qubain, *Education and Science in the Arab World;* and Massialas and Jarrar, *Education in the Arab World.*

17. This is a particularly important asset for women students, given West Bank sensibilities about family honor and the difficulty that single women have in obtaining rental accommodations in the neighboring Arab countries. The recent opening of a law faculty in the University of Jordan in Amman (which graduated its first class in 1983), where most West Bankers have relatives, will probably widen access to legal education for women and less-well-to-do residents of the West Bank.

18. The twenty or so lawyers from the area who had studied in the Soviet Union or other Eastern Bloc countries had all received scholarships from the host state. This information was given to me by two informants who had studied in Eastern Bloc countries, one in the Soviet Union and the other in Czechoslovakia (the latter having received his doctorate there). Although it was not made explicit, it seemed apparent that these grants were channeled through local political parties sympathetic to the granting countries.

19. In the case of England and the United States, both common law jurisdictions, incompatibility with civil law traditions and systems of legal education followed in the Arab world are also discouraging factors. Of the roughly five hundred lawyers in the West Bank, a scant two had studied in England, a third in the United States, (for both undergraduate and law studies), and a fourth had studied in France (obtaining a doctorate). Three of the four Western-trained lawyers were Christians.

20. Some of the last group are recent secondary school graduates whose families cannot forgo their immediate earning power, while others are older persons, often married and with dependents, striving for upward mobility. These second careerists form an important subgroup, which will be discussed later in this chapter.

21. The figures on higher degree holders among the striking faction are from an article on the strike in the Jerusalem Arabic journal *al-ʿawdeh,* volume 2, no. 41 (May 24, 1984). In the cases of some of these higher degree holders, the strike was a direct factor in their decision to continue studies beyond the BA. Higher study seemed the most beneficial use of time pending the outcome of the strike, or simply a better alternative to returning to the West Bank to professional inactivity, or a step in the direction of a career in the teaching of law (a practice compatible with the terms of the strike). I was aware of only one working lawyer who had dabbled in academia, teaching business law at a local university for several terms.

22. Few informants, especially those of the working contingent, evinced interest in extending their theoretical knowledge of the law or in keeping abreast of developments in other jurisdictions by reading. Contemporary legal practice in the West Bank apparently provides little incentive for continuing theoretical study, as cases are said to be simple, and sophisticated legal argument is seen as wasted on corrupt and incompetent judges (chapter 8 addresses the issue of judicial corruption). In addition, current legal sources are difficult to acquire, since the West Bank itself is not a locus for

the production or publishing of legal journals or treatises, and the complications involved in travel and the importation of written materials in Arabic into the Occupied Territories constitute significant obstacles to their acquisition there.

23. Again let us note the West Bank community's sensitivity to actions that appear to signal resignation to the continuation of the occupation, and so a form of acceptance of its legitimacy. During the period of my research, several young working lawyers who were among my most helpful informants were agonizing over the decision to study Hebrew. In the end, practical considerations won out, and they had begun language sessions with a tutor by the time I left the area.

24. An important exception to the rule are the lawyers trained either in the Jerusalem Law Classes (who are fluent in English), in Eastern Europe, or in the West. Next to Hebrew, English is the most useful as a professional tool, facilitating dealings with foreign clients and aiding argument in military courts. The official languages of the military courts are Arabic and Hebrew, but military judges who are fluent in English permit West Bank lawyers to use it.

25. Two military orders passed since 1967 have introduced minor changes in the training requirements laid down in Jordanian law. The first authorizes the Israeli officer in charge of the judiciary to permit an apprentice lawyer (*muhami mutadarrib*) to perform part of his or her apprenticeship in a Judicial Department office. The second order grants discretion to the same official to shorten the period of apprenticeship for particular individuals to a minimum of six months.

26. The decision to work or strike is not irreversible, however, and it is not uncommon for an individual to begin to train with a striking lawyer and then to switch to a working lawyer, or vice versa, even though, in either case, this can involve restarting the two-year period of apprenticeship.

27. The term *"istaaz"* (or *"ustaadh"* in literary Arabic) is a general form of address used for intellectuals. Employed by a subordinate in reference to a mentor, it connotes substantial deference.

28. A number of informants complained that their mentors had taken virtually no interest in them and that essentially they had been in practice for themselves from the outset of their *tadrib*. Others highly praised the conscientiousness of their mentors and attributed to them their own usually high professional achievements.

29. In at least one case of which I am aware, a master lawyer had dispatched his trainee to an office located in the latter's home town, doubtless, to aid the master in securing business in an area in which he had no family ties of his own.

30. The "service ethic," of course, is one of the classical features of Western professions. See Magali Sarfatti Larson, *The Rise of Professionalism*, for example.

31. At this point, it is not uncommon for the master lawyer to award gratuities to an *estagiare* from the proceeds of cases on which he or she has worked.

32. Religious court cases tend to be neither lucrative nor intellectually and professionally stimulating, according to most informants. One of the striking lawyers most active in the Islamic courts from Hebron described his practice to me as "basically social work, a service I offer to a needy public, not true legal practice."

33. Despite its format, the function of this ritual, which may last up to two hours, is in reality purely ceremonial. Trainees cannot fail, as the panel has no power to reject the submitted research. I was told of one case, however, in which a member of the panel protested the poor quality of a piece of research by refusing to participate in the public interrogation. In a defense I attended, it rapidly became evident that the *estagiare* had plagiarized egregiously from the two major Arab jurists of administrative law. This was cause for relatively gentle chiding by the panel, which concluded the session by praising the research as a "good" piece of work.

34. Charles Morrison, "Kinship in Professional Relations: A Study of North Indian District Lawyers," *Comparative Studies in Society and History* 14 (1972): 100–125, describes an interesting contrast in India, where father-son relationships within the legal profession appear to engender greater tensions than those between non-kin.

35. Prosecutors are required to hold law degrees, so those who moved from such a post to private practice had studied law prior to entering government service. Reporters and other clerks who had made their way into law practice had typically studied law by correspondence while working their civil service jobs.

36. For some, temporary acceptance of the low salary of a civil servant was part of a conscious long-term strategy according to which former public position would be parlayed at a later stage into a lucrative private practice. Others, however, joined the judiciary after having risen to prominence as independent lawyers.

37. Some of these are older lawyers who practiced in Amman before the West Bank fell under Israeli occupation. Others are younger lawyers who spent several years following their graduation from the university working as lawyers in Amman or as legal advisers to government bureaucracies or private corporations in one of the Arab states of the Gulf. Rarer are lawyers who practiced for some time in the West Bank, left for a period of years to engage in a law-related profession outside the area, and then returned to resume legal work.

38. Another small group has retained its ties to the field by teaching law in local universities. Two doctors of law were full-time instructors at an-Najah National University in Nablus in the Faculty of Business Administration, and a holder of a Master's degree taught part-time in the Department of Political Science. A third doctor of law was a full-time instructor of Islamic law at Hebron University, while a fourth had recently left the West Bank to teach in Jordan at the new University of Mu'ta.

39. Technically, many of them are in contravention of the Law of the Union of Nizami Lawyers' strictures against the pursuit of certain other vocations. Presumably in recognition of the special circumstances surrounding

the strike, the JLU has elected, in most cases, to overlook these infractions.

40. In addition to the aforementioned deportations, a number of West Bank lawyers were imprisoned, disbarred, put under house arrest, had their international travel restricted, among other sanctions, for political activities alleged by the military government to have violated security regulations.

41. Bastedo, "Law Colleges"; Nash, "The Philadelphia Bench and Bar"; and Reuschemeyer, *Lawyers and Their Society.*

6. The Organization of the Legal Profession

1. Young lawyers commonly form partnerships to handle the expense of setting up practice and surviving the early lean years, during which income is typically low and they are fighting to establish themselves professionally.

2. I learned of only three Israeli lawyers who made somewhat regular appearances in the civil courts of the West Bank, as they have been permitted to do since 1968, and as many more had done during the early years of the strike. One of these was a Palestinian from within the "Green Line" (the term often used for the boundary between Israel and the Occupied Territories). The second was an Armenian from Jerusalem who had been practicing since the Mandate period. The third was a Jewish immigrant from Iraq who was fluent in Arabic. Most Israeli lawyers with whom I spoke refrained from practice in West Bank civil courts, citing their ignorance of Jordanian law and the problem of corruption in the local judiciary.

3. The law of the military courts is laid down in special security regulations and is not precisely the law applicable in Israel itself or that which is studied in Israeli law schools. On the other hand, the security regulations import much Israeli law. The laws of evidence relied upon in the military courts are the same as those employed in criminal proceedings in Israeli courts. The only compilations of decisions of the military courts, which end in 1976, are in Hebrew, and military orders are often more easily obtained in Hebrew than in Arabic.

4. The former military prosecutors now defending Palestinians before the military courts, otherwise repugnant characters to most in the West Bank community, trade on this notion.

5. Another manifestation of the prejudice in favor of Jewish lawyers is the willingness of Palestinian clients to pay higher fees to Jewish lawyers than to Arab lawyers for the same work. Many of my Palestinian informants complained bitterly about this fact.

6. The effective loss of access to Jerusalem's market for legal services has been particularly telling. The one hundred thousand or so Arab residents of the city equal approximately one-eighth of the West Bank population. Nor do sheer numbers tell the entire story: Jerusalem was and continues to be the major metropolitan center of the West Bank, with a more highly educated population and a concentration of businesses and headquarters of churches, associations, and other prime consumers of legal services.

7. In the year of my research, a Committee for the Defense of Prisoners' Rights was formed to publicize a prisoners' strike at Jneid prison outside of Nablus. The group included the prominent Jewish Israeli "political" lawyers and a number of Israeli Arab lawyers. They were joined by an organization representing West Bank working practitioners called the Committee of Arab Lawyers (lajnat al-muhamiin al-ʿarab), which will be discussed in chapter nine. This was the first cooperation among these groups of which I am aware, although much informal cooperation had preceded it.

8. This is not the proper place to examine the backgrounds of Israeli lawyers who practice in the West Bank nor the role of this group within the Israeli legal profession. Suffice it to note that there are interesting parallels between them and legal professionals in other societies. For example, in the nineteenth-century United States, young, minority, and lower-middle-class lawyers took over the less desirable practices in the circuit courts and in frontier regions. See Morton Horwitz, *The Transformation of American Law, 1780–1860;* and Dennis R. Nolan, *Readings in the History of the American Legal Profession.*

9. Sometimes civil cases that must be brought in Israeli courts (such as insurance compensation cases) are referred by West Bank lawyers to Israeli lawyers. One lawyer I interviewed in Tulkarm regularly sent road accident cases to an Israeli Arab lawyer with an office in nearby Tayyibeh. I encountered only one lawyer who had anything approaching a standing relationship with any other foreign lawyers or law offices. He practiced in Ramallah, a town that has sent thousands of emigrants to the United States, and occasionally would cooperate with a law office in Detroit. These cases typically involved inheritance of real property in Ramallah by emigrant-heirs living in the Detroit area.

10. Considering the limited uses to which clerical helpers are usually put, for many attorneys it probably is not cost effective to hire them. Secretaries are paid in the range of seventy-five to one hundred JD monthly, an extravagance for many of the less successful lawyers, who are both long on their own time and short on disposable income.

11. In one case, however, in which the residents of a refugee camp south of Jerusalem had sought an injunction to halt the operations of a cement factory that spewed dust into the air over the adjacent camp, the lawyer for the plaintiffs submitted into evidence an environmental impact report prepared by a French engineering firm.

12. "Key money" payments may run into thousands of JD. The choicest locations in East Jerusalem, according to some informants, command a price of up to fifteen thousand JD.

13. The waiting list for new telephone service in the Occupied Territories in 1984–1985 was three to four years, creating yet another obstacle to effective practice with which new lawyers must cope.

14. The laws in force in the West Bank are the Jordanian laws as they stood in 1967 or as amended by the military government, but *not* as they have been amended in Jordan itself since 1967. The Jordanian government prints

statutes only as they are currently amended, and not as they stood in 1967 or earlier. In consequence, there are no new printings of the Jordanian laws as they are applied in the West Bank available to West Bank practitioners.

15. The expenses are considerable. One lawyer with whom I attended court sessions in Nablus at a northern extreme and Hebron at a southern extreme and all points in between in the space of two days had logged forty-six thousand kilometers in his car in the space of nine months and ran monthly gas expenses equivalent to $250 to $300. He was, however, one of the more successful of the younger attorneys in practice at the time.

16. Of course, such arrangements vest lawyers with an interest in stringing out litigation into a multitude of sessions. There is no doubt that suspicion about this tactic hovers in the minds of clients and accounts in part for the negative image that some hold of the profession.

17. The fees in military court cases are very high in relation to the incomes of the families of most defendants, an inordinate share of whom are camp residents and thus members of the most impoverished sector of West Bank society. Relief is sometimes available from two sources. The American Friends Service Committee runs a legal aid office based in Jerusalem, which provides partial financial support to needy families to defend members incarcerated by the military government. Beginning in 1978 and until the early eighties, the Joint Committee was willing to reimburse families fully for attorney fees in military court cases on presentation of receipts to the committee in Amman. This gave rise to a scam of sorts; some attorneys would vastly inflate fees in the knowledge that they would not ultimately be borne by the parties themselves.

18. Since it is the more prominent and founding clans that possess the greatest amount of land in many Palestinian towns and villages, the lawyers who hold many of the general retainerships for migrants are themselves members of the same clans and, simultaneously, of the professional elite. In Ramallah, for example, a lawyer holding many general retainerships from migrants was a member of one of the seven putative founding clans of the town, a status he claimed to be crucial to his success in this particular area of practice.

19. As I have noted, for a number of years, the West Bank community was insulated from the effects of local economic stagnation by remittances earned by local emigrés working in the Gulf and daily migrant workers in Israel. But at the time of my research, and for the first time since occupation, downturns in both the Gulf and the Israeli economies had occurred simultaneously, causing a rather severe economic crisis in the Occupied Territories.

20. The stipend given by the JLU to striking lawyers had risen by the time of my research from an initial 40 JD's to 130 JD's monthly (roughly $3.30 U.S./JD). This income was supplemented in greatly varying amounts according to individual lawyers' personal assets, remittances from relatives working abroad, and level of active participation in the profession.

21. For purposes of rough comparison, the average monthly income of petty civil servants and clerks is probably close to 100 dinars. University

professors earn between 250 and 700 dinars per month in the better-paying local institutions, depending on the degrees they hold. A few upper-level independent businesspeople may earn as much as 5,000 dinars per month or even more. Needless to say, individual conditions differ considerably. Some lawyers have many dependents; others are not the sole wage earners in the household.

22. One young rising star in the profession proudly toured me around his hometown, pointing out rental residential property and two sharecropped orange orchards that he had purchased from the proceeds of his law work.

7. The Content of Legal Practice

1. Michael J. Meeker, *Literature and Violence in North Arabia*, is one among many who have noted the pronounced valorization of spoken language and oratory in Arab culture. Another manifestation of this in the legal realm is the greater weight accorded oral testimony over documentary evidence in traditional Islamic law. See Liebesny, *The Law of the Near and Middle East.*

2. Christian lawyers often do not work on Sunday. Military courts also function six days a week, but observe the Jewish Sabbath, Saturday.

3. Early or otherwise expedient scheduling of cases is one of the advantages enjoyed by elite lawyers or others who have ingratiated themselves with court personnel.

4. Striking lawyers gather at union headquarters in Beit Hanina, a suburb north of Jerusalem, or in lawyers' offices in the various towns.

5. After only a few weeks of frequenting the lawyers' lounge in the Ramallah court building, I, having been mistaken for a local lawyer, began to be queried by laypeople about their legal problems.

6. Many West Bankers assume that all telephone service in the region is monitored by the Israeli military intelligence. Transactions of any significance are preferably conducted in person.

7. Robert Kidder ("Formal Litigation and Professional Insecurity: Legal Entrepreneurship in South India," *Law and Society Review* 9, no. 1 [1974], 11–37), suggests that Indian lawyers are deliberately erratic in their behavior, as part of a strategy of cultivating images as "eccentric geniuses."

8. Because of the legal difficulties encountered by landlords in raising rents to keep pace with inflation, the magistrate courts have in recent years been clogged with eviction cases, which often involve values greatly disproportionate to the general civil jurisdiction of these courts. The judges in the magistrate courts continue to be the lower-ranking, less experienced members of the judiciary. Many of my lawyer informants thought that eviction cases should be removed from the jurisdiction of the magistrate courts and vested in the higher courts. These and similar problems are explored more fully in chapter 8.

9. Jordanian civil procedure is liberal in permitting interlocutory appeals, and it is common for cases to travel back and forth between the lower courts and the court of appeals before final resolution.

10. The legal profession's concentration on land-related cases is apparently typical in many Third World countries with similar economic structures. See Dias et al. (eds.), *Lawyers in the Third World.*

11. It is common in the West Bank for grocers and other small retailers to run monthly lines of credit for regular customers. The amounts seldom exceed one hundred dinars. In the straitened economic conditions that the West Bank was enduring at the time of my research, defaults on this type of credit arrangement were said to be multiplying.

12. Accordingly, despite the existence of torts law, there is no significant field of torts practice. One informant claimed that there had been only one case of compensation for personal injury filed in the civil courts in the region since 1945.

13. Purely Arab administrative authorities, such as elected municipalities, may still be sued in the West Bank court of appeals sitting in its capacity as a high court. But according to one knowledgeable informant, the number of these cases does not exceed two or three per year.

14. In this respect, the West Bank civil court system is similar to the civil law jurisdictions from which it has taken much inspiration. See John H. Merryman, *The Civil Law Tradition.*

15. In regard to routine cases, the decision to hold sessions in chambers or in open court appeared to be a matter of the judge's whim. In one magistrate court, the obliging judge volunteered to hold an open court session for my benefit. Another young, rather stern, judge told me that he insisted on always holding open sessions "to avoid the appearance that justice is something that is arranged behind closed doors."

16. An exception to this are the sessions of the court of appeals. All of these I attended were held in chambers and were extremely formal.

17. Beneath the veneer of courtesies, the actual relations between judges and lawyers vary widely according to individual personalities. But there is a strong tendency for them to become antagonistic. I once witnessed a verbal fray in the magistrate court in Tulkarm between the lawyer I had accompanied and the judge. Later in his office, the lawyer informed me that he had filed a complaint with the officer in charge of the judiciary against the judge for calling him an "*az'ar*" (something worse than a scoundrel) in open court. Other lawyers subsequently told me that this judge had a reputation for being weak and easily intimidated and that, as a result, the Tulkarm lawyers had gotten in the habit of shouting and carrying on in an unseemly manner.

18. In fact, this example represents only one species of a diverse genus of court delays. Others are mentioned in chapter 8.

19. A number of books and periodicals labeled by the military government as "hostile propaganda" are banned from the West Bank and possession of them is a chargeable offense.

20. In 1980, in an effort to regulate the inflow of the Steadfastness Funds and so to better control their political impact, the military government decreed that no more than three thousand dollars or the equivalent in other currencies could be brought into the West Bank at one time. Amounts in excess of that could be declared and deposited in a special account, to be

disbursed under the supervision of the military government. Many young Palestinian men returning from sojourns in the Gulf with their savings, either unaware of the regulations or attempting to circumvent them, are apprehended by Israeli authorities at the bridge from Jordan on their reentry to the West Bank.

21. This account is based on my attendance at the sentencing hearing and background information provided to me by the lawyer representing Rafiq.

22. Residents of Jerusalem who are charged with violations of security regulations are tried within a parallel military court system, which functions in Israel. Unlike the military court system in the West Bank and Gaza, within Israel the system includes a military court of appeals.

23. A *qadi* in one *shariʿa* court proudly displayed to me the stationery of the court, headed by the seal of the Hashemite Kingdom of Jordan, and made a point of mentioning to me that the order by which he held his appointment was issued "in the name of King Hussein."

24. Here and in what follows I am referring mostly to the *shariʿa* courts, not to the ecclesiastical courts, all of which are located within the walls of the Old City of Jerusalem.

25. Not once did I see a lawyer wearing a *hatta* in any place other than an Islamic court.

26. The military administration also regularly withholds driving licenses and other governmental benefits from individuals convicted or suspected of having committed security offenses.

8. Deterioration of the Formal Court System

1. West Bank lawyers have also been cut off from serving clients in the East Bank. Prior to 1967, a number of prominent West Bank lawyers had flourishing clienteles in Amman.

2. Shamgar, *Military Government*, p. 449.

3. Figures from the West Bank conform to a pattern identified in postcolonial African courts by Richard Abel ("Western Courts in Non-Western Settings: Patterns of Court Use in Colonial and Neo-Colonial Africa," in *The Imposition of Law*, ed. Sandra Burman and Barbara Harrell-Bond), who suggests that civil litigation may decrease *because* criminal prosecutions increase, as citizens increasingly view the state courts as hostile and intrusive agencies rather than as appropriate forums for the airing of their disputes.

4. The order actually culminated a series of decrees altering the process and composition of authorities responsible for such disputes as specified in Jordanian law.

5. The frequency of such incidents had been steadily increasing since 1979, when the military government lifted a moratorium on purchases of West Bank land by private Israeli interests. Prior to that, only the Jewish National Fund (a quasi-governmental agency dedicated to promoting Zionist settlement) and its subsidiary land development company, Hamnuta, and the Israel Lands Administration (a government department) had been permitted to purchase land in the Occupied Territories.

6. The suspicions of my informants were not entirely ungrounded. After my departure from the field, the Israeli press reported the arrests of Israeli military and civilian officials for participation in shady land deals in the West Bank.

7. In Tulkarm, for example, the man appointed magistrate court judge had been a leading activist in the Village Leagues. During the period of my fieldwork, he had taken a leave of indefinite duration to work further on league organizing. In Qalqilya, the recently appointed magistrate judge was the son of the local Village League head and had spent four undistinguished years in private law practice before his appointment.

8. These figures were provided by Nihad Jarallah, president of the district court of Hebron just prior to occupation. After 1967, he served as president of the district court in Ramallah until his appointment as president of the court of appeals in 1970. He remained in that capacity until his resignation in 1981.

9. The magistrate court of Qalqilya also sat in Salfit, some thirty to forty kilometers distant, for two days each week.

10. Court clerks have also substituted for vacationing prosecutors under a similar provision.

11. I have already noted that early in the occupation, the civil courts shied away from asserting their jurisdiction over claims against the occupation authorities and were subsequently barred from doing so by military decree.

12. The president of the court of appeals, the highest judicial officer in the civil court system under occupation, is also the Judicial Department's chief administrator and thus is responsible for hiring clerks and other department employees.

13. Military Order No. 841 of May 15, 1980, authorizes the closure of criminal case files at any stage of investigation or court proceedings before civil authorities or their transfer to military authorities by specified officers of the military government.

14. Some lawyers speculated that narcotics cases were being tried in military courts because they provided military intelligence with opportunities to recruit drug offenders as informers on the political activities of others both within and outside of prisons.

15. The *mafateeh* are of no particular social category and include religious leaders, petty civil servants, and others. The *miftaah* for the town of Beit Jala, for example, is a baker. Their identities are part of common though semicovert social knowledge.

16. The extent to which corruption penetrates to the higher levels of administration in the West Bank to include Israeli overseers of civilian departments is unknown. Lawyers widely believe that many Israeli officials receive bribes, and they claim to know with certainty of the participation of a few specific Israelis.

17. In Jordan, meanwhile, judicial salaries now start at two hundred dinars monthly and escalate according to position and seniority to a maximum of seven hundred dinars. This information was provided by Fuad

Khuri, court inspector for the Ministry of Justice, in an interview in Amman in February 1985. Judges were the only former Jordanian civil servants in the West Bank who did not continue to receive salaries from the Jordanian government after 1967 in addition to their salaries from the military government. Lawyers pointed out that this situation had severed any means of restraint Jordan may have exerted over the judges and had left them more amenable to Israeli influence.

18. Once when I accompanied a lawyer to the Hebron court, his session was delayed for the third consecutive time because of the failure of the police to deliver his client from the jail to the court.

19. In Jenin, for example, one person was performing the tasks of chief court reporter, notary public, and treasurer, while another was acting as an executive officer, assistant to the prosecutor, and process server. In Hebron, the chief court reporter served regularly as the notary public and occasionally stood in for an absent prosecutor. I was informed of similar situations in other courts in the region.

20. This occurred, for example, in "priority" (*awlawiya*) cases. Jordanian real property law confers a right of priority on the holder of land adjacent to a parcel that is being sold. He or she may match the price offered by any purchaser, posting it with the court, and, under certain conditions examined by the court in an action, gain title. Sums posted in this manner are now converted from Jordanian dinars to Israeli shekels at the rate on the day of deposit and then disbursed on termination of the proceedings either to the vendor or to the unsuccessful adjacent owner in shekels, at the rate of exchange on the date of the disbursement. With the rapid devaluations of the shekel that have occurred since the mid-seventies, the real value of amounts held by the court for the duration of litigation that usually lasts several years is constantly decreasing and authorities are accordingly paying out less in real value than they receive.

21. Among them, according to figures delivered in a press conference held by lawyers in Jerusalem, were the records of some 330 land cases, 250 of which had been decided but not yet executed, while the remaining 80 were still pending. A number of these cases were against Israeli land purchasers and involved allegations of forgery of the kind described earlier in this chapter. As Jordanian procedural law prohibits the use of photocopies, many irreplaceable documents concerning landownership were lost in the fire.

22. The most important sources for the law of belligerent occupation are the Hague Convention of 1907 and the Fourth Geneva Convention of 1949. The Israeli High Court has held the first but not the second of these bodies of law to limit the actions of the Israeli military government in the Occupied Territories. The Israeli government has consistently claimed to observe the provisions of the Geneva Convention as a matter of principle.

23. In a few cases, at least, highly successful legislation has resulted. For example, on the initiative of the Bethlehem municipal council, a military order drafted by its legal adviser (a striking lawyer) was issued that authorized the constitution of "municipal courts" to enforce municipal regula-

tions. A court was established to serve the municipalities of Beit Sahour, Beit Jala, and Bethlehem, and city officials were pleased with their speedier and more effective enforcement powers.

24. On occasion, military officers have given oral expropriation orders for lands identified by little more than the sweep of an arm, assigning village *makhateer* responsibility for notifying landowners directly.

25. Some forms of collective punishment, such as curfews and house demolitions, are permitted under a set of Defense Emergency Regulations originally implemented by the British in 1945. The Israeli military government claims that the regulations were in force in the West Bank when the occupation began in 1967, and hence are legitimate. Military orders also establish the principle of collective responsibility for some criminal acts, such as rockthrowing in the course of a demonstration. Other punishments, such as fines, are individual in form but, in many instances, collective in impact.

26. Excerpts from the Landau Commission Report were printed in English in the *Jerusalem Post* of November 1, 1987. The commission was appointed in the wake of two scandals within the Israeli intelligence community. In April 1984, three armed Palestinians hijacked a bus carrying Israeli civilians along the coastal highway. The bus was stormed by Israeli troops, with the loss of several lives. Initially, it was reported that all three hijackers died in the assault on the bus. However, an Israeli newspaper, defying government censors, published pictures showing Israeli soldiers leading away two live hijackers. It was later discovered that the hijackers had been taken into a field and beaten to death, apparently under orders of the head of Shin Bet. The second scandal involved revelations that several members of the intelligence service had conspired to frame an Arab Druze member of the Shin Bet for espionage and treason. The man had already spent a number of years in prison before his innocence was revealed.

27. Much legal detail, inappropriate to this study, was painstakingly provided by informants to substantiate these claims.

28. See, for example, Shamgar, *Military Government*. The same work includes the text of Military Order No. 172, which establishes the objections committees and governs their operation.

29. Informants with experience before the military objections committees also pointed out the difficulties in preparing for cases when they were uncertain as to the kinds of evidence that would be admissible and what weight would be accorded that evidence.

30. In contrast, a military order has been issued that provides for mutual recognition of judgments between the civil courts of Israel and the Occupied Territories.

31. One lawyer described to me a meeting that he had attended with the officer in charge of the judiciary in which the latter had shown him the bank statement of a court of appeals judge in Amman, where his harvest of bribes had been secreted.

32. Shehadeh, *Occupier's Law*, reports a 1981 attempt by the authorities to form a judicial appointments committee for the civil courts with members of the judiciary and legal profession. Nominated individuals declined to

participate because the proposed committee would have been in violation of Jordanian law and represented a move in the direction of an overall autonomy scheme for the West Bank, to which the community was thoroughly opposed.

33. In Jordanian law, the court inspector investigates complaints against civil court judges, examines their decisions for consistency and quality, and acts as a general overseer of the administrative functions of the courts. The court inspector is based in Amman and therefore, since the advent of occupation, has not enjoyed access to West Bank civil courts. The functions of the position had been assumed by the president of the court of appeals, in retrospect, a situation akin to the proverbial fox guarding the henhouse.

34. I encountered several lawyers who had been solicited for the position, but had declined it. One, a former judge, had apparently been pursued fairly persistently by the officer in charge of the judiciary. According to him, he had settled the discussion when he asked the officer, "If I discovered a problem and made a recommendation, would you enforce it?" and had received the frank answer, "No."

9. Disintegration of the Profession

1. In the direct aftermath of the June war, the Palestinian community was paralyzed by the totally unanticipated Arab defeat. Few expected anything but a rapid Israeli withdrawal. A major turning point in local consciousness was reached with the annexation of Jerusalem, the first clear indication that temporary occupation might be transformed into something longer-lived. Widespread, organized community opposition to the occupation dates to that rude awakening. See Jan Metzger, Martin Orth, and Christian Sterling (eds.), *This Land Is Our Land: The West Bank under Israeli Occupation.*

2. Some of the earliest lawyers exiled were Kamal Dajani, ʿAbd al-Muhsin Abu Maizer, Ibrahim Bakr, and Yahya Hammoudeh.

3. Passage of the Israeli Foreign Attorney's Examination (in Hebrew) was required, however. Few East Jerusalem lawyers have acquired the necessary proficiency in Hebrew or Israeli law, for reasons I have already noted.

4. The details of the origin of the fund are unclear, but at some point early on, stipends began to be paid by the Jordanian government, probably out of the budget of the Ministry for the Occupied Territories, set up after 1967. Responsibility for the management of the fund shifted to the Joint Committee on its establishment in 1978.

5. These figures were given to me by Nihad Jarallah, president of the court of appeals from 1970 until 1981. Another source claims that only eight returned to their offices after the war (Israeli National Branch, International Commission of Jurists, *The Rule of Law*).

6. Shehadeh and Kuttab, *The West Bank*, p. 46.

7. The fact that a number chose the first of these options suggests that, for some claimants and for some kinds of disputes, informal modes of dispute processing were unsuitable or inadequate. Of course, many citizens—

those charged with criminal or security offenses—were not before the courts by their own will, and their choice was between representation by an Israeli lawyer or no representation at all. Considering the stakes, it is not surprising that most chose to hire a lawyer.

8. Lawyer Ali Safarini, interviewed by Abdul Karim Sammara, "15 ʿaam ʿala idraab al-muhaamiin fi ʾl-ard al-muhtalla" [15 Years of the Lawyers' Strike in the Occupied Territory], *al-ʿawdeh* (Jerusalem weekly), no. 3 (1982).

9. All of these developments were accompanied by vitriolic debate conducted in the local press by members of the working and striking factions, supported variously by professional journalists and other community leaders. In this early stage, working lawyers generally found most sympathy for their position among municipal leaders, members of chambers of commerce, and prominent conservative and pragmatist political personalities. The striking lawyers were defended by other unions and forces of the growing Palestinian national movement in the region.

10. This is demonstrated by the relative sizes of the two contingents (250 striking master lawyers; 165 working). The continuation of the trend was also evident in the ratio of striking *estagiares* (70) to working *estagiares* (23) at the time of my fieldwork.

11. This situation was partially altered in 1977, when the Jordanian government, citing budgetary shortages, limited the number of stipends paid to then-current levels. From that point onward, new lawyers have queued for a spot on the roster, moving up only as openings occur because of deaths, emigrations, or other losses of professional status among those registered before them. West Bank officials were somewhat reticent to reveal the precise number of stipends being paid. I estimate approximately 180. At the time of my research, the amount of each stipend had reached 140 Jordanian dinars per month.

12. The diversity of political tendencies within both groups (including those sympathetic to Jordan, or to various Palestinian or pan-Arab political parties and organizations) is related to the fact that neither Jordan nor the PLO and affiliated organizations has taken a definitive stand with regard to the strike in recent years. This is discussed further later in this chapter.

13. Nidal Amir Taha, "Azmat al-idraab wa ʾl-ʿamal" [The Crisis of the Strike and Work], *al-bayadir* (Jerusalem weekly); "Muqtarahat liʾl-khuruj min azmat al-idraab wa ʾl-ʿamal" [Suggestions for a Resolution of the Crisis of the Strike and Work], *al-bayadir* 5, no. 4 (1980); "At-tariq liʾl-khuruj min azmat al-idraab wa ʾl-ʿamal" [The Way to a Resolution of the Crisis of the Strike and Work], *al-bayadir* 5, no. 5 (1981). The volume and number of the first in this series of articles were illegible on my copy, but the second article refers to them as having appeared in the previous issue of the journal.

14. Most of the information that follows is derived from interviews with members of the Steering Committee of the Committee of Arab Lawyers and from the various internal documents they kindly provided me.

15. A notice placed in the East Bank press by the *naqib* (head) of the union and reprinted in the West Bank media charged CAL participants with the "crime of cooperation with the enemy" for their initiative to found "an

independent union" and advocated that they be jailed and stripped of their Jordanian passports should they travel to the East Bank.

16. It should be recalled that much of internal politics in the West Bank in recent years has consisted of resisting perceived attempts by Israel, Jordan, and the United States to coax out a leadership in the Occupied Territories amenable to the process proposed in the "Camp David scheme." In the political parlance of the contemporary West Bank, those three words possess almost talismanic power, bearing the strongest negative associations.

17. In fact, even had the JLU supported the establishment of a branch union in the West Bank, cooperation of Israeli authorities would have been necessary for its effective operation. But the negative stance of the JLU toward CAL efforts further weakened the latter's legal and political position vis-à-vis the Israeli authorities.

18. The Law of the Jordanian Lawyers' Union permits the formation of branches of the JLU in each judicial district, but nothing on the order of a regional branch that might encompass the West Bank.

19. This was the much-protested decree that transferred jurisdiction over disputes concerning first-time registrations of land from the magistrate courts to the military objections committee.

20. In 1985, membership of the JLU stood at about 1,000, of whom 245 were located in the West Bank. I was present in Amman in February of that year during the biannual elections for JLU offices. Newspapers recounted the strident avowals of all contestants of their support for the striking lawyers of the West Bank.

21. Those solicited declined the invitation, arguing that the proposed committee had no foundation in Jordanian law, which, on the contrary, provided for such functions through the JLU.

22. On a reduced scale, this tactic paralleled the general Jordanian policy adopted after the 1974 Rabat Arab summit of mouthing that meeting's endorsement of the PLO as the "sole legitimate representative of the Palestinians" while quietly attempting to lay the groundwork for the reassertion of Jordanian sovereignty over the West Bank.

23. According to several working lawyers and nonlawyer informants, the booklet was the outgrowth of a 1983 meeting between a delegation of striking lawyers and representatives of the Joint Committee in Amman. The delegation sought an increase in the amount of the stipends paid to its constituents, evoking a challenge from the Joint Committee to produce something concrete to justify the support being provided them.

24. A memorandum issued by the striking lawyers to the community in 1980 likened the group to the "unknown soldier" (*al-jundi al-majhoul*) on the local political scene, stalwart yet unappreciated.

25. The sole development suggesting otherwise occurred after I departed from the field. A number of ostensibly striking lawyers were struck from the stipend roster for having been absent from the West Bank or for having engaged in disallowed vocations. The action hints at the financial difficulties of the Joint Committee, dependent as it is on the contributions of the oil states. Were the source of funds for stipends to dry up, there is little

question that many striking lawyers would be compelled to resume practice, no matter how unfavorable the market. Almost all other indicators, however, militate in favor of the status quo.

26. I do not propose that this represents the *conscious* strategy of the strike, but merely the reflexive impulse underlying it.

27. M. G. Smith, *Corporations and Society,* p. 94, defines a "corporate group" as "an enduring, presumably perpetual group with determinate boundaries and membership, having an internal organization and unitary set of external relations, an exclusive body of common affairs, and autonomy and procedures adequate to regulate them." Corporate group status is not an either/or proposition, but represents a continuum along which groups are ranged; some possess more or fewer of some ideal or typical traits and in greater or lesser degrees of formality, intensity, and so on (Smith's definition implies no exclusion of these qualifications, but does not state them), thus my preference for the term "erosion" over "loss" to describe the West Bank legal profession's corporate group status.

10. Conclusions

1. This capacity has been a fundament of the legitimacy of the legal profession in a number of other societies. See David Sills (ed.), *International Encyclopedia of the Social Sciences,* vol. 9, p. 63.

2. An increase in the prosperity of the legal profession would surely follow improvements in the general economic conditions in the West Bank. This might be partially stimulated by the revival of the Arab oil economies, which some experts are forecasting for the early to mid-nineties.

3. According to reports I received in early 1987, the morale in the courts and among lawyers has improved dramatically since the arrest and conviction of the corrupt judges and their replacement with appointees from among the respected members of the legal profession. Several of the latter, especially the new president of the court of appeals, appear to be distinguishing themselves with their competence and integrity.

Appendix

1. The term "dispute processing" replaced the earlier "dispute settlement" as scholars recognized that much behavior formerly categorized as directed toward "settlement" was often simply another mode of disputing (William Felstiner, "Influences of Social Organization on Dispute Processing," *Law and Society Review* 9, no. 1 [1974]: 63–94).

Many scholars were convinced to pursue these questions by Max Gluckman, who proposed that understanding the social relationships between parties would permit one to predict the type of procedure to which they would resort to resolve their dispute. Individuals in small-scale societies, typically enmeshed in cross-cutting "multiplex" relationships, tend to seek conciliatory outcomes so as to maintain ongoing relations and obligations. Individuals in larger-scale societies are more likely to be bound only by single-stranded, or "simplex," relationships and with consequently less interest in their preservation, tend to seek adjudicated settlements (Max Gluckman, *The Judicial Process among the Barotse of Northern Rhodesia*). Stewart Macaulay, "Non-contractual Relations in Business," later demonstrated that interest in the preservation of ongoing relations may account for resort to conciliatory outcomes in complex societies as well.

2. Nader and Todd, *The Disputing Process*, p. 9, delineate an intendedly exhaustive continuum that includes "adjudication, arbitration, mediation, negotiation, coercion . . . avoidance, and 'lumping it.'" A sample of works that examine some of these procedures are P. H. Gulliver, "Negotiations as a Mode of Dispute Processing," *Law and Society Review* 7, no. 4 (1973): 667–691 (negotiation); idem, "On Mediators," in *Social Anthropology and Law*, ed. Ian Hamnett (mediation); Andrew Strathern, "When Dispute Procedures Fail," in *Contention and Dispute*, ed. A. L. Epstein (coercion or self-help); James Woodburn, "Minimal Politics: The Political Organization of the Hadza of Northern Tanzania," in *Politics in Leadership*, ed. William Shack and Percy Cohen (avoidance); and Felstiner, "Influences of Social Organization" ("lumping it").

3. Nader and Todd, *The Disputing Process*, p. 16. Moore also advocates a "processual" approach, maintaining that "the continuous making and re-iterating of social and symbolic order is seen as an active process, not as something which, once achieved, is fixed. The view is taken that existing orders are endlessly vulnerable to being unmade, remade, and transformed, and that even maintaining and reproducing themselves, staying as they are, should be seen as a process" (Sally Falk Moore, *Law as Process: An Anthropological Approach*, p. 6). This, of course, involves a somewhat different notion of "process" than that proposed by Nader and Todd, implying accordingly different directions for study.

4. There are many such examples. One of the more recent is Witty, *Mediation and Society*, the introductory chapter of which refers to similar works, including a number treating Middle Eastern societies. Most of the contributors to the Nader and Todd volume, *The Disputing Process*, including Canter, Lowy, Parnell, Rothenberger, and Ruffini, are in the same vein, although some (notably, Rothenberger) express reservations about the feasibility of distinguishing in reality between the various forms of dispute procedures, and note the fluidity of the roles of negotiator-mediator-adjudicator and the rapidity with which a single actor may move between them.

5. Gulliver, "Negotiations as a Mode of Dispute Processing."

6. J. O. Starr and J. Pool, "The Impact of a Legal Revolution in Rural Turkey," *Law and Society Review* 8, no. 4 (Summer 1974): 533–560.

7. Jane Collier, *Law and Social Change in Zinacantan*.

8. Witty, *Mediation and Society*; Lowy, in Nader and Todd, *The Disputing Process*.

9. J. L. Gibbs, "The Kpelle Moot: A Therapeutic Model for the Informal Settlement of Disputes," *Africa* 33 (1963): 1–11.

10. In my view, far too much has been made of the supposed associations of formal institutions adjudication-zero-sum outcomes and informal proce-

dures-negotiations/mediation-compromise outcomes. Kidder, "Formal Litigation and Professional Insecurity," points out that formal litigation can be a vehicle for negotiations and compromise outcomes. My West Bank data confirm this and also suggest that non–state-sponsored procedures can be highly "formal" and adjudicative, at least at certain stages, and may also impose zero-sum solutions.

11. For example, my data confirm that *speed* of process and *predictability* of outcome are important elements where individuals enjoy freedom to choose among modes of dispute processing. Disputants who have options may also "award" cases to some mediators or withhold them from others, as more or less conscious symbolic statements about the relative legitimacy of the various mediators and the institutions they represent.

12. Although I will not pursue the point here, there are, to my mind, always questions raised by game theory–influenced explanations of behavior in anthropology (of which F. G. Bailey was a leading proponent), which concern the level of access to consciousness and manipulability that sometimes are at the core of the actor's persona and psyche, such as senses of identity, honor, and personal dignity. See F. G. Bailey, *Stratagems and Spoils.*

13. Moore, *Law as Process,* p. 107, argues that the principle of collective responsibility in societies that observe it may be selectively applied according to, among other things, the "desirability of the confrontation from the point of view of the social units potentially involved." Robert Kidder, "The End of the Road? Problems in the Analysis of Disputes," *Law and Society Review* 15, nos. 3–4 (1981): 719, claims that the very term "dispute," conjuring up images of dyadic confrontations between free acting individuals, belies a covert influence from Western legal theory and tends to obscure the "systematic inequalities and institutionalized asymmetrical developments" in a society's relationships (p. 719).

14. For example, Richard Canter, "Dispute Settlement and Dispute Processing in Zambia: Individual Choice versus Societal Constraints," in *The Disputing Process—Law in Ten Societies,* ed. Laura Nader and Harry Todd, Jr.; Collier, "Political Leadership"; and Gulliver, "On Mediators."

15. Keebet von Benda-Beckmann, "Forum Shopping and Shopping Forums: Dispute Processing in a Minangkaban Village in West Sumatra," *Journal of Legal Pluralism,* no. 19 (1981): 117.

16. Some authors, even while acknowledging the state's "legitimacy" interest in dispute processing, at other points use language that construes "forum shopping" as a simple matter of individual choice. See, for example, Phillip Parnell, "Village or State? Competitive Legal Systems in a Mexican Judicial District," in *The Disputing Process—Law in Ten Societies,* ed. Laura Nader and Harry Todd, Jr.; Canter, "Dispute Settlement and Dispute Processing in Zambia," discusses the influence of the remedy agent on the direction of disputes, but refers to "societal constraints" on disputant choice. These sometimes impart a sense of impersonality to forces that are often no more than the will of other involved actors.

17. Very few anthropologists have bothered to speculate as to *why* the function of dispute processing and political legitimacy may be so closely in-

tertwined. Sally Falk Moore ("Individual Interests and Organizational Structures: Dispute Settlements as 'Events of Articulation,'" in *Social Anthropology and Law*, ed. Ian Hamnett) begins such an analysis, examining court cases as occasions for symbolic representations of the corporate and authoritative qualities of the state. I will not digress at length to explain my own views on this matter, but I would suggest than one might start from the premise that the function of mediation (in the broad sense of any third party facilitation of dispute resolution) in many societies is something like a "core attribute" of legitimate authority, and that to pose as a mediator is to contend symbolically for sovereignty. During the 1936–1939 Arab revolt against British rule in Palestine, for example, the revolutionaries established "popular courts," which tried civil and criminal cases. British officials, recognizing their symbolic significance, were especially galled by the existence of these courts and tried mightily to stamp them out. Another work that highlights the political symbolism of courts is Daniel Lev, *Islamic Courts in Indonesia*. Magali Morsy ("Arbitration as a Political Institution: An Interpretation of the Status of Monarchy in Morocco," in *Islam in Tribal Societies*, ed. Akbar Ahmad and David Hart, argues that the Moroccan state is largely derived from and dependent on the institution of arbitration.

18. See, for example, G. Sidney Silliman, "A Political Analysis of the Philippines' Katarangang Pambarangay System of Informal Justice through Mediation," *Law and Society Review* 19, no. 2 (1985): 279–301; and A. Paliwala, "Economic Development and the Legal System of Papua New Guinea," *African Law Studies* 16 (1978): 3–79. Richard Abel, *The Politics of Informal Justice*, points out that the tactic of "delegalization" through the establishment of informal institutions of justice may function to extend the ambit of state control. Of course, the foundation of new institutions of dispute processing or changes in the structure and jurisdiction of existing ones may also result in unintended shifts in local community power. See Leopold Posposil, "Legally Induced Culture Change in New Guinea," in *The Imposition of Law*, ed. Sandra Burman and Barbara Harrell-Bond.

19. Abel, *The Politics of Informal Justice*, p. 270, argues that even informal systems of justice in the United States have spawned specialists who "ensure that informal institutions foster dependence on paraprofessional mediators, counselors, and advocates, notwithstanding the rhetoric of disputant participation and self-reliance."

20. Moore, "Individual Interests and Organizational Structures."

21. See M. B. Hooker, *Legal Pluralism*; and Metzger, "Legal Services Programs in Asia."

22. Sandra Burman and Barbara Harrell-Bond, *The Imposition of Law*.

23. Abel, "Western Courts in Non-Western Settings."

24. Galanter, "The Study of the Indian Legal Profession," p. 201.

25. Chapter 2 concerns the imposition of the modern Palestinian legal profession. It suffices to mention at this point that the profession emerged in the late Ottoman period coincident with the establishment of a secular, Western-inspired court system in the empire and then crystallized into its

contemporary form during the British Mandate period. It may be noted parenthetically that the imposition of the legal profession was not limited to the Third World; the formation of the profession in nineteenth-century Russia closely parallels its development in the Ottoman Empire. See Kucherov, *Courts, Lawyers, and Trials.*

26. Lawrence Friedman, "Legal Culture and Social Development," *Law and Society Review* 4, no. 1 (1969): 29–44. See also Merryman, *The Civil Law Tradition.*

27. See Johnson, "Imperialism and the Professions."

28. Sally Lloyd-Bostock, "Explaining Compliance with Imposed Law," in *The Imposition of Law,* ed. Sandra Burman and Barbara Harrell-Bond, p. 23.

29. Robert Kidder, "Toward an Integrated Theory of Imposed Law," in *The Imposition of Law,* ed. Sandra Burman and Barbara Harrell-Bond, p. 297.

30. A number of students of other societies with imposed law and legal institutions have examined the cultural distance and dissonance between indigenous values and beliefs and Western legal culture. See, for example, Rudolph and Rudolph, "Barristers and Brahmans in India," and Khare, "Indigenous Culture."

31. Nearly exclusive focus on litigation is a feature characteristic of many Third World legal professions. See the various contributions in Dias et al. (eds.), *Lawyers in the Third World;* Committee on Legal Services to the Poor in Developing Nations, *Legal Aid and World Poverty;* and *Law and Society Review* 3, wholly devoted to studies of the Indian legal profession. The absence of complex corporations (economic or other), which typically fuel the demand for legal planning in Western societies, is also a critical factor in this phenomenon.

32. See Larson, *The Rise of Professionalism.*

33. This "missionary" sense has been fostered by their Western mentors, one might add. Much of the literature on the non-Western legal profession was spawned by the "law and development" movement, which swept the North American legal academic imagination in the sixties and seventies, and which singled out lawyers as the prospective torchbearers of modernity in Third World societies. A classic example is Committee on Legal Services to the Poor in Developing Nations, *Legal Aid and World Poverty.* A review of the "law and development" movement and an extensive bibliography of the voluminous literature it produced is given in Francis G. Snyder, "Law and Development in the Light of Dependency Theory," *Law and Society Review* 14, no. 3 (Spring 1980): 723–804. Another useful review is that by John H. Merryman, "Comparative Law and Social Change: On the Origins, Style, Decline, and Revival of the Law and Development Movement," *American Journal of Comparative Law* 25 (1977): 457–491.

34. Bernard Cohn, "Anthropological Notes on Disputes and Law in India," *American Anthropologist* 67, no. 6 (1965): 82–122; Starr and Pool, "The Impact of a Legal Revolution in Rural Turkey."

35. On the latter point, see Luckham, "Imperialism." On the Indian legal profession, see Galanter, "The Aborted Restoration."

Glossary

'agal: ropelike fastener, part of traditional Arab male headaddress, used to secure the cloth portion, *hatta*, to the head.

ahwal shakhsiya: category of court cases pertaining to personal status (marriage, adoption, inheritance, and the like), which falls within the jurisdiction of the religious courts in the West Bank.

al-lajna al-mushtaraka: the Joint Committee composed of Jordanian government and PLO representatives established in the Baghdad Conference of Arab states in 1978 to administer the *amwaal as-sumud*, or Steadfastness Fund.

al-qada' al-'asha'iri: tribal adjudication.

'amama: headdress of an Islamic court *qadi*, or judge; a fezlike hat, the base of which is wrapped with a white cloth.

'amdi: used in the language of tribal adjudication to describe an intentional wrong against another.

amwaal as-sumud: a fund established by the Arab states in the Baghdad Conference in 1978 to support the *sumud*, or "steadfastness," of the Palestinian residents of the Israeli-occupied territories, administered by the Joint Committee of Jordanian and PLO representatives.

Arab Higher Committee: the principal organization through which Palestinian resistance to British rule and aspirations for national independence were expressed in the Mandate period, 1923–1948.

'arad: colloquial Palestinian word for honor. When used as *qadiyat-'arad*, a case of honor, connotes a sexual offense against a woman.

'ardhaljis: petition writers, generally of ill-repute, who represented citizens in the courts of the Ottoman Empire prior to formal regulation of the legal profession in the late nineteenth century.

'ashira, pl. **'asha'ir:** clan or tribe.

ʿatweh: the three-day truce period negotiated between the families of an injured party and of an offender, which is the first phase of tribal adjudication.

awlawiya: the right, stemming from Ottoman law and preserved in Jordanian civil law, for an owner of land to have "priority" (*awlawiya*), under specified circumstances, in the purchase of an adjacent plot.

az-ʿar: scoundrel, pimp.

Baʿth party: a political party founded in Syria in the late forties, with the ideal of unifying the Arab countries into a single nation. The party later spread throughout the Eastern Arab world, in the fifties and sixties claiming many followers in Jordan, including the West Bank.

Baghdad Conference of Arab states: the summit of Arab states held in 1978 to promote the *sumud,* or steadfastness, of the Palestinian residents of the Israeli-occupied territories. It established both the *amwaal as-sumud* (Steadfastness Fund) and the *al-lajna al-mushtaraka* (Joint Committee) to administer the fund.

Border Police: the unit of the Israel Defense Forces responsible for internal security. Its soldiers are identified by their green berets.

British Mandate: the administration created when the League of Nations charged Great Britain with temporary rule of Palestine and the task of helping its residents achieve independence. The Mandate was formally ratified in 1923, six years after British military occupation, and ended with the withdrawal of British administrators and troops from Palestine in 1948.

Camp David Accords: the term frequently given to two distinct pacts negotiated between Israel, Egypt, and the United States at Camp David, Maryland, and signed in 1979. The first was a peace treaty between Israel and Egypt and resulted in Israeli withdrawal from the Sinai Peninsula. The second envisioned a five-year "transitional" period in the West Bank and Gaza Strip, during which Palestinians of those regions would enjoy some form of self-rule or autonomy. The ultimate destiny of the occupied territories was to be determined through further negotiations. The second agreement has never been implemented.

chambers of commerce: business associations present in major West Bank towns. During Israeli occupation, the chambers have often represented the interests of the business community in dealings with the military government.

court of appeals: *mahkamat al-istiʾnaaf,* the highest civil court currently functioning in the West Bank. It hears appeals from decisions of both the magistrate and district courts. It also sits as a high court, reviewing allegedly illegal or unjust acts by nonmilitary government officials.

court of cassation: the Jordanian Supreme Court. Located in Amman, it is the highest appellate court in the Jordanian judicial system, reviewing decisions from the courts of appeal and also functions as a high court. Since 1967, residents of the West Bank have had no recourse to the court of cassation in either its appellate or high court capacity.

court of first instance: *mahkamat al-bidaya,* commonly called simply district courts. These have jurisdiction over a limited category of appeals from the magistrate courts, as well as original jurisdiction in all cases that exceed the jurisdictional limits of the magistrate courts.

custodian of absentee property: the officer within the military government who controls lands declared to have been abandoned by Palestinian owners who fled the West Bank in the 1967 war.

daar: house or family.

Defense Emergency Regulations: a set of laws initially promulgated by the British mandatory government, granting it extensive extrajudicial powers to deal with political unrest. These laws were never explicitly repealed by Jordan, and the Israeli military government continues to apply them in the West Bank today.

district court. *See* court of first instance.

diya: blood money; the amount paid in compensation to the victim of a wrong or to his or her family through tribal adjudication.

estage: the French term, often used in the West Bank, for the two-year apprenticeship undergone by novice lawyers, or *estagiares.*

execution department: the branch of the civil court system charged with enforcing, or executing, judgments of the civil and religious courts.

fasaad: corruption.

fellah, pl. *fellahin:* peasant.

Fertile Crescent: the large fertile region arching from the Mediterranean coast in the west, including Palestine, around the Syrian desert to Iraq in the east.

ghurfat al-ʿasafeer: "room of the sparrows," where imprisoned Palestinians claim to be placed with informers, "sparrows," who attempt to elicit incriminating statements from them.

Green Line: common term for the border between Israel and the West Bank.

hadari: town dweller.

hatta: the cloth portion of traditional Arab male headdress.

hamula, pl. *hamayil:* extended lineage.

High Court: in the legal systems of both Jordan and Israel, a capacity normally vested in the Supreme Court. Sitting as a high court, the Supreme Court reviews complaints against government officials claimed to be illegal or unjust. Since 1967, the high court powers of the Jordanian Supreme Court have been vested in the court of appeals in Ramallah. The Israeli Supreme Court exercises high court jurisdiction over all Israeli government officials, including military government officials acting in the West Bank.

Higher Planning Council: an agency composed of Israeli military government and nonmilitary civil servants that is responsible for land-use planning in the occupied territories.

Hukuk Mektebi: the first Ottoman law school, established in Istanbul in 1871.

ijtima-ʿi: sociable.

intifada: the uprising in the occupied territories against Israeli rule that began in December 1987.

intisab: correspondence system of university education.

ʿird: classical Arabic for "honor."

Israel Defense Forces (IDF): the Israeli army.

Israeli High Court. *See* High Court.

istaaz: general term for an especially learned or educated person; *muhami istaaz,* a master lawyer.

istishara qanuniya: legal advice or counsel.

Istiqlal party: the pan-Arab "Independence" party founded by lawyer ʿAwniʿAbd al-Hadi in 1932.

jaha wa al-wajaha: procession of town or village notables who accompany representatives of an offender's family to the family of a victim to sue for peace through tribal adjudication.

Joint Committee. *See al-lajna al-mushtaraka.*

Jordanian Lawyers' Union (JLU): established by the Law of the Union of Nizami Lawyers in 1952 to regulate the affairs of the legal profession. Members of the striking faction of West Bank lawyers continue to be licensed by and to be members of the JLU.

Judicial Department: the division of the Ministry of Justice responsible for administration of the courts.

kafil: a guarantor or sponsor of a party involved in tribal adjudication.

katib al-istid-ʿaʾat: petition writer.

khataʾa: used, in the language of tribal adjudication, to describe an unintentional wrong against another.

lajiʾ: refugee.

lajnat al-muhamiin al-ʿarab: the Committee of Arab Lawyers (CAL), founded by the working faction of West Bank lawyers to represent their interests.

Land Law: the code of laws pertaining to real property adopted by the Ottoman government in 1858 as part of the general reform movement of the nineteenth century, or Tanzimat.

magistrate court: lowest-level court in the Jordanian civil court system, with jurisdiction over petty crimes, civil disputes with small amounts in controversy, and a limited category of real property disputes, including those involving lease agreements.

mahkama, pl. *mahakim:* court.

mahkamat al-bidaya. See court of first instance.

mahkamat al-istiʾnaaf. See court of appeals.

makhamat as-sulh: magistrate court.

Majalla: the Ottoman civil code adopted in the late nineteenth century.

Mandatory Government: the British government of Palestine, 1923–1948 (*see also* British Mandate).

manqaʿ-al-damm: "blood judge" of tribal adjudication.

manshad: the highest in the hierarchy of tribal judges, uniquely qualified to hear cases of honor (*qadiyatʿarad*).

mazalim: a form of extraordinary justice recognized in Islamic law and stemming from the absolute authority of the caliph to right all wrongs and from his obligation to protect the community in accord with religious principles.

miftaah, pl. *mafateeh:* "key," the popular term for a person who conveys bribes to government officials.

muʾassassaat wataniyeh: nationalist institutions founded in the occupied territories by Palestinians to strengthen the community against pressures for migration.

muhami istaaz: master lawyer.

muhami mutadarrib: apprentice lawyer or *estagiare.*

mukhabarat: military intelligence.

mukhtar, pl. *makhateer:* appointed village officials who, since Ottoman times, have served as intermediaries between their *hamayil,* or clans, and government authorities.

murafaʿa: oral argument in court.

mutasarrif: district governors under Jordanian administration. The office was abolished in 1967 by the Israeli military government.

muzawwirun: "forgers," the pejorative reference to the petition writers of late Ottoman-era Egypt.

nafaqa: "maintenance," a sum a Muslim husband is obligated by Islamic law to provide his wife periodically for her support and for the support of any children during the marriage.

nahal: paramilitary civilian settlements established by the Israeli government in the occupied territories, especially in border areas.

naqib: head of a union.

National Guidance Committee: the informal leadership of the Palestinian community in the occupied territories, founded in 1978. The committee was outlawed and disbanded by the military government in the early 1980s.

nizamiyeh courts: "regulatory" secular courts established in the late nineteenth century throughout the Ottoman Empire as part of the Tanzimat, or reforms.

objections committees: tribunals created by the Israeli military government to consider claims by West Bank residents of a generally civil nature, including those concerning expropriation or new registration of lands, tax assessments, customs, civil service pensions, and so on.

Occupied Territories: the areas formerly controlled by Syria, Jordan, and Egypt that were occupied by Israel in the June 1967 war.

Ottoman Empire: the Turkish empire, which ruled many parts of the Middle East, including Palestine, until its collapse in World War I.

piastre: one one-hundredth of a dinar.

qadi: judge.

qadi-ʿashaʾiri: tribal judge.

qadi sulh: magistrate court judge or magistrate.

qadiyat-ʿarad: a case of honor, typically a sexual offense against a woman.

qanun: law.

qarawi: villager.

qaza: Ottoman judicial district.

rawabit al-qura. See Village Leagues.

rizqa: the amount sometimes offered a tribal judge by parties to a dispute in payment for his services.

rural council: a Jordanian village administrative unit.

sahib al-damm: in the language of tribal adjudication, the offended party.

sanjaq: Ottoman administrative unit between a *qaza,* or judicial district, and a *vilayet,* or province.

shariʿa: Islamic law.

sheikh: an older male head of a lineage or clan.

shurta: police.

sijill: record book of the Islamic courts, which previously functioned as public records offices.

simsaar, pl. *samasira:* a middleman or broker; often used pejoratively in reference to Palestinians who act as intermediaries between Israeli purchasers of land in the Occupied Territories and Palestinian landowners.

siyadat al-qadi: "your excellency the judge," the form of address used by lawyers in addressing judges.

Steadfastness Fund. *See* amwaal as-sumud.

souq: market.

sulh: a final peace between offending and aggrieved parties achieved through tribal adjudication.

sumud: steadfastness.

sura: a verse from the Qurʾan.

taʿassub: partisanship, clannishness.

tabaqa, pl. *tabaqat:* class; *at-tabaqa al-adna,* lower class; *at-tabaqa al-wusta,* middle class; *at-tabaqa al-ʿulya,* upper class.

tadrib: the two-year obligatory apprenticeship undergone by novice lawyers.

tahkim: arbitration.

Tanzimat: a movement of broad reforms undertaken by the Ottomans, beginning in the mid-nineteenth century, that aimed to "modernize" and Westernize the laws and administration of the empire.

thawrat sitti wa tlateen: the Revolution of '36; the three-year revolt of the Arab residents of Palestine against Zionist colonization and British rule in Palestine, 1936–1939.

'urf: "customary" law applied in tribal adjudication.

vilayet: Ottoman administrative unit composed of several subunits, or *sanjaqs;* equivalent to a province.

Village Leagues: voluntary organizations that sprang up in the West Bank in the late seventies and early eighties and were briefly promoted by the Israeli military government as possible Palestinian representatives in peace negotiations.

wakala: general contract of agency; *wakala-ʿama,* general retainership.

wakil: agent; a term employed to describe legal representatives in the Ottoman courts prior to formal regulation of the legal profession.

wasta: "intermediary" or "intermediation"; influence through personal ties that a person may bring to bear to gain special privileges or consideration from government officials.

waqf, pl. ***awqaaf:*** a trust in Islamic law, matters of which fall within the jurisdiction of the *shariʿa,* or Islamic courts.

wujuh: village or town notables.

Bibliography

Abdel-Malik, Anouar. *Egypt: Military Society*. New York: Vintage Books, 1968.

Abed, Shukri. *Israeli Arabism: The Latest Incarnation of Orientalism*. Washington, D.C.: International Center for Research and Public Policy, 1986.

Abel, Richard, ed. *The Politics of Informal Justice*. Vol. 1. New York: Academic Press, 1982.

———. "Western Courts in Non-Western Settings: Patterns of Court Use in Colonial and Neo-Colonial Africa." In *The Imposition of Law*, ed. Burman and Harrell-Bond, pp. 167–200.

Abrahams, Sidney. "The Colonial Legal Service and the Administration of Justice in Colonial Dependencies." *Journal of Comparative Legislation* 30 (1948): 1–11.

Abu-Ghazaleh, Adnan. *Arab Cultural Nationalism in Palestine during the British Mandate*. Beirut: Institute for Palestine Studies, 1973.

Abu-Lughod, Janet. "The Demographic Consequences of Occupation." In *Occupation: Israel over Palestine*, ed. Aruri, pp. 255–268.

Anabtawi, Samir N. 1986. *Palestinian Higher Education in the West Bank and Gaza*. New York: Methuen and KPI.

el-ʿAref, ʿAref. *Bedouin Love Law and Legend*. Jerusalem: Cosmos Publishing, 1944.

Aruri, Naseer, ed. *Occupation: Israel over Palestine*. Belmont, Mass.: Arab-American University Graduates, 1983.

Asad, Talal. "Anthropological Texts and Ideological Problems: An Analysis of Cohen on Arab Villages in Israel." *Review of Middle East Studies*, no. 1 (1975): 1–40.

Ayoub, Victor. "Conflict Resolution and Social Reorganization in a Lebanese Village." *Human Organization* 24, no. 1 (Spring 1965): 11–17.

Badran, Nabil. "The Means of Survival: Education and the Palestinian Community, 1948–1967." *Journal of Palestine Studies* 9, no. 4 (1980): 44–74.

Baer, Gabriel. "The Office and Functions of the Village Mukhtar." In *Palestinian Society and Politics*, ed. Migdal.

Bailey, F. G. *Stratagems and Spoils*. New York: Schocken Books, 1969.

el-Barguthy, Omar Effendi. "Judicial Courts among the Bedouin of Palestine." *Journal of the Palestine Oriental Society* 2 (1922): 35–65.

Bastedo, T. G. "Law Colleges and Law Students in Bihar." *Law and Society Review* 3, no. 2 (1968): 269–294.

Beattie, Kirk James. "Egypt: The Struggle for Hegemony, 1952–1981." Ph.D. dissertation, University of Michigan, 1985.

Beaumont, Peter, Gerald Blake, and J. Malcolm Wagstaff. *The Middle East: A Geographical Study.* New York: John Wiley & Sons, 1976.

Bentwich, Norman. "The Legal System of Palestine under the Mandate." *Middle East Journal* 2 (1948): 33–46.

Benvenisti, Meron. *The West Bank Data Project.* Washington, D.C.: American Enterprise Institute, 1984.

Bill, James. *The Politics of Iran: Groups, Classes, and Modernization.* Columbus, Ohio: Charles Merrill, 1972.

Bourdieu, Pierre. "The Sentiment of Honour in Kabyle Society." In *Honor and Shame,* ed. J. G. Peristiany, pp. 191–241.

Bujra, Abdullah. *The Politics of Stratification.* Oxford: Clarendon Press, 1971.

Burdick, William. *The Bench and Bar of Other Lands.* Brooklyn: Metropolitan Law Book Co., 1939.

Burman, Sandra, and Barbara Harrell-Bond, eds. *The Imposition of Law.* New York: Academic Press, 1979.

Canter, Richard. "Dispute Settlement and Dispute Processing in Zambia: Individual Choice versus Societal Constraints." In *The Disputing Process—Law in Ten Societies,* ed. Nader and Todd, pp. 247–280.

Cobban, Helena. *The Palestine Liberation Organization: People, Politics, and Power.* Cambridge: Cambridge University Press, 1984.

Cohen, Abner. *Arab Border Villages.* Manchester: Manchester University Press, 1965.

Cohen, Amnon. "The Changing Pattern of West Bank Politics." *Jerusalem Quarterly,* no. 5 (Fall 1977): 105–113.

———. *Palestine in the 18th Century.* Jerusalem: Magnes Press, 1973.

Cohn, Bernard. "Anthropological Notes on Disputes and Law in India." *American Anthropologist* 67, no. 6 (1965): 82–122.

Collier, Jane. *Law and Social Change in Zinacantan.* Stanford: Stanford University Press, 1973.

———. "Political Leadership and Legal Change in Zinacantan." *Law and Society Review* 11, no. 1 (Fall 1976): 131–163.

Committee on Legal Services to the Poor in Developing Nations. *Legal Aid and World Poverty.* New York: Praeger, 1974.

Coulson, N. J. *A History of Islamic Law.* Edinburgh: Edinburgh University Press, 1964.

Cygielman, Victor. "Voices from the West Bank." *New Outlook,* 17 (August–September 1974): 45–48.

Dakkak, Ibrahim. "The Transformation of Jerusalem: Juridical Status and Physical Change." In *Occupation: Israel over Palestine,* ed. Aruri, pp. 67–96.

Demant, Peter. "Israeli Settlement Policy Today." In *Occupation: Israel over Palestine*, ed. Aruri, pp. 143–166.

Dias, C. J., R. Luckham, D. O. Lynch, and J. C. N. Paul, eds. *Lawyers in the Third World: Comparative and Developmental Perspectives*. New York: International Center for Law in Development, 1981.

Doumani, Beshara. "Palestinian Islamic Court Records: A Source for Socioeconomic History." *Middle East Studies Association Bulletin* 19, no. 2 (1985): 155–172.

Drori, Moshe. "The Israeli Settlements in Judea and Samaria: Legal Aspects." In *Judea, Samaria, and Gaza: Views on the Present and Future*, ed. Elazer, pp. 49–80.

———. "Local Government in Judea and Samaria." In *Military Government in the Territories Administered by Israel, 1967–1980: The Legal Aspects*, ed. Shamgar, pp. 234–284.

Eickelman, Dale. *Moroccan Islam: Tradition and Society in a Pilgrimage Center*. Austin: University of Texas Press, 1976.

Elazar, Daniel, ed. *Judea, Samaria, and Gaza: Views on the Present and Future*. Washington, D.C.: American Enterprise Institute, 1982.

Evans-Pritchard, E. E. *The Sanussi of Cyrenaica*. Oxford: Clarendon Press, 1949.

Farrag, Amina. "The Wastah among Jordanian Villagers." In *Patrons and Clients*, ed. Ernest Gellner and John Waterbury, London: Duckworth, 1977.

Felstiner, William. "Influences of Social Organization on Dispute Processing." *Law and Society Review* 9, no. 1 (1974): 63–94.

Friedman, Lawrence. "Legal Culture and Social Development." *Law and Society Review* 4, no. 1 (1969): 29–44.

Galanter, Marc. "The Aborted Restoration of 'Indigenous' Law in India." *Comparative Studies in Society and History* 14 (1972): 53–70.

———. "The Study of the Indian Legal Profession." *Law and Society Review* 3, no. 2 (1968): 201–217.

Geertz, Clifford, Hildred Geertz, and Lawrence Rosen. *Meaning and Order in Moroccan Society*. New York: Cambridge University Press, 1979.

Gellner, Ernest. *Saints of the Atlas*. Chicago: University of Chicago Press, 1969.

Gibbs, J. L. "The Kpelle Moot: A Therapeutic Model for the Informal Settlement of Disputes." *Africa* 33 (1963): 1–11.

Gluckman, Max. *The Judicial Process among the Barotse of Northern Rhodesia*. Manchester: Manchester University Press, 1955.

Goadby, Francis, and Moses Doukhan. *The Land Law of Palestine*. Tel Aviv: Shoshany's Printing Co., 1932.

Graham-Brown, Sarah. "The Economic Consequences of Occupation." In *Occupation: Israel over Palestine*, ed. Aruri, pp. 167–222.

———. "Impact on the Social Structure of Palestinian Society." In *Occupation: Israel over Palestine*, ed. Aruri, pp. 223–254.

Gulliver, P. H. "Negotiations as a Mode of Dispute Processing." *Law and Society Review* 7, no. 4 (1973): 667–691.

———. "On Mediators." In *Social Anthropology and Law*, ed. Hamnett.

Hadar, Zvi. "The Military Courts." In *Military Government in the Territories Administered by Israel, 1967–1980: The Legal Aspects,* ed. Shamgar, pp. 171–216.

Halabi, Rafik. *The West Bank Story.* Rev. ed. New York: Harcourt Brace Jovanovich, 1981.

Hamnett, Ian, ed. *Social Anthropology and Law.* New York: Academic Press, 1978.

Hardy, M. J. L. *Blood Feuds and Blood Money in the Middle East.* Beirut: Catholic Press, 1963.

Harris, William W. *Taking Root.* New York: Research Studies Press, 1980.

Heller, Mark A. "Foreign Occupation and Political Elites: A Study of the Palestinians." Ph.D. dissertation, Harvard University, 1976.

———. "Politics and Social Change in the West Bank since 1967." In *Palestinian Society and Politics,* ed. Migdal, pp. 185–211.

Hill, Enid. *Mahkama!* London: Ithaca Press, 1979.

Hooker, M. B. *Legal Pluralism.* Oxford: Clarendon Press, 1975.

Horwitz, Morton J. *The Transformation of American Law, 1780–1860.* Cambridge, Mass.: Harvard University Press, 1977.

Hudson, Michael C. *Arab Politics: The Search for Legitimacy.* New Haven: Yale University Press, 1977.

Israeli National Branch, International Commission of Jurists. *The Rule of Law in the Areas Administered by Israel.* Tel Aviv, 1981.

Johnson, Terence. "Imperialism and the Professions." In *The Sociological Review Monograph,* no. 20, ed. Paul Halmos. Keele University, December 1973.

"Karp Report." Press bulletin. Jerusalem: Government Press Office, February 7, 1984.

Kennett, Austin. *Bedouin Justice: Law and Custom among the Egyptian Bedouin.* Cambridge: Cambridge University Press, 1925.

Khare, R. S. "Indigenous Culture and Lawyers' Law in India." *Comparative Studies in Society and History* 14 (1972): 71–96.

Kidder, Robert. "The End of the Road? Problems in the Analysis of Disputes." *Law and Society Review* 15, nos. 3–4 (1981): 717–727.

———. "Formal Litigation and Professional Insecurity: Legal Entrepreneurship in South India." *Law and Society Review* 9, no. 1 (1974): 11–37.

———. "Toward an Integrated Theory of Imposed Law." In *The Imposition of Law,* ed. Burman and Harrell-Bond, pp. 289–306.

Kucherov, Samuel. *Courts, Lawyers, and Trials under the Last Three Tsars.* New York: Praeger, 1953.

Laqueur, Walter, and Barry Rubin, eds. *The Israel-Arab Reader.* 4th ed. New York: Penguin Books, 1984.

Larson, Magali Sarfatti. *The Rise of Professionalism.* Berkeley: University of California Press, 1977.

Lavine, Avraham. "Social Services in the Administered Areas." In *Judea, Samaria, and Gaza: Views on the Present and Future,* ed. Elazar, pp. 145–170.

Layish, Aharon. *Women and Islamic Law in a Non-Muslim State.* New York: John Wiley & Sons, 1975.

Lesch, Ann Mosely. *Arab Politics in Palestine, 1917–1939.* Ithaca, N.Y.: Cornell University Press, 1979.

———. *Political Perceptions of the Palestinians on the West Bank and the Gaza Strip.* Washington, D.C.: Middle East Institute, 1979.

Lev, Daniel. *Islamic Courts in Indonesia.* Berkeley: University of California Press, 1972.

Levi, Sasson. "Local Government in the Administered Territories." In *Judea, Samaria, and Gaza: Views of the Present and Future,* ed. Elazar.

Lewis, Bernard. *The Emergence of Modern Turkey.* 2d ed. New York: Oxford University Press, 1968.

Liebesny, Herbert. 1955. "The Development of Western Judicial Privileges." In *Law in the Middle East,* ed. Liebesny and Khadduri, pp. 309–333.

———. *The Law of the Near and Middle East.* Albany: State University of New York, 1975.

Liebesny, Herbert, and M. Khadduri, eds. *Law in the Middle East.* Washington, D.C.: Middle East Institute, 1955.

Lloyd-Bostock, Sally N. A. "Explaining Compliance with Imposed Law." In *The Imposition of Law,* ed. Burman and Harrell-Bond, pp. 9–25.

Lowy, Michael J. "A Good Name Is Worth More Than Money." In *The Disputing Process—Law in Ten Societies,* ed. Nader and Todd, pp. 181–208.

Luckham, Robin. "Imperialism, Law, and Structural Dependence: The Ghana Legal Profession." In *Lawyers in the Third World: Comparative and Developmental Perspectives,* ed. Dias et al., pp. 90–122.

Lustick, Ian. *Arabs in a Jewish State.* Austin: University of Texas Press, 1980.

———. "Israel and the West Bank after Elon Moreh: The Mechanics of De Facto Annexation." *Middle East Journal* 35, no. 4 (1981): 557–577.

Lutfiyya, Abdulla. *Baytin: A Jordanian Village.* The Hague: Mouton, 1965.

Macaulay, Stewart. "Non-contractual Relations in Business: A Preliminary Study." *American Sociological Review* 28 (1963): 55–67.

Ma'oz, Moshe. *Palestinian Leadership on the West Bank.* London: Frank Cass, 1984.

Massialas, Byron, and Samir Jarrar. *Education in the Arab World.* New York: Praeger, 1983.

Matar, Ibrahim. "Israeli Settlements and Palestinian Rights." In *Occupation: Israel over Palestine,* ed. Aruri, pp. 117–142.

Medcalf, Linda. *Law and Identity: Lawyers, Native Americans, and Legal Practice.* Beverly Hills: Sage Publications, 1978.

Meeker, Michael J. *Literature and Violence in North Arabia.* New York: Cambridge University Press, 1979.

Merryman, John H. *The Civil Law Tradition.* Stanford: Stanford University Press, 1969.

———. "Comparative Law and Social Change: On the Origins, Style, Decline, and Revival of the Law and Development Movement." *American Journal of Comparative Law* 25 (1977): 457–491.

Metzger, Barry. "Legal Services Programs in Asia." In *Legal Aid and World Poverty*, by Committee on Legal Services to the Poor in Developing Nations.

Metzger, Jan, Martin Orth, and Christian Sterling, eds. *This Land Is Our Land: The West Bank under Israeli Occupation*. London: Zed Press, 1983.

Migdal, Joel, ed. *Palestinian Society and Politics*. Princeton: Princeton University Press, 1980.

——. "State and Society in a Society without a State." In *The Palestinians and the Middle East Conflict*, ed. Gabriel Ben-Dor, pp. 377–402. Ramat Gan: Turtledove Press, 1978.

Milson, Menahem. "How to Make Peace with the Palestinians." *Commentary* 71, no. 5 (May 1981): 25–35.

Mishal, Shaul. *West Bank/East Bank: The Palestinians in Jordan, 1949–1967*. New Haven: Yale University Press, 1978.

Mogannam, E. T. "Developments in the Legal System of Jordan." *Middle East Journal* 2 (1952): 194–206.

Moore, Sally Falk. "Individual Interests and Organizational Structures: Dispute Settlements as 'Events of Articulation,'" In *Social Anthropology and Law*, ed. Hamnett, pp. 159–188.

——. *Law as Process: An Anthropological Approach*. London: Routledge & Kegan Paul, 1978.

Morrison, Charles. "Kinship in Professional Relations: A Study of North Indian District Lawyers." *Comparative Studies in Society and History* 14 (1972): 100–125.

Morsy, Magali. "Arbitration as a Political Institution: An Interpretation of the Status of Monarchy in Morocco." In *Islam in Tribal Societies*, ed. Akbar Ahmad and David Hart. London: Routledge & Kegan Paul, 1984.

Nader, Laura, and Harry Todd, Jr., eds. *The Disputing Process—Law in Ten Societies*. New York: Columbia University Press, 1978.

Nakhleh, Emile. *The West Bank and Gaza: Toward the Making of a Palestinian State*. Washington, D.C.: American Enterprise Institute, 1979.

Nash, Gary. "The Phliadelphia Bench and Bar, 1800–1861." *Comparative Studies in Society and History* 7, no. 2 (1965): 203–220.

Nashif, Taysir. *The Palestine Arab and Jewish Political Leaderships: A Comparative Study*. New York: Asia Publishing House, 1979.

Nathan, Eli. "The Power of Supervision of the High Court of Justice over the Military Government." In *Military Government in the Territories Administered by Israel: The Legal Aspects*. ed. Shamgar, pp. 109–170.

Negbi, Moshe. "The Israeli Supreme Court and the Occupied Territories." *Jerusalem Quarterly*, no. 27 (Spring 1983): 33–47.

Nisan, Mordechai. *Israel and the Territories: A Study in Control*. Ramat Gan: Turtledove Press, 1978.

Nolan, Dennis R. *Readings in the History of the American Legal Profession*. New York: Bobbs & Merrill, 1980.

Odenyo, Amos. "Professionalism and Change: The Emergent Kenyan Lawyer." In *Lawyers in the Third World: Comparative and Developmental Perspectives*, ed. Dias et al., pp. 177–203.

Ottenberg, Simon. "Local Government and the Law in Southern Nigeria." In *Traditional and Modern Legal Institutions in Asia and Africa*, ed. D. C. Buxbaum, pp. 26–43. London: E. J. Brill, 1967.

Paliwala, A. "Economic Development and the Legal System of Papua New Guinea." *African Law Studies* 16 (1978): 3–79.

Parnell, Phillip. "Village or State? Competitive Legal Systems in a Mexican Judicial District." In *The Disputing Process—Law in Ten Societies*, ed. Nader and Todd, pp. 315–350.

Peristiany, J. G., ed. *Honour and Shame*. Chicago: University of Chicago Press, 1966.

Pipes, Daniel. *Slave Soldiers and Islam: The Genesis of a Military System*. New Haven: Yale University Press, 1981.

Pitt-Rivers, Julian. *Mediterranean Countrymen: Essays in the Social Anthropology of the Mediterranean*. The Hague: Mouton, 1963.

Porath, Yehoshua. *The Palestinian Arab National Movement: From Riots to Rebellion*. New York: Frank Cass, 1977.

Posposil, Leopold. "Legally Induced Culture Change in New Guinea." In *The Imposition of Law*, ed. Burman and Harrell-Bond, pp. 127–145.

Qubain, Fahim. *Education and Science in the Arab World*. Baltimore: Johns Hopkins University Press, 1966.

Raphaeli, Nimrod. "Military Government in the Occupied Territories: An Israeli View." *Middle East Journal* 23, no. 2 (1969): 177–190.

———. "The West Bank: Governing without Administration." *Public Administration in Israel and Abroad* 10 (1970): 27–36.

Reid, Donald. *Lawyers and Politics in the Arab World, 1880–1960*. Chicago: Bibliotheca Islamica, 1981.

———. "The Rise of Professions and Professional Organization in Modern Egypt." *Comparative Studies in Society and History* 16, no. 1 (1974): 24–57.

Reuschemeyer, Dietrich. *Lawyers and Their Society*. Cambridge: Harvard University Press, 1973.

Rudolph, Lloyd, and Susanne Hoeber Rudolph. "Barristers and Brahmans in India: Legal Cultures and Social Change." *Comparative Studies in Society and History* 8, no. 1 (1965): 24–49.

Said, Edward. *Orientalism*. New York: Pantheon Books, 1978.

Schmida, Leslie, ed. *Education in the Middle East*. Washington, D.C.: Amideast, 1983.

Schmitthener, Samuel. "A Sketch of the Development of the Legal Profession in India." *Law and Society Review* 3, no. 2 (1968): 337–382.

Shamgar, Meir, ed. *Military Government in the Territories Administered by Israel, 1967–1980: The Legal Aspects*. Jerusalem: Hebrew University, 1982.

Shehadeh, Raja. "The Legal System of the Israeli Settlements." *International Commission of Jurists Review*, no. 27 (1981): 59–74.

————. *Occupier's Law*. Washington, D.C.: Institute for Palestine Studies, 1985.

Shehadeh, Raja, and Jonathan Kuttab. *Civilian Administration in the Occupied West Bank*. Ramallah: Law in the Service of Man.

————. *The West Bank and the Rule of Law*. Geneva: International Commission of Jurists, 1980.

Shemesh, Moshe. "The West Bank: Rise and Decline of the Traditional Leadership, June, 1967 to October, 1973." *Middle East Studies* 20, no. 3 (July 1984): 290–324.

Silliman, G. Sidney. "A Political Analysis of the Philippines' Katarangang Pambarangay System of Informal Justice through Mediation." *Law and Society Review* 19, no. 2 (1985): 279–301.

Sills, David, ed. *International Encyclopedia of the Social Sciences*. Vol. 9. New York: Macmillan & Free Press, 1968.

Smith, M. G. *Corporations and Society*. London: Duckworth, 1974.

————. "Historical and Cultural Conditions of Political Corruption among the Hausa." *Comparative Studies in Society and History* 6, no. 2 (1964): 164–194.

Snyder, Francis G. "Land Law and Economic Change in Rural Senegal: Diola Predge Transactions and Disputes." In *Social Anthropology and Law*, ed. Hamnett, pp. 113–157.

————. "Law and Development in the Light of Dependency Theory." *Law and Society Review* 14, no. 3 (Spring 1980): 723–804.

Starr, J. O., and J. Pool. "The Impact of a Legal Revolution in Rural Turkey." *Law and Society Review* 8, no. 4 (Summer 1974): 533–560.

Starr, J. O., and B. Yngevesson. "Scarcity and Disputing: Zeroing in on Compromise Decisions." *American Ethnologist* 2, no. 3 (1975): 553–566.

State of Israel, Ministry of Defense, Coordinator of Government Operations in Judea-Samaria and the Gaza District. *Judea-Samaria and the Gaza District: A Sixteen-Year Survey (1967–1983)*. Jerusalem, 1983.

Strathern, Andrew. "When Dispute Procedures Fail." In *Contention and Dispute*, ed. A. L. Epstein. Canberra: Australian National University Press, 1974.

Tamari, Salim. "In League with Zion: Israel's Search for a Native Pillar." *Journal of Palestine Studies* 12, no. 4 (Summer 1983): 41–56.

Taqqu, Rachelle. "Peasants into Workmen: Internal Labor Migration and the Arab Village Community under the Mandate." In *Palestinian Society and Politics*, ed. Migdal, pp. 261–285.

Teveth, Shabtai. *The Cursed Blessing*. London: Wiedenfeld & Nicolson, 1970.

Tibawi, A. L. *Arab Education in Mandate Palestine*. London: Lusacs, 1936.

Turner, Bryan. *Weber and Islam*. London: Routledge & Kegan Paul, 1974.

Tyan, Emile. "Judicial Organization." In *Law in the Middle East*, ed. Liebesny and Khadduri, pp. 236–278.

Van Arkadie, Brian. *Benefits and Burdens*. New York: Carnegie Foundation for International Peace, 1977.

von Benda-Beckman, Keebet. "Forum Shopping and Shopping Forums: Dispute Processing in a Minangkaban Village in West Sumatra." *Journal of Legal Pluralism*, no. 19 (1981): 117–160.

Wittfogel, Karl. *Oriental Despotism.* New Haven: Yale University Press, 1957.

Witty, Catherine. *Mediation and Society: Conflict Management in Lebanon.* New York: Academic Press, 1980.

Woodburn, James. "Minimal Politics: The Political Organization of the Hadza of Northern Tanzania." In *Politics in Leadership,* ed. William Shack and Percy Cohen, pp. 244–264. Oxford: Clarendon Press, 1979.

Ziadeh, Farhat. *Lawyers, the Rule of Law, and Liberalism in Modern Egypt.* Stanford: Hoover Institution, 1968.

Zureik, Elia. "Theoretical Considerations for a Sociological Study of the Arab State." *Arab Studies Quarterly* 3, no. 3 (1981): 229–257.

Index

administration of justice, in the West Bank, 52, 65

administrative detention, 1. *See also* Defense Emergency Regulations

administrative law, cases involving, 110; before West Bank court of appeals, 210 n.13; military decrees affecting, 126

Ain Shams University, 77

Alami, Musa, 25

Allon Plan, 199 n.53

al-Masri, Zafir, 55, 196 n.30

annexation, of Jerusalem by Israel, 49; and changes in *shariʿa* courts, 197 n.41; implications for legal profession, 146, 206 n.6; protests by lawyers against, 145; and resistance to Israeli occupation, 215 n.1

apprentice lawyers, 80–82, 204 nn.28,29

apprenticeship: arrangement of, 79; changes in terms of, 204 n.25; in Jordanian law, 79; as requirement for entry to legal profession, 74; role in legal training, 78, 79; among striking lawyers, 81, 205 n.33; supervision of, 79–80; of West Bank lawyers, 79–82

Arab Higher Committee, 25, 27, 185 n.26; lawyers in, 185 n.28

Arab-Israeli War of June 1967, 5, 49;

impact on West Bank economy, 52; lawyers in West Bank after, 58

Arab nationalism, 27. *See also* Baʿth party

ʿashira, 41

attorney general, Israeli, 60, 65

autonomy, state, 48, 193 n.3

Baghdad Conference of Arab States, 13

banking, in West Bank, 134

Bar Association, Arab, 26, 185 nn.32,33,34. *See also* Committee of Arab Lawyers; Jordanian Lawyers Union

Bar Association, Israeli, 74

Baʿth party, 28

Begin, Menachem, 63

Beirut Arab University, 77

blood money, 40, 191 n.34. *See also* tribal adjudication

Border Guards, 51, 116

bribery. *See* corruption

British Mandate: court system, 21–22, 183 n.15; establishment and structure, 21, 183 n.14; lawyers during, 6, 24–26; legal reforms, 22; obligation to promote independence, 23, 184 n.20

building codes, cases involving, 110

businesses, Israeli, dealings in West Bank, 60, 181 n.20

businesses, West Bank, 187 n.6, 189 n.18